JAMES LUTHER MAYS

HOSEA

THE OLD TESTAMENT LIBRARY

General Editors

JAMES LUTHER MAYS

HOSEA

A Commentary

The Westminster Press

PHILADELPHIA

Standard Book No. 664–20871–1

Library of Congress Catalog Card No. 75–79618

Published by The Westminster Press®

Philadelphia, Pennsylvania

PRINTED IN THE UNITED STATES OF AMERICA

6 7 8 9 10

CONTENTS

PREFACE

ONCE A commentary is in print, the opinions and judgments contained therein take on a certainty and finality which at places exceeds the confidence felt by the exegete who wrote them. The demands of a manuscript rob one of the luxury and honesty of remaining tentative and undecided before ambiguous problems. That is particularly true for a commentary on Hosea. The book is notorious for the difficulties of its text, and the way in which Hosea's sayings were committed to literature raises formidable problems for literary analysis. A better understanding of many of the obscurities will be reached by the rapidly developing study of Hebrew philology, but for the present a number of problems are subject to no confident solution. As the reader will discover, there are points at which interpretation has to proceed on the basis of quite tentative decisions about the meaning of the text. The writer could do no more than warn the reader at the worst places, since the nature of the commentary precludes extended technical discussion.

The exegetical literature on Hosea has been enriched in recent years by several notable contributions; their value as partners in conversation about the meaning of Hosea is gratefully acknowledged. The commentaries of H. W. Wolff and W. Rudolph merit special mention; their comprehensiveness and depth make them inevitable and invaluable resources. James M. Ward's *Theological Commentary* has also been a stimulating companion. These, along with other works, have contributed to this attempt to understand Hosea far more than scattered references indicate. Unfortunately there was no chance to profit from Walter Brueggemann's just appearing *Tradition for Crisis: A Study in Hosea* or the anticipated Anchor Bible volume on Hosea from David Noel Freedman.

Though he hopes that this volume will find some usefulness among a broad clientele, the author has had a specific audience in mind during its preparation – the minister and theological student as they work on the interpretation and understanding of Scripture. This orientation explains some things about the commentary. The comment has been written with the intention of putting the reader in touch with the intention of the text and clearing the way for him to consider its significance as language of faith. Other literature has been referred to only where the reader might profit from further material or where the author wants to indicate direct contact with the work of another. The bibliography is quite selective and is intended primarily to serve the study of the message of Hosea.

The author cannot conclude his work on the volume without expressing his gratitude to several who have played a significant role in the history of its preparation. He wishes with this volume particularly to greet Professor H. H. Rowley, whose skill and encouragement as a teacher introduced him to research in Hosea studies. Apart from the initiation and confidence of the author's senior colleague in Old Testament, Professor John Bright, the project would never have been undertaken. And finally, it is a pleasure to acknowledge with appreciation the unflagging persistence and high competence of Mrs Franklin S. Clark, the editorial secretary of *Interpretation*, whose labours and enthusiasm have made a real contribution to the entire project.

ABBREVIATIONS

ANEP	*The Ancient Near East in Pictures Relating to the Old Testament*, ed. J. B. Pritchard, 1954
ANET	*Ancient Near Eastern Texts Relating to the Old Testament*, ed. J. B. Pritchard, 1955²
ATD	Das Alte Testament Deutsch
BASOR	*Bulletin of the American Schools of Oriental Research*
BDB	F. Brown, S. R. Driver and C. A. Briggs, *Hebrew and English Lexicon of the Old Testament*, rev. ed., 1953
BH	Biblia Hebraica, ed. R. Kittel (referring to the critical notes)
Bibl.	*Biblica*
BJRL	*Bulletin of the John Rylands Library*
BL	H. Bauer and F. Leander, *Historische Grammatik der hebräische Sprache*, 1922
BK	Biblischer Kommentar
BO	Biblica et Orientalia
BZAW	Beiheft zur *Zeitschrift für die alttestamentliche Wissenschaft*
CAT	Commentaire de l'Ancien Testament
CBQ	*Catholic Biblical Quarterly*
EB	Études Bibliques
ET	English translation
EvTh	*Evangelische Theologie*
G	Greek
GK	Gesenius' *Hebrew Grammar*, ed. E. Kautsch, English ed. by A. E. Cowley, 1910²
HAL	*Hebräisches und aramäisches Lexikon zum Alten Testament*, W. Baumgartner with B. Hartmann and E. Y. Kutscher, first part 1967
HAT	Handbuch zum Alten Testament
IB	*The Interpreter's Bible*
ICC	International Critical Commentary
IDB	*The Interpreter's Dictionary of the Bible*
Interpr.	*Interpretation*
JBL	*Journal of Biblical Literature*

JPS	Jewish Publication Society
JTC	*Journal of Theology and Church*
KAT	Kommentar zum Alten Testament
KB	L. Köhler and W. Baumgartner, *Lexicon in Veteris Testamenti Libros*, 1958
MT	Massoretic Text
OTL	Old Testament Library
RHPR	*Revue d'Histoire et de Philosophie Religieuses*
RSV	The Revised Standard Version of the Bible
S	Syriac
SBT	Studies in Biblical Theology
T	Targum
TB	Torch Bible Commentaries
Th. Büch.	Theologische Bücherei: Neudrucke und Berichte aus dem 20. Jahrhundert, Altes Testament
TLZ	*Theologische Literaturzeitung*
TWNT	*Theologisches Wörterbuch zum Neuen Testament*
TZ	*Theologische Zeitschrift*
VT	*Vetus Testamentum*
VTS	Supplements to *Vetus Testamentum*
WMANT	Wissenschaftliche Monographien zum Alten und Neuen Testament
WO	*Die Welt des Orients*
ZAW	*Zeitschrift für die alttestamentliche Wissenschaft*

JAMES LUTHER MAYS

HOSEA

I

INTRODUCTION

To THE END of the book of Hosea (14.9), an Israelite of a period long after the prophet has affixed a recommendation: 'Whoever is wise, let him understand these things. . . .' His assumption that meditation upon the sayings of Hosea ben Beeri is a part of Wisdom may stand as fitting conclusion to the heritage left by the prophet. As spokesman for God and because of his role in the history of Israel's religion Hosea is a crucial figure in the Old Testament. He stands near the source of a current of faith and tradition that flows to Jeremiah and Deuteronomy. None surpasses him in the passion and creativeness of his prophecy. He spoke out of a feeling of identification with his God that carries a convincing authenticity. He was a man of tremendous emotional range, able at least to reflect in his own feelings the gamut of divine wrath and compassion. Through his sayings and person Yahweh, the God of Israel, wages his final battle against Baal for the soul of Israel.

1. THE MAN

The book of Hosea contains little direct information about the man Hosea. Indeed, his name appears only in the title of the book (1.1) and the heading (1.2a) for the narrative in 1.2b–9; after that it is never mentioned again. The title tells us his father's name was Beeri, but adds nothing further. We do not know where his home was, what he did before he became a prophet, or how and when he was called to his mission. There can be, however, little question that he came from the kingdom of Israel and carried out his mission there. Certain peculiarities of his language are derived from the dialectal individuality of the north. His sayings are directed for the most part to Ephraim. He knows the political and religious situation of Israel in detail. The places most frequently mentioned in his sayings are the

I

royal city of Samaria (7.1; 8.5f.; 10.5, 7; 14.1) and the cultic centres at
Bethel (4.15; 5.8; 10.5; 12.5) and Gilgal (4.15; 9.15; 12.12). Probably these were the places where most of his oracles were spoken. It is
obvious from the quality of his sayings that Hosea was a man of
ability and culture. He drew on the resources of Wisdom, was skilled
in using a variety of literary devices in the formulation of his speeches,
knew the historical traditions of Israel in depth, and was even
acquainted with occasional esoterica like the graveyards of Memphis
(9.6). But there is no evidence that would aid in the reconstruction of
his life before he became a prophet.

Hosea probably became a prophet while he was still young; 1.2
suggests that it was about the time he was of marriageable age. His
career stretched over some twenty-five years. The view of the prophetic
office which surfaces in Hosea's sayings is a high one that finds its
later advocates in Jeremiah and Deuteronomy. Hosea knew the
prophet as the primary instrument of Yahweh in his dealing with
Israel. The office went back to Moses and had served Yahweh to keep
and punish Israel (12.10, 13; 9.8; 6.5). It was probably through the
traditions of this prophetic succession that Hosea received his understanding of Israel's history as composed of two distinct phases (wilderness and Canaan) and his conception of the prophet as one who
fought for Yahweh against Baal and king and foreign alliances and
secular military power. What the manner of his contact with the
older $n^e b\bar{\imath}$'$\bar{\imath}m$ was is not known, but it was surely a close and significant one for him.[a] It must have been this high view of his calling, as
well as the immediacy of the experience of serving as the mouth of
Yahweh, that saw him through the decades of opposition and disappointment as his calls to Israel to return to Yahweh were ignored,
and the nation moved nearer the fulfilment of his prophecies of doom.
Only once does a rather opaque window open on his relations with
his contemporaries (9.7–9). After he had interrupted a festival
celebration with commands that it cease, he is driven to bitter rejoinder at the attack upon him, and speaks of the scorn and hostility
with which his hearers surround his way. The incident was hardly
isolated; it can be taken as a clue to the tension and pain that must
have accompanied his entire career.

We are told of course that Hosea was married (1.2f.) and that he
'bought an adulteress' (3.1f.). Whatever trouble Hosea may have had

[a] See R. Rendtorff, 'Reflections on the Early History of Prophecy in Israel', *JTC*
4, 1967, pp. 17ff.

personally with the women in his life, the difficulty of interpreting the record of their role in his prophecy has far surpassed it. The only narratives in the book are the two stories about these women and they are both reports of symbolic acts. Therein lies the problem; they were written to extend and expound the significance of Hosea's relation to the woman as a prophetic message from Yahweh but not to furnish data for a reconstruction of Hosea's biography. Adhering closely to the form that belongs to such reports, the stories serve their purpose well. There is no doubt about the basic message in them. But agreement about the details of Hosea's life on which the stories are based is not likely. According to the first story (1.2–9) Hosea received a divine command early in his prophetic career to marry a harlotrous woman as a symbolic demonstration of Yahweh's situation in his relation to faithless Israel. The Gomer bat Diblaim whom he chose was probably one of the sacred prostitutes of the fertility cult. Three children were born to the couple and to each the prophet gave a name which was an announcement of judgment. The second story (3.1–5) reports that Hosea received a second command, this time to love a woman living in adultery with a paramour, to show that Yahweh still loved the Israelites in spite of their apostasy. To carry out the command he acquires an unnamed woman and shuts her away from himself and all men as a dramatization of Yahweh's chastisement through which he seeks the return of the people to him. Whatever implications for the life of Hosea may lie in those stories, it is certain that these symbolic acts brought his whole life into public view and involved his total existence in the hostility provoked by his message. He had to incarnate in his own personal life the word of Yahweh. That he could and did is evidence of his profound identification with his God, an identification which, if we can judge from his sayings, allowed him even to feel and experience 'the emotions of Yahweh'.

2. THE TIME

The prophetic career of Hosea began during the prosperous and peaceful years of Jeroboam II and closed as the history of the northern state of Israel moved toward its tragic finale. The events and conditions of that quarter of a century (c. 750–722) are reflected everywhere in the sayings of Hosea. When Hosea named Jezreel as a prophecy against the house of Jehu (1.4), the great-grandson of Jehu, Jeroboam II (786–746), was obviously still on the throne. His marriage and the birth of three children apparently took place during Jeroboam's reign (1.2–9), so the beginning of his career could be dated around 750. Much of the material in the first chapters of the book mirrors those early years of stable rule, economic prosperity, and flourishing religion (1.2–9; 2.2–15; 4.1–5.7). But the idyll was not to last; Hosea's oracles foretold the doom that hung over the confident kingdom. Jeroboam's son, Zechariah (746–745), was murdered by the usurper Shallum who in turn died at the hand of Menahem (745–738). The bloody art of politics by conspiracy and murder which marked Israel's waning history had begun (7.7; 8.4).

In 745 Tiglath-pileser III ascended the throne of Assyria and the mills of international history that ground out the fall of Israel were set in motion. The new monarch was an ambitious and talented ruler whose goal was empire. By 743 he was campaigning in the west. Menahem quickly decided that submission was the best policy and paid a heavy tribute that sorely taxed the landholders of Israel.[a] The strategy of seeking safety by vacillation between accommodation to Assyria and resistance with Egyptian connivance was inaugurated (Hos. 7.11). When Pekahiah (738–737) succeeded his father, the patriots of Israel who bitterly resented Menahem's submission, rallied to a military clique led by Pekah ben Remaliah. Pekah murdered the young king, seized the throne (737–732), and set about the formation of an anti-Assyrian coalition. The so-called Syrian-Ephraimite war against Judah (Isa. 9.8–12) was an episode in this venture (Hos. 5.8–11). In 733 Tiglath-pileser came to settle accounts with the rebels. He ravaged the land, deported much of the poulation, and appropriated most of Israel's territory, leaving only the capital city of Samaria and the hill country of Ephraim to the reduced kingdom. The remnant was saved when Pekah was murdered by Hoshea ben Elah who promptly surrendered, paid tribute,[b] and assumed Israel's throne as a vassal of Tiglath-pileser (Hos. 5.13; 8.9f.?).

For a time Hoshea (732–724) was subservient and Israel had a breathing space of relative quiet. Many of the oracles in chs. 9–12 would fit into this interval. But Hoshea was not content to remain a vassal and began to seek Egyptian support for revolt (Hos. 9.3; 11.5; 12.1). When Shalmaneser V (727–722) succeeded Tiglath-pileser, Hoshea withheld tribute. Chapters 13–14 echo the disastrous consequences of the revolt. In 724 Shalmaneser was in Palestine. Hoshea

[a] II Kings 15.19f.; see *ANET*, p. 283.
[b] *ANET*, p. 284.

became his captive (Hos. 13.10). Israel's armies were defeated and the capital was besieged. Hosea's latest prophecy still anticipates the fall of Samaria (13.16); nothing of its fall is reflected in his words. The preservation of his messages in Judean circles indicates that he or some of his associates escaped to the southern kingdom during the final months of Israel's existence.

3. THE SAYINGS

Except for the two narratives in 1.2–9 and 3.1–5 the book is composed of sayings originally prepared for oral delivery to an audience. For several reasons the analysis and interpretation of the sayings is more difficult than in other prophetic books. The first is the state of the text. It has the well-deserved reputation of being the worst preserved in the Old Testament. At a number of places exegetical decisions must rest on reconstructions of MT and are therefore tentative.[a] The state of the text may be due to the circumstances of its preservation and removal to Judah during the hectic days of Israel's collapse. Even at the most difficult places, however, there is a hesitation simply to call the text corrupt. Hosea is the only native of the northern area whose sayings have been preserved, and some of the resistance of the text to normal philological analysis is probably due to the dialectal distinctiveness of syntax and vocabulary that has persisted in the text in spite of its having been preserved in Judahistic circles.[b] It is a curious and so far unexplained fact that the degree of difficulty varies from place to place. Chapters 1–3 contain few real problems. In chs. 4–14 there are sections of equally clear text. The quite difficult places are scattered (4.4f., 17–19; 6.7–9; 7.4–6, 14–16; 8.9f., 13; 10.9–10; 11.12; 13.9–10).

Beyond the difficulties posed by the text are those created by a combination of the collector's practices and Hosea's own style. Together the two result in a blurring of the edges of the individual units of speech. The messenger formulae, so helpfully frequent in other eighth-century prophets, are almost completely absent; the oracle formula ('a saying of Yahweh') appears only in 2.13, 16, 21; 11.11 (probably a contribution by the editor) and the proclamation formula only in 4.1 and 5.1. Hosea was not given to following the structures

[a] See the collection of data and proposals up to 1900 in ICC, the probings of H. S. Nyberg (*Studien zum Hoseabuch*, 1935), and the full recent discussion in BK and KAT.
[b] See the full list of peculiarities compiled by W. Rudolph, KAT, pp. 20f.

of speech-types; the clear announcement of judgment is rare. Instead, there is a bewildering practice of shifting from direct address to third-person reference to the audience or vice versa (e.g. 2.2, 4; 4.4–10, 11–14). At the first stages of the collection of Hosea's sayings, individual units were woven together into integrated compositions that are held together by a common theme or setting; examples are 2.2–15; 5.8–6.6; 8.1–14.[a] The identification of oral units within the collector's compositions must depend on the appearance of vocatives, new subjects, shifts in personal style.

Hosea thought of the prophet as the mouth of God (6.5); accordingly his sayings are predominantly spoken in the first person of divine speech (e.g. 2.2ff.; 4.1–14; 5.10–15; 11.1ff.). On occasion he speaks in his own right in prophetic sayings (e.g. 4.6; 5.3–7; 9.1–9, 13f., 17; 12.2–6), but one frequently has the feeling that Hosea is so personally identified with his God that shifts to third-person references to Yahweh do not fundamentally interrupt the actuality of his function as God's spokesman. Most of his sayings are messages of judgment which combine reproach and announcement of punishment (e.g. 4.1–3; 5.1–2, 10; 13.4–8); sometimes these elements appear independently. He uses the announcement of a 'complaint' (*rîb*; cf. 2.2; 4.1, 4; 12.2) frequently enough to suggest that in many other cases the style of his message of judgment may be drawn from forms used in legal proceedings in the court in the gates; it is possible, for instance, that the shift in persons for speaker and addressee may reflect different moments and situations of Israelite trial procedure.[b] On two occasions Hosea formulates a 'prophetic liturgy' (5.15–6.6; 14.1–8) in which he delivers an oracle that is a divine answer to the penitence of the people (6.4–6 is negative; 14.4–8 is positive); the salvation-oracle given by the prophet in the cult as a response to laments of the people may well be the analogy for some of the other salvation-oracles in Hosea (1.10f.; 2.16–23).

Hosea could turn a neat proverb, and several times he uses folk sayings to enforce the logic of his message of judgment (4.11, 14b; 8.7). At the practice of conveying meaning through comparisons, so

[a] H. W. Wolff in BK calls these compositions 'kerygmatic units' because he thinks they are made up of sayings (divine and prophetic) which derived from one appearance of the prophet and were spoken in sequence, sometimes in response to reactions of the audience. But composition by similar theme or catchword, or perhaps the same general period in the case of 5.8–6.6, explains the larger units adequately; and so much does not have to be imagined.

[b] See H. J. Boecker, *Redeformen des Rechtslebens im alten Israel* (WMANT 14), 1964.

beloved by the wise, he was a past master. Metaphors pour from his mouth. There is hardly an oracle which does not contain at least one, and often they are multiplied within a simple saying as Hosea throws up one image after another to heighten the impact of his speech (see the list below under 'The Message'). He was also skilled in formulating and using word-plays; correspondence of sound, spelling, and meaning of words juxtaposed within a saying is a rather regular feature of his style. Unfortunately it is a device usually lost in translation because it is perceptible only in Hebrew.[a]

Beyond all discussion of forms and techniques of speech lies a profounder dimension of Hosea's language that is perceived only through empathy with its intention and the man behind it. It emerges from a psychological intimacy of prophet and God. It articulates a passion whose range runs the gamut of emotions from hate to love, from anguish to anger. There is in it a feeling for and of 'the divine pathos' (A. Heschel), the inner tragedy and glory of the God who by his own choice struggles for the soul of his people.

4. THE MESSAGE

Hosea's theology is a very articulate and specific understanding of Yahweh as God of Israel and Israel as the people of Yahweh. These two foci of his faith belong to the same ellipse; they are inseparably related. Yahweh is known through his acts for Israel and his declaration of his will for them. Israel is defined, identified, and judged in the context of those deeds and instructions. This history of Yahweh's relationship with Israel is the sphere within which the thought of Hosea moves. Unlike Amos, Isaiah, and Jeremiah he appears to have spoken no oracles about foreign nations. Assyria, and in a secondary way Egypt, come within the horizons of his concern; but they only appear in connection with Yahweh's dealings with Israel. The theology which finds expression in the speech of Hosea is a direct descendant of the all-Israel Yahwist faith of the old tribal league.

The God who speaks through Hosea bears the proper name Yahweh, the name revealed to Moses as the sign of the Exodus. Hosea even knows the 'I AM' variation on the name (1.9) from the story of the call of Moses (Ex. 3.14). Yahweh inaugurated his relationship with Israel in Egypt; there he chose them (11.1), from there he

[a] See the comment on 8.7, 9; 9.15; and the full list gathered by Rudolph, KAT, pp. 21f.

delivered them and Israel knows no other God or Saviour (13.4). In the wilderness Yahweh nurtured the young nation and tended its needs (13.5; 11.3f.; 9.10). Israel's residence in Canaan is due to Yahweh's help. In Hosea the conquest-tradition is a direct sequel of Exodus and wilderness (11.2; 13.6). The land belongs to Yahweh (9.3) so it is called 'the house of Yahweh' (9.5, 8; 8.1). The people reside in the land as the tenants of their God, and the wine and grain and oil which they enjoy are his gifts (2.8; 10.11; 11.2; 13.6). Hosea does not mention Sinai, but he speaks explicitly of Yahweh's covenant with Israel (6.7; 8.1). Even where the covenant is not mentioned, it is constantly presupposed. The covenant binds Israel to obey the instruction of Yahweh (8.1), the stipulations of his will for Israel which Hosea knows in a written (8.13) and in a decalogic form (4.2).

Loyal as he is to the old traditions about Yahweh and Israel, Hosea is far from being a traditionalist. There is in his thought and speech an exciting combination of traditional and contemporary, of ancient and modern. He was a provocative and creative figure in the history of Israel's faith. Three features of his spoken messages stand out in this respect: his dialogue with the fertility religion of Canaan, the freedom with which he theologizes by the use of metaphorical images, and his knowledge and use of history as a source of meaning. These three features are combined in his oracles to create a dramatic, colourful, and urgent prophecy of great force in its impact on mind, senses, and emotion.

From the opening verses of ch. 1 to the concluding oracle in ch. 14, the cult and mythology of the god Baal is the foil of most of Hosea's sayings. Through Hosea Yahweh wrestles to win his people free from this other god and from the way of viewing themselves and reality which goes with his cult. In this, Hosea is successor to the great Elijah. In the encounter Hosea is both polemicist and apologist. His condemnation of Israel's commerce with Baal and of any syncretistic modification of Yahwism by the influence of Baalism is unyielding. But he also adapts the motifs and rubrics of the fertility cult to portray the relation of Yahweh and his people, to diagnose Israel's sin, and to describe the future which God will create. With daring skill he appropriates the language and thought of Canaanite religion while rejecting Baalism itself. By this strategy Hosea achieves a fresh modernism that plunges into the contemporaneity of his audience.[a]

[a] See E. Jacob, 'L'Héritage Cananéen dans le livre du prophète Osée', RHPR 43, 1963, pp. 250–9.

Just how he executed this assault on contemporary culture can best be seen by looking at his unending use of comparisons and images to extend the range of the traditional language of faith. One overlooks the most characteristic method of his thought if Hosea's metaphors are regarded as merely decorative.[a] They participate in the theological dimension of his oracles and constitute an important element of the revelation of Yahweh through the prophet. By them he intensifies the personal quality of Yahweh's relation to Israel. The normative history and the covenant are translated into a drama of persons in which the issues and values at stake are those of personal relations. The most effective and influential in later thought is the portrayal of the covenant in terms of Yahweh as husband and Israel as wife, presented in 2.2–15 and in the prophetic symbolism of chs. 1 and 3. It is a prime example of his appropriation of themes from the fertility cult. Yahwism had always avoided sexual motifs in its speech about its God precisely because the sexual idiom was central in the mythology of the fertility cult. Baal was the owner-husband of the land; his sexual life created its fertility. But Hosea probably adopted the image because at the beginning of his career he was commanded by Yahweh to enact his relation to Israel through marriage (1.2ff.). On the authority of the divine revelation he spoke of Yahweh as the lawful husband of Israel. In Hosea's hands the myth of the divine marriage became an allegory of Yahweh's experience with Israel in Canaan; and the context in which the relation was understood was removed from the magical and cultic world of Canaan to the moral structure of the covenant. The deities worshipped at the state and local shrines became Israel's illicit lovers whom she pursued to gain a harlot's hire of wine, grain, and oil (2.5, 7, 10). 'Harlotry' was coined as the term for every unfaithfulness of Israel to Yahweh (see comment on 1.2). Yahweh's punishment is aimed at the reform of the wife (2.6f., 14, 16) and his saving restoration takes place as reconciliation (2.15, 19). From this matrix love is drawn as the term for Yahweh's dealing with Israel (3.1). When Hosea looks back beyond Israel's life in the land to the Exodus, he presents Yahweh as a father watching over the first steps of his son Israel (11.1ff.). In his help to Israel Yahweh is physician (14.4; 7.1; 11.3) and shepherd (13.5). In his judgment he is hunter (7.12), carnivore (5.14; 13.7f.), wound and infection (5.12). As Saviour he is like dew (14.5) and fruitful tree (14.8). Yahweh looks on Israel as herd (13.5–8), heifer (10.11), vine

[a] See H. W. Wolff, BK, pp. xv–xvi, xviii.

(10.1), grapes and early fig (9.10). In her sin and suffering Israel is like the sick (5.13); a fickle bird (7.11f.); a stubborn cow (4.16); an unborn child (13.13); a cake of bread (7.8); morning mist (6.4); chaff, smoke and dew (13.3). In restoration Israel is compared to the flourishing plant life of Lebanon (14.5–7) and sown ground (2.21ff.). The metaphors drawing on plant life are surprising, and most probably are more incursions in the sphere of fertility cult; they are a way of claiming that the whole realm of growth belongs to Yahweh alone, but that his real interest is not the fertility of crops but the obedience of persons.

Against the cyclical thought-world of Canaan Hosea sets the historical traditions of Yahwism. For him they are not mere tradition or isolated items of faith, but a guide to understanding and a way to put things in the right perspective. No prophet is better informed than Hosea about Israel's history, or uses historical tradition more for the stuff of his kerygma. The definitive period of Israel's existence was the time of the Exodus and wilderness and conquest (2.14f.; 9.10; 11.1; 13.4f.). In those days Yahweh was the exclusive subject of Israel's history and the people received their true identity as they were shaped and defined by Yahweh's acts. But with the nation's entry into the land, a counter-history began of which the people themselves were the subject. This second period had its own beginnings which supplied a perspective for understanding the present. At the land's very edge, at the shrine of Baal-peor, Israel began a flirtation with Baal (9.10). The significant sites which came within Israel's horizons as she entered the land all became points of departure for a history of sin that still continued. Gilgal (9.15; 4.15; 12.11) and Gibeah (9.9; 10.9) and Jezreel (1.4) were the sources of Israel's faithlessness. Hosea even reaches back to traditions about the patriarchs to find material for the diagnosis of Israel's failure (12.3f., 12). The imminent action of Yahweh proclaimed by Hosea was in a real sense a strategy calculated to blot out this second history and wrench the course of Israel's existence back into the channels of the first. By his punishment Yahweh would bring the career of faithlessness to a disastrous conclusion so that it could not possibly continue. Then he would take the people back to their primary history, to the wilderness, where they would learn again to be his people (2.14f.). From there he would give them the land again. In portraying this recapitulation by which Israel would be reconstituted as the true people of Yahweh, Hosea draws the themes and hopes of salvation belonging to Canaan's fertility

religion into the rubrics of history and covenant. The cultic marriage between God and land is replaced by a remarriage between Yahweh and his people (2.16, 19). The cycle of the year with its hopes of the renewal of fertility is translated into an expected renewal of Israel (2.21ff.; 14.5ff.). Nature is pre-empted by history as the sphere of God's action. The *Urzeit* of a mythical paradise which furnished the model for an *Endzeit* in mythical thinking is shifted to the salvation-history which is to be resumed once and for all by the work of Yahweh's mercy, faithfulness, and love.

Against the background of the normative past Hosea drew his indictment against Israel. Reduced to its simplest terms the indictment was that Israel had broken Yahweh's covenant and rebelled against his instruction (8.1). The entire corporate life of the people in cult and politics was a rejection of their God and a betrayal of the identity which he had created for them by the old history of salvation. Their faithless sin was nothing new; from the time they had entered the land of Canaan they had fashioned a history of their own, adding one sin to another until their evil deeds became the sum of their character (7.1f.; 4.12). Now they were a virtual prisoner of their sin, trapped by the identity which they had created (5.4). This faithlessness had reached such dimensions that Yahweh must pronounce over them the name which they have earned: 'Not-my-people' (1.9).

The reproaches of Hosea were aimed at two primary targets; in his eyes the failure of Israel was manifested in its cultic and political life. In the first part of the book there is a virtual preoccupation with Israel's involvement with the fertility religion of Canaan. Baal is the great antagonist in the struggle for the soul of Israel. In Jeroboam's kingdom the long process of syncretism had reached a culmination in which the worship and understanding of Yahweh had been Canaanized and there was outright practice of the Baal cult. Baals were adored as deities of the land at state shrines and local high places (2.13, 17; 9.10; 11.2; 13.1). Baal's devotees believed him to be the creator of the land's fertility and divine source of crops, flocks, and children (2.5, 8, 12; 7.14; 9.1f., 11f.). The appropriate ritual of sympathetic magic to ensure the effectiveness of the deity's procreative powers dominated the cult; sexual rites with the use of sacred prostitutes and bacchanalian celebration marked the festivals (4.11–14, 18). Sacrifice was understood as a means of influencing God to procure his material blessings (4.13; 5.6; 8.11, 13; 10.1). The old aniconic purity of Yahwism had been abandoned; images were all

over the land (8.4–6; 10.5; 11.2; 13.2; 14.3, 8). In all this apostasy the priests who were responsible for the knowledge of God in Israel bore a particular guilt; their avarice and corruption infected the very sources of faith for the people (4.4–10; 6.9).

The royal court and its policies was the second target of Hosea's reproaches. Israel's leaders were party to the national apostasy; their international stratagems were a substitute for turning to Yahweh. Guilt for the blood of Jezreel was on the head of Jeroboam II (1.4). His successors, who reached the throne by conspiracy and assassination, turned bloodshed into a normal technique of politics (7.3–7). Once on the throne these men saw the monarchy as the source of Israel's strength (7.16; 8.14; 10.13). In the recurrent crises of the period they turned to Egypt and Assyria in an attempt to build national security by clever diplomacy (5.13; 7.8f., 11; 8.9f.; 14.3). All these kings and leaders were the creatures of Israel's sin; Yahweh had no part in their tenure (8.4). Indeed, they were the instruments of his wrath (13.11). The texts do not furnish unambiguous evidence concerning Hosea's attitude toward kingship *per se*. The reference to Gilgal in 9.15 has been read as an assertion that all Israel's evil started with the inauguration of Saul; but this construction is uncertain. Yet, one gets the impression that Hosea thought Israel's experience with the monarchy was little better than their involvement with Canaanite religion. Israel should have no other saviour but Yahweh (13.4, 10). These kings had come between Yahweh and Israel, corrupted covenant (10.4), entangled the nation in deceptive alliances to evade Yahweh's punishment, created false hopes of independent security. Though 1.10f. is not certain to be from Hosea, it is the one political oracle of salvation in the book; it looks for a reconstitution of the people under a chief along the lines of the tribal league. The reference to 'David their king' (3.5) is the work of a Judean editor.

When Hosea uses normative terms to specify what is demanded of Israel, he bypasses *righteousness* and *justice* emphasized by Amos and Isaiah (justice only in 12.6) in favour of *knowledge of God*, *devotion*, and *faithfulness* (4.1; 6.4, 6; 12.6). On the meaning of these terms in Hosea, see the commentary on 4.1. The place of Yahweh's instruction (*tōrā*) as a measure of Israel's obedience was crucial (4.1, 6; 8.1, 12). But in characterizing Israel's disobedience Hosea is not content merely to cite infractions in a legal manner. He prefers the terms and metaphors which interpret the disobedience as personal betrayal and

estrangement. In his vocabulary *faithfulness, devotion,* and *knowledge of God* are the qualities of living in relation demanded by Yahweh. It is this breakdown at the personal level which grieves the prophet most. So he portrays Israel as an adulterous wife (2.2ff.) and rebellious son (11.1ff.); for verbs to describe Israel's sin he constantly chooses those which speak of one person's rejection and evasion and desertion of another. In Hosea's thinking the history of Yahweh and Israel was meant to be a living dialogue of love and loyalty between committed persons.

In his many announcements of impending punishment Hosea speaks generally of two kinds of public, concrete disaster which appear to correspond to the two basic sins of the fertility cult and the monarchy with its politics. The richness of the land's produce which Israel thought to obtain from Baal will be taken away (2.9–13). Not only the land, but the populace itself will be barren (4.3, 10; 8.7; 9.2, 11–14, 16). Whether by drought, or pestilence, or loss of the land, the blessings for those who keep the covenant will be replaced by the curses of famine, hunger, and childlessness, so that Israel can learn in terrible finality who is the source of good for them. As Assyrian pressure more and more overshadows the political existence of the kingdom, Hosea speaks of the suffering and devastation and humiliation of military defeat and political collapse (7.16; 8.3, 13f.; 10.6–10, 14; 11.6; 13.15f.). Every political stratagem will fail, every alliance prove futile, the king and his princes be swept away. The people will end up in exile (9.3, 6, 15, 17; 11.5). In these various disasters Israel suffers the consequences of its faithlessness. The past and present sins of Israel have become its fated, inexorable future. The spirit of harlotry has possessed the people and they, surrounded by their deeds, are prisoner to them (5.4; 7.2); they must reap the whirlwind they have sown (8.7). Hosea speaks of their sins as though they were an objective instrument wielded against them (1.4; 2.13; 9.9; 12.14). The inbreaking calamities are also the direct action of Yahweh who in them expresses his anger and wrath at Israel's betrayal (5.10; 13.11). Ordinary language would not suffice to express the furious rage into which Yahweh's love had been driven, so Hosea resorts to theriomorphisms to depict Yahweh's punishment (13.7f.; 5.14 and 12). And when he views Israel's tribulation in terms of its helplessness because Yahweh no longer acts as covenant God (1.6, 9), Hosea speaks of Yahweh's withdrawal and absence (5.6, 15).

In and through Israel's punishment Yahweh works as chastiser, seeking to discipline and correct his people (5.2, 9; 10.10). Yahweh's wrath will not exhaust itself in simple revenge; his harshest measures of judgment are the extremes of a struggle for the soul of Israel. In the speeches of Hosea, Yahweh laments over, and threatens the nation. The procedures of the court trial (*rib*, 2.2ff.) where the settlement between estranged parties is sought are transacted in the arena of history. Yahweh pleads with Israel and wrestles with the people's recalcitrance (6.4) seeking an answer, a response – that they return to him (5.15; 7.7, 10). In face of their bondage to their sin the occasional imperatives by which the nation is summoned to mend its ways are really interpretations of the intention of Yahweh's punishment (2.2f.; 4.15; 12.6). In 11.8 and 13.14 the tension between Yahweh's anger at Israel's rebellion and passion for a reconciliation breaks out into an agonizing struggle with himself. Punishment takes up the function of the unrequited exhortation. In sayings in the first part of the book, Hosea looks for chastisement to bring Israel back to Yahweh (2.6f.; 14f.; 3.4f.; 5.15). When Israel fails to respond, even in the midst of terrible suffering, Yahweh draws back from the nation's annihilation (11.8f.). The exhortation which Hosea offers Israel in 14.1–3 presupposes the collapse of every resort but return.

Israel's return to Yahweh (see commentary on 3.5) is thus gathered up into Hosea's programme of salvation. It is the product of Yahweh's chastisement. All the terrible suffering which he brings on Israel is not so much judicial and legal punishment as the assault of his love as husband and father of the people upon their unfaithfulness. The land is ravaged only to remind Israel of days of loyalty to Yahweh (2.7). The loss of state and cult will leave the nation no future except return (3.4f.). Yahweh will bring his people again into the wilderness where he can win back the wife lost to Baal by re-enactment of the original salvation-history (2.14f.). The series of salvation-oracles brought together in 2.16–23 depict the restoration which will occur as Yahweh resumes the role of Israel's husband. He will never again be confused with Baal (2.16f.). He will give them back the land and establish it as a sanctuary of peace against the marauding of beasts and men (2.18). As Israel's bridegroom he himself will pay the bridal price; it will be his righteousness, justice, devotion, compassion, and faithfulness which establish the new marriage (2.19f.). In that day of restoration Yahweh will completely pre-empt the role of Baal, endowing land and people with fertility. The old history of election and compassion will resume as the people take up the original dialogue ('My people' . . . 'my God', 2.21–23).

The questing love of Yahweh finds its most poignant expression in the oracle of Yahweh and his son (11.1–9, 11). The poem belongs to a time when the shattering blows of Assyrian invasion had already begun without awakening the expected return to Yahweh (vv. 5–7). The wrestling with Israel then becomes a struggle within God over the future of his people – a contest won by the overwhelming compassion of God. He takes the redemption of Israel wholly upon himself. In the final tragic days of Israel's existence Hosea gave Israel a prayer as a way to return to their God (14.1–3) who never gave up his desire to be their Saviour (vv. 4–8).

5. THE BOOK

Hosea's prophetic activity apparently ceased shortly before the fall of Samaria in 721; at that time the record of his prophecy was brought to Judah, and it is to that rescue operation that we owe the existence of the book. The book reached its present form in the south; the hand of the Judahistic redactors is evident at several places (see below). But the process of assembling and arranging the material must have begun during Hosea's ministry, which after all lasted at least a quarter of a century. Moreover, there is a loose chronological order in the sayings in chs. 4–14 which means that the final collectors were acquainted with Hosea's career in one way or another.

The book falls into two easily recognized sections which are distinct in size and plan. The first is chs. 1–3. It serves as a kind of introduction to the book. The collector set out to bring together all the material which seemed to him to deal with the relation between Hosea's life, particularly his marriage and children, and his prophecy. He had the autobiographical unit (3.1–5) written by Hosea and the composition in 2.2–15 already at hand. He gathered the salvation oracles in 2.16–23 because they contained themes which fit the marriage-children scheme. Lacking a historical introduction for the whole he probably composed 1.2–6, 8f. himself. He then arranged this material so that messages of punishment and salvation alternate (1.2–9 and 1.10–2.1; 2.2–15 and 2.16–23) and set the autobiographical unit which combines both themes at the conclusion.

The second section, chs. 4–14, lacks the clear plan of the first. Here the collector is working simply to arrange the rest of the material available to him and he is using common themes and catchwords to organize it. Oracles of hopeful outlook (11.1–11 and 14.1–8) are set at the end of series of words of judgment, suggesting that the alternation of punishment and salvation evident in chs. 1–3 may have played a role in shaping two sub-sections, chs. 4–11 and 12–14. So far as the historical setting of the individual sayings can be ascertained, the material seems to have a general chronological sequence. 4.1–5.7 reflects the stability of Jeroboam's reign. 5.8–6.6 came from the Syrian-Ephraimite war and its aftermath. Chapters 10–14 fit best into the reign of Hoshea. The rest of the material can be placed in the years between Jeroboam and Hoshea. Within the limits imposed by the shape of his material and the other methods he is using, the collector seeks to preserve a profile of Hosea's career. Some of the material may have already been assembled into larger units before the collector began his work. 5.8–6.6, a series of sayings during the Syrian-Ephraimite war, is probably a case in point. It is impossible to say who is responsible for the arrangement of other sequences by theme and catchword; we can only observe the result. 4.1–3 is used as an introduction because of its opening formula and broad scope. 4.4–10 contains two themes ('complaint', 'knowledge of God') that appeared in 4.1–3 and itself establishes the 'harlotry' theme which appears in one way or another in 4.11–5.7, where all the sayings focus on cultic apostasy. The Syrian-Ephraimite war sequence is followed by oracles which illustrate the transiency of devotion mentioned in 6.4 (6.7–7.:6). Chapter 8 opens with a general charge that Israel has broken covenant (8.1–3) followed by sayings which cite specific violations (8.4–14). 9.1–9 is held together by a situation, the prophet's preaching at a cultic festival. With 9.10 a series of sayings begins which feature the use of historical references to interpret the present, a device that continues to appear through ch. 13.

It is entirely possible then that the book was created largely in its present form and scope by an editor or group working in Judah in the years after the fall of Samaria. They must have had direct guidance from Israelites who knew Hosea and were sympathetic to his mission. It is not inconceivable that the prophet himself was a refugee in Judah. Very little material that did not originate with Hosea has been added in the formation and the use of the book. The origin of 1.10–11 is a problem; in spite of its lack of similarity to other salvation-oracles of Hosea, it may have come from him. 2.1 is the contribution of the compiler of chs. 1–3, who also wrote 1.2–6, 8f. as its introduction. A number of small additions and revisions are due to an interest in using the book in Judah (1.7; phrases in 3.5; 4.15?; 5.5b; 6.11a;

Judah in 10.11b; 11.12b; 12.2). The title (1.1) is the contribution of Deuteronomic circles who collected and edited the prophetic tradition as a whole. 11.10 updates the picture of hope to the exilic situation. 14.9 is the final addition, the comment of a follower of Wisdom who at his distance finds the book a guide to the man that seeks to walk in the commandments of Yahweh.

BIBLIOGRAPHY

COMMENTARIES IN SERIES

W. R. Harper, 1905 (ICC)
A. van Hoonacker, 1908 (EB)
E. Sellin, 1929[2,3] (KAT XII/1)
T. H. Robinson, 1954[2] (HAT 14)
J. Mauchline, 1956 (IB VI)
G. A. F. Knight, 1960 (TB)
A. Weiser, 1964[5] (ATD 24)
H. W. Wolff, 1965[2] (BK XIV/1)
E. Jacob, 1965 (CAT XIa)
W. Rudolph, 1966 (KAT XIII/1)

INDIVIDUAL COMMENTARIES AND BOOKS

J. Wellhausen, *Die kleinen Propheten* (Skizzen und Vorarbeiten V), 1893[2]
G. A. Smith, *The Book of the Twelve Prophets* Vol. I, rev. ed., 1928
J. Lindblom, *Hosea, literarisch untersucht*, 1927
H. S. Nyberg, *Studien zum Hoseabuch*, 1935
H. W. Robinson, *The Cross of Hosea*, 1949
G. Östborn, *Yahweh and Baal. Studies in the Book of Hosea and Related Documents*, 1956
N. Snaith, *Mercy and Sacrifice. A Study of the Book of Hosea*, 1953
J. M. Ward, *Hosea. A Theological Commentary*, 1966

ARTICLES

A. Alt, 'Hosea 5.8–6.6. Ein Krieg und seine Folgen in prophetischer Beleuchtung', *Kleine Schriften* II, 1953, pp. 163–87
W. Eichrodt, 'The Holy One in Your Midst, the Theology of Hosea', *Interpr.* 15, 1961, pp. 259–73
G. Fohrer, 'Umkehr und Erlösung beim Propheten Hosea', *TZ* 11, 1955, pp. 161–85

E. Jacob, 'Der Prophet Hosea und die Geschichte', *EvTh* 24, 1964, pp. 281–90

'L'Héritage cananéen dans le livre du prophète Osée', *RHPR* 43, 1963, pp. 250–9

J. L. McKenzie, 'Divine Passion in Osee', *CBQ* 17, 1955, pp. 287–99

'Knowledge of God in Hosea', *JBL* 74, 1955, pp. 22–27

H. W. Wolff, '"Wissen um Gott" bei Hosea als Urform von Theologie', *EvTh* 12, 1952/3, pp. 533–54, reprinted in *Gesammelte Studien zum Alten Testament* (Th. Büch. 22), 1964, pp. 182–205

'Hoseas geistige Heimat', *TLZ* 81, 1956, pp. 83–94, reprinted in Th. Büch. 22, pp. 232–50

'Guilt and Salvation. A Study of the Prophecy of Hosea', *Interpr.* 15, 1961, pp. 274–85

II

COMMENTARY

1. THE TITLE: 1.1

1 ¹The word of Yahweh which came to Hosea ben Beeri, in the time of Uzziah, Jotham, Ahaz, and Hezekiah, kings of Judah, and in the time of Jeroboam ben Joash, king of Israel.

The superscription is a title for the entire book. Similar titles appear as the headings of other prophetic books (Zeph. 1.1; Micah 1.1; Joel 1.1; Jonah 1.1; Jer. 1.1f.; Ezek. 1.3); this similarity in form indicates that such titles were the work of the circles who edited the prophetic works during the exilic and post-exilic period.[a] The heading is more than a mere name for the book; the final redactor states in it his theological understanding of the work so that it will be properly read and understood. The book as a whole is 'the word of Yahweh', the message of the God of Israel. The category of 'word' (*dābār*) is extended to include the total tradition deriving from a prophet, all his oracles and the narratives which tell of his activity (cf. 1.2–9 and ch. 3). The reader is to find in the sum and variety of the material the one unified 'word of the Lord'. That word is not the product of human speculation or wisdom; it 'came' (*hāyā 'el*), happened, as an event of revelation to a particular man, and his proclamation is reflex and expression of that event. The revelation had a setting in the history of Israel; it took place during the reigns of certain kings. The word was an occurrence in the history of Yahweh and Israel, and therefore is relevant to all who live in the ongoing stream of that history. The title furnishes precious little biographical information about the man who was instrument of the word. His name was Hosea, mentioned in the book for the second and last time in the next

[a] J. Lindblom, *Prophecy in Ancient Israel*, 1962, pp. 279ff.

verse. The name appears also in Num. 13.8; I Chron. 27.20; II Kings 15.30; Neh. 10.23; the first two texts associate the name with Ephraimites, which some have read as a clue to the tribal heritage of Hosea. His father was Beeri, a name found also in Gen. 26.34. Apparently the redactor knew no tradition about the home or occupation of this prophet of the north, as the redactor of the Amos book did about him (Amos 1.1). The list of kings by which the activity of Hosea is dated also indicates the remoteness of the redactor. The Judean kings are given the preferred place by being listed first, a clue to the Judean provenance of the editor. In naming Uzziah, Jotham, Ahaz, and Hezekiah, the editor allows for a period which stretches from the accession year of Uzziah in 783 to the death of Hezekiah in 687. Since the reigns of Uzziah (783–742) and Jeroboam ben Joash (786–746) covered roughly the same period, the beginning of Hosea's ministry can be dated before 746 (cf. 1.4). But what of the lower limits of Hosea's ministry? The accession year of Hezekiah is hotly debated because the biblical data concerning the reign of Hezekiah given by the Deuteronomistic historian in II Kings are confused and pose one of the worst problems in the chronology of the monarchy.[a] Apparently the redactor of the book of Hosea shared that confusion. The fact that Jeroboam II is the only king of Israel mentioned raises another question, because a number of the sayings of Hosea are set in the midst of events during the reigns of Menahem, Pekah, and Hoshea. Either the redactor was misinformed on this matter as well, or the tradition mentioning Jeroboam alone originally applied only to the material in chs. 1–3, which seems to belong in large part to this early period in Hosea's ministry. In any case nothing in Hosea's sayings hints that he was active after the fall of Samaria in 721.

2. DIVINE WORD AND HUMAN LIFE: 1.2–9

1 [2]The beginning of Yahweh's speaking through[b] Hosea.
    Yahweh said to Hosea, 'Go take yourself a harlotrous wife and harlotrous children, for the land is surely committing harlotry, turning away from Yahweh.' [3]So he went and took Gomer, daughter of Diblaim. She conceived and bore him a son, [4]and Yahweh said to him 'Name

[a] D. N. Freedman, 'The Chronology of Israel', in *The Bible and the Ancient Near East*, ed. G. E. Wright, 1961, pp. 211f.
[b] For *dibber b-* as 'speak through', see I Kings 22.28.

him Jezreel, for it will not be long before I visit the bloodshed of Jezreel upon Jehu's house and bring the kingdom in Israel's house to an end. [5]It will come to pass on that day that I will break Israel's bow in the valley of Jezreel.' [6]She conceived again and bore a daughter, and he said to him, 'Name her Unpitied, for I will not continue to have pity on Israel's house,[a] but will surely remove them.[a] [7]But on Judah's house I will have pity and I will save them by Yahweh their God. I will not save them by bow or sword, by battle or horses or riders.' [8]When she had weaned Unpitied, she conceived and bore a son, [9]and he said, 'Name him Not-my-people, for you are not my people, and [b]I am not I-AM for you.'[b]

This narrative of Hosea's marriage to Gomer and of the three children born to them tells about four separate acts of prophetic symbolism. Occasions on which God commanded a prophet to do something as a dramatic enactment of a divine word are a common feature of prophetic activity (e.g. Isa. 8.1ff.; 20; Jer. 27.1ff., etc.).[c] Chapter 3 is another story of a symbolic act. The reports typically contain the divine command to perform a specific act, the interpretation of the act's symbolic significance, and the obedient performance of the act. All three elements are present here only in the case of the marriage itself whose conclusion is reported (v. 3a); but since the next three symbolisms involve a name given to a child already born, the report simply assumes that the divine command is obeyed. The marriage is an indictment against Israel, a way of disclosing their sin. The names of the children, on the other hand, are all sentences of judgment, announcing decisions of Yahweh because of that sin. But, apart from certain expansions (vv. 5 and 7) of the account, the report itself is a literary unity. A basic formal structure, repeated four times, integrates the sequence: Yahweh (or 'he') said to Hosea (or 'him'), 'Go/name . . .' always followed by 'for' (*kī*) introducing the interpretation. The fact of the marriage is obviously presupposed in the account of the births; after v. 4a no proper names are used for God, prophet, or wife, as successive sentences grow more economical in expression. The indictment stated in the marriage's symbolic mean-

[a-a] Read *nāśā'* as 'remove, take away' (KB *s.v.* 17; BDB *s.v.* 3) and *lāhem* as acc. obj. The text is relatively certain, but the locution is subject to various constructions: 'that I should forgive them' (ICC, RSV); 'but instead I will withdraw it (i.e. my pity) from them' (BK); 'to show them any favour at all' (an ellipsis for *nāśā' pānīm*, Ward).

[b-b] The sentence could be translated 'and I! I am not yours'; see the comment.

[c] Cf. J. Lindblom, *Prophecy in Ancient Israel*, 1962, pp. 165ff.

ing creates the context for the verdict announced in the names of the children.[a]

Disagreement about the nature of this family narrative is as old as the interpretation of the early Church Fathers. Is the story an allegory whose only reality is the meaning, or do marriage and births represent actual episodes in the life of Hosea? The majority of recent commentators agree that the latter is correct. The very character of prophetic symbolism requires that the divine word be actualized in a representative event. The narrative itself gives clues to the factual human history of which it tells. Gomer and Diblaim are personal names, not sign-language for some reality other than a person. The story is laconic and matter-of-fact. The children come in the irregular succession of son-daughter-son. The narrative notes that the third child was conceived just after the second was weaned. The story reports the real. And yet it is not, indeed cannot be, approached as though it were biography. The interest is not in Hosea and the experiences of his life, and perhaps it was the recognition of this which led to the allegorical approach before prophetic symbolism was properly understood. There is a severe concentration on the divine word through the prophet's family life. The very genius of the formal, repetitive style is that it excludes almost everything which does not serve the pattern of command and interpretation. The narrative is kerygmatic, not biographical. Through it, as well as oracle, the word of Yahweh is known – and that is its sole purpose. The details of Hosea's family life are hidden behind the word-function of the

[a] The problem of Hosea's marriage has produced a bewildering variety of theories to interpret the material in chs. 1–3. While most proposals have their individual features, discussion has focussed primarily on three basic issues: the nature or type of the reports in chs. 1 and 3, the character or status of Gomer, and the relation between the events in the biographical report (ch. 1) and the autobiographical one (ch. 3). Some have contended that either one or both of the narratives are allegorical, though most modern studies take them as accounts of real events in Hosea's life. Concerning Gomer's character or status it has been argued that 'woman of harlotry' (1.2) is simply a symbolic description designating Gomer as a member of an apostate people; that the term is proleptic, describing her in terms of what she later became; that she was a common prostitute, or a temple prostitute, or a woman whose virginity had been offered to the deity in the cult. Of the relation of the events recounted in the two reports it has been said that chs. 1 and 3 are parallel accounts of the same event taken from different sources; that the woman in ch. 3 is another person, not Gomer; that the narratives are to be read in sequence as different stages of Hosea's relation to Gomer. For a discussion of all the proposals with bibliography, see H. H. Rowley, 'The Marriage of Hosea', *BJRL* 39, 1956–7, pp. 200–33 (reprinted in *Men of God*, 1963, pp. 66–97); and the more recent bibliography in BK[2], p. 6.

narrative. Modern questions formed out of legitimate curiosity about just what happened are frustrated and will never be answered with final certainty because the data are missing.

The events in the story belong to the earliest phase of Hosea's prophetic activity. His public appearance as a spokesman for Yahweh began with his marriage to Gomer (cf. the comment on 2a below). The announcement of judgment against the dynasty of Jehu presupposes that Jeroboam II (died 746) or at least his son Zechariah, who only reigned six months, was king of Israel. The entire sequence of events could have covered as little as five years, though the interval between the first and second children is not stated. The third-person style, in contrast to the first person in which ch. 3 is written, suggests that Hosea did not compose the account himself. But it must have been written by a disciple and contemporary who was adept at the formally appropriate style and knew at first hand the facts of Hosea's early career. The motive for its composition doubtless lay in the desire to give an account of this crucial part of Hosea's activity not represented directly by words of his own, and what is equally important, to furnish the setting in Hosea's life which is an indispensable background to the family metaphors in the oracles of ch. 2 and to the report of another prophetic symbolism in ch. 3.

[2a] 'The beginning of Yahweh's speaking through Hosea' is a title introducing the entire narrative of 1.2–9 rather than a temporal clause connected only with the rest of v. 2. MT carefully separates it from the words which follow it with an emphatic device of punctuation, and its syntax best fits this construction. As such, it is the narrator's interpretation of what follows. The marriage and the succession of children mark the opening phase of Hosea's work as a prophet. The story of Hosea and his family is to be told as an instance of Yahweh's speaking *through* him. The narrator excludes with this characterization any proleptic interpretation of the marriage as a normal marital contract which Hosea came to regard as revelation in the light of subsequent experience. The marriage was not a way for Yahweh to speak *to* Hosea but *through* him; it was from the first an enterprise of declaring the revelation of Yahweh, the God of Israel. Thus, the title requires that any hypothesis about Hosea's relation to Gomer satisfy the requirements of public kerygmatic act. No story of a call in the strict sense of Isa. 6; Jer. 1; Ezek. 1–2 has been preserved in the Hosea tradition. All that the title implies is that his first public action in the office of a spokesman for Yahweh was his marriage to Gomer.

[2b] The marriage is an act of obedience to Yahweh's command undertaken to dramatize the divine indictment of Israel. Hosea is to display the predicament of Yahweh in his covenant with Israel by wedding a harlotrous woman! The theme of command and interpretation-word is harlotry (*zānā*), sexual promiscuity, a theme which is a dominant motif in Hosea's oracles (verbs in Qal: 2.5; 3.3; 4.12ff.; 9.1; Hiphil: 4.10, 18; 5.3; nouns: 2.2, 4; 4.12; 5.4; 6.10). The key to its power and poignancy in Hosea's oracles and actions is not his own private life with his wife, but the religious situation of Israel. The foil for Hosea's use of marriage as a model of Yahweh's relation to Israel and of sexual promiscuity as the *leit-motif* of his portrayal of Israel's sin is to be found in the fertility cult of Canaanite religion.[a] The ritual of Canaan's indigenous shrines was devoted to the divinity named Hadad who was customarily called by his epithet Baal (lord, husband, owner). The Baals of the local shrines throughout Canaan were manifestations of this deity. He was the god of the late autumn and winter rain storms upon which the peasant farmer was utterly dependent for water, pasture, and crops. The believer thought of the land as the wife which the god fertilized with rain. The cult was based on sympathetic magic. To anticipate, induce, and participate in Baal's intercourse with earth, sexual rites were used, the *hieros gamos* celebrated in the cult by representative protagonists. The theme of 'harlotry' is a distinctly Yahwist interpretation of Israel's involvement in the cult of Baal. The Canaanite god in his multiple manifestations at local shrines is the male figure in the drama. Israel is cast as a woman lured to give herself to the Baals in return for their gifts through the fertility of the land. Yahweh because of his covenant with Israel becomes the legitimate husband; the rigid exclusivism of the Yahwist faith against every syncretism furnishes the basis for the cry of 'harlotry/adultery'. And of course the cry was more than theological metaphor. The cult of Baal involved both men and women in sexual rites; the men lay with sacred prostitutes, and the women as devotees of Baal possibly made themselves available to male worshippers to receive fertility through the cult (cf. the commentary on 4.13f.). Here metaphor and reality are almost synonymous. It is this cultic environment which furnishes the key to the most likely interpretation of

[a] The interpreter may consult among others: W. F. Albright, *Archaeology and the Religion of Israel*, 4th ed. 1956, pp. 68–94; J. Gray, *The Legacy of Canaan*, 1957; C. H. Gordon, 'Canaanite Mythology' in *Mythologies of the Ancient World*, ed. S. N. Kramer, 1961.

the two expressions 'a woman/wife of harlotry' and 'children of harlotry'. 'Harlotry' ($z^e n\bar{u}n\bar{\imath}m$, a plural of abstraction) denotes a category of person, their class more than their activity. Hosea was to select a woman who was recognizable as harlotrous in the sense of the word in his prophetic vocabulary. She could not have been simply a woman of unknown promiscuous tendencies; that would not serve as conscious obedience to the command. A common prostitute would satisfy the public symbolism, but not as eloquently as one whose sexual promiscuity was a matter of the very harlotry of Israel in the cult of Baal. The more likely category is that of the sacred prostitutes ($q^e d\bar{e}\check{s}\bar{o}t$; cf. 4.14). Such a maiden had played the harlot in the harlotry of Israel! The theory has been advanced that it had become general practice in Israel for young women to offer their virginity to the deity in preparation for marriage, and that Gomer had done so,[a] but serious objections to the hypothesis have been raised[b] which leave it in a precarious position. The 'harlotrous children' are not a brood already belonging to the woman before marriage with Hosea. The abbreviated divine command has the sense: 'Take a harlotrous wife and beget harlotrous children.' The story of the births in vv. 3b–9 fills out that part of the command. That the children are harlotrous has nothing to do with their own character; nothing is made of them except their naming. Rather they are harlotrous because of their mother. Coming from her womb which has been devoted to the cult of Baal, they are religiously the offspring of harlotry. See 'sons of harlotry' in 2.4 as a designation of Israelites and the contextual description of their mother, Israel.

[3] In obedience to the divine command Hosea selected Gomer bath Diblaim for a wife. Since the woman is only named and not described in any way, the assumption is that she fitted the required classification and was a 'woman of harlotry'; apparently Hosea was left to select any individual from the specified group. 'Gomer' appears to be the short form of a theophoric name formed with the verb *gmr*; see Gemariah (Jer. 29.3). The vocalization could be a derogatory transfer of the vowels of *bōšet*, 'shame' (so Rudolph). Diblaim is not found in the OT as a personal name, but it is not likely to be a corruption of the place-name Diblathaim (Num. 33.46; Jer. 48.22) which would be unexpected in the expression 'daughter of –'. The unusual dual form has led to suggestions that the word means

---

[a] H. W. Wolff, BK, pp. 13f.
[b] W. Rudolph, 'Präparierte Jungfrauen', *ZAW* 75, 1963, pp. 65ff.

'fig-cake' (*d*ᵉ*bēlā*) and identifies Gomer as a prostitute who could be
had for the cheap price of two cakes, or that it indicates a cultic
attachment (cf. cakes used in the Ishtar cult, Jer. 7.18). Diblaim is
more likely an intentional corruption of the personal name *Dᵉbalyām*,
a theophoric which contains the name of the Canaanite deity Yam
(so Rudolph). Without hesitation the narrator goes on to report that
a son was born to the couple, and thus moves forward to the second
element of Hosea's assignment, the children of harlotry.

[4] By divine command the newborn son is incorporated into the
prophetic message of his father. A word of God becomes his identity,
so that one cannot call his name without repeating the terse revelation
from Yahweh. The form of vv. 3b and 4 appears in Isa. 8.3f. when
Isaiah's second son is given a similar message-name; cf. also Isa. 7.3.
Jezreel is the name both of the valley-plain between the mountain
ranges of Samaria and Galilee (Josh. 17.16; Judg. 6.33) and of a
town at the valley's southern edge on the north-west spur of Mount
Gilboa, the modern village of *Zerʿīn*. Well known as it was, Jezreel
must have had an enigmatic ring as the name of a child, a tantalizing
opaqueness – it could mean weal or woe! It is a theophoric, meaning
'God sows', an omen of fertility and blessing (cf. 2.22); and the valley
was the site of Gideon's famous victory over the Midianites (Judg.
6–7; cf. 6.33). But the interpretation points in the opposite direction;
the name is a sentence of death upon the dynasty (house) of Jehu and a
portent of the end of kingship (for *mamlᵉkūt* meaning the royal office
instead of realm, cf. I Sam. 15.28; II Sam. 16.3; Jer. 26.1) in Israel.
The expression 'blood(-shed)' of Jezreel evokes ominous historical
memories of incidents in that city which overshadowed and stained
the promise of its name. The city had been a place of violence, murder,
and the shedding of much blood – all of it associated with the machin-
ations of royal politics. The famous Ahab, son of Omri, had a second
palace there (I Kings 21.1), and it was there that his queen Jezebel
plotted the judicial murder of Naboth. When Jehu overthrew the
Omride dynasty, blood ran in its streets as the entire royal court was
assassinated (II Kings 9–10). Now the descendant of Jehu, Jeroboam
II, was to be punished on account of the blood crying out from
Jezreel's soil for revenge. What Israel's rulers had done in being and
becoming king qualified the holder of the kingship as the first to be
condemned in Hosea's message of judgment. Throughout Hosea's
messages the institution of kingship is regarded as a manifestation of
Israel's revolt against Yahweh (3.4; 7.3; 8.4); where Amos announced

the coming death of Jeroboam (Amos 7.9), Hosea foretold the end of kingship itself in Israel – and within decades the prophecy was fulfilled. The blood-bath with which Jehu had baptized his revolt against the Omrides had been instigated by the prophetic guild under Elisha (II Kings 9.1–10). Hosea stands in a tradition which has a different view of kingship and another evaluation of Jehu's 'reform'.

[5] The introductory formula, 'It will happen in that day . . .' (cf. 2.16 and 21) separates this verse from the preceding interpretation of the name Jezreel. In v. 5 Jezreel is the name of the valley-plain instead of a city stained with blood – a place instead of a guilt (cf. 1.11). The subject of the judgment announced in it is the entire nation rather than the king as in v. 4. The verse is probably a Hosea fragment introduced by a redactor into the narrative because of the common catch-word, Jezreel. The burden of this fragment is simply that the military might of Israel would be broken on the famous battle ground of Jezreel's open plain. For 'bow' as a metaphor for military strength cf. Gen. 49.24; I Sam. 2.4. The prophecy was substantially fulfilled in 733 when Tiglath-pileser swept across the entire Galilean territory of Israel and left the state a helpless vassal.[a]

[6] With strict economy in words the narrative moves to the birth of the next child, a daughter; the form of v. 4 is repeated so as to focus attention on the one matter of interest, the symbol-names and their meaning. The failure of the narrative to state explicitly here and in v. 8 that the child was born to Hosea is hardly an implication that the second and third children were the result of Gomer's adultery. The style grows more terse, omitting also the name of Yahweh as subject of 'said'. The names of the children are not constructions of their status, but explicitly applied to the nation. The daughter is to be named 'Unpitied'; in Hebrew the name is a sentence: 'She has found no pity.' The verb (rḥm) means far more than 'to feel sorry for'; it stands for the personal identity with their children which moves parents to tenderness, the helping affection of kinsmen to one another, the compassion of the strong upon the weak. It is the love stirred in the emotions by the need and dependence of another.[b] A daughter called 'Un-cared-for' would be a scandal; every time her name is called it speaks of a child whose father would not play his rightful role. Because she is a prophet's child the scandal would be known to be a word to the people. It is the nation (house) of Israel which is

---

[a] J. Bright, *A History of Israel*, Philadelphia: 1959; London: 1960, p. 257.
[b] Cf. *TWNT* II, p. 477.

left without compassion before their God. The announcement of God's verdict in the interpretation implies that till now Israel has lived in the compassion of God; his feeling for them in the covenant bond has endured all their follies and failures. But now that fatherly indulgence is to be withdrawn. Cf. the similar statement in 2.4, and the reversal of the name in 2.23.

[7] This development of the significance of the name 'Unpitied' into a prophecy of salvation for Judah is certainly a secondary expansion of the narrative. 'Yahweh's withdrawal of his compassion applies only to the northern kingdom,' comments this editor who is concerned that the harsh word to Israel be read correctly and in the light of the later unfolding of the salvation-history. The emphasis on divine intervention apart from any military defence points to the marvellous escape of Jerusalem from Sennacherib in 701 (cf. II Kings 19.32–37). It was probably added to the Hosea material after that date, but before the fall of Jerusalem at the beginning of the sixth century.

[8] In Israel a child was not weaned until after two or three years, and the occasion was important in the life of the family (Gen. 21.8; I Sam. 1.24). This allusion to the timing of the third child is a touch of the human story behind the account. The name designated for the second son strikes at the foundation of Israel's religion. [9] 'My people' ('ammî) is an expression drawn from the vocabulary of Yahweh's covenant with Israel. The basic relational formula which describes the covenant founded at Sinai is: 'You are my people, and I am your God' (cf. Ex. 6.7; Lev. 26.12; Deut. 26.17ff.; II Sam. 7.24; Jer. 7.23; 11.4; etc.). The name and the sentence which interprets it is an outright declaration by Yahweh that the covenant is no longer in force. In formulating the strict parallelism in the interpretative sentence Hosea uses a verbal form for the divine name which is found only in Ex. 3.14 where the name Yahweh is revealed to Moses. Literally the second member reads 'and I am not your I-AM ('ehyeh)'. The use of this interpretation of the divine name, instead of the expected 'your God', heightens the radical character of the declaration, for it points beyond the formal covenant to the mysterious, powerful person of the I-AM whose being-there was the reality upon which Israel's salvation rested. The shift to second person and the style of direct address is due to the tenacity of terms in a formula fixed in its usage as a declaration addressed to the people. The negative formulation corresponds to a legal action of divorce and opens the way to the sentence at the beginning of the allegory which portrays Yahweh and

Israel as husband and wife (2.2). Just as the customary structure of mutual responsibility in marriage is cancelled by divorce, the entire cultic and legal structure of the people's relation to their God is abolished by Yahweh's declaration. They can no longer expect security and blessing to follow because Yahweh is bound to them by covenant. This does not mean that Yahweh is done with Israel, but now he deals with them as the enforcer of the covenant's curses on those who break it, and as the God who having been betrayed by his 'bride' must find a way beyond 'marriage' to overcome their faithlessness. All the decisions and actions of Yahweh announced by Hosea belong to this situation and lead toward this goal.

3. THE DAY OF JEZREEL: 1.10–2.1 (Heb. 2.1–3)

1 [10]Yet[a] the number of the sons of Israel shall be like the sand of the sea
that can be neither measured nor counted.
[b]In the place where[b] they were called 'You are not my people,'
they shall be called 'sons of the living God'.
[11]The sons of Judah and the sons of Israel shall assemble in unity,
and select one chief for themselves,
and go up from the land.
Yea, great shall be the day of Jezreel!
2 [1]Call your brothers 'My people',
and your sisters 'Pitied'.

In contrast to the judgment and rejection foretold by the names of Hosea's children in 1.2–9, this oracle speaks of a future when Israel's population shall become too numerous to be counted, their relationship to God be reconstituted, the divided north and south reunite, establish one leader over them, go up from the land – all on the day of Jezreel. The description unfolds in the style of rhythmic narration, telling about the events of time quite different from the present; it evokes a picture which faith can contemplate and anticipate in the terrible contrasts of the present. Here neither God nor prophet speaks to the people in direct address, nor is Yahweh specifically named as

[a] In its context the opening *waw* is an adversative, setting vv. 10f. in contrast to 1.2–9.
[b-b] The current preferred translation of *bimqōm 'ašer* is 'instead of' (cf. *KB*, p. 560, 6; *BDB*, p. 880, 7b), but there are no valid parallels for equating the phrase to *taḥat 'ašer*. The problem is contextual; what 'place' could the text have in mind? See the comment.

the actor. In contrast to the usual style of Hosea the piece is woven in an impersonal idiom so as to concentrate on the events themselves as the truly significant revelation. 1.10–2.1 was set in its present position following 1.2–9 by the arranger of chs. 1–3 in accord with his design of alternating the themes of judgment and salvation. The piece seemed appropriate because it contained themes that echoed the symbol-names of Hosea's children; 'not my people' in v. 10 picks up the name of the third child in v. 9 and Jezreel (v. 11) points to v. 4. The direct address in 2.1 sets it apart from the impersonal style of 1.10f. It is probably the composition of the collector who felt that the mention of Jezreel in v. 11 called for the reversal of the other two names from 1.2–9 also; he possibly had 2.23 before him as a model for the addition. Whether 1.10f. is an oracle of Hosea is difficult to say. In style and conception of the drama of salvation, it is without parallels in the book of Hosea. Yet it has many connections with undoubtedly authentic oracles and draws on traditions with which Hosea was at home. If it does not derive from Hosea, it must come from his period and the circles sympathetic to his prophecy. The salvation promised in the oracle presupposes an Israel in desperate circumstances. The people are reduced in number; the covenant is abrogated; Israel and Judah are divided, without a leader, and denied the security and blessing of the promised land. All of these features correspond to elements in Hosea's conception of Yahweh's judgment on Israel; because with Israel's increase they sinned the more, their growth shall cease (4.10; 9.12, 16; 14.1); Yahweh has abrogated the covenant (1.9; 8.1); the hostility between Judah and Israel is the cause of divine wrath (5.8–14); the blessing of the land will be denied them (2.9, 12; 4.3). The events of salvation follow the time of wrath. This picture of hope then offers no easy escape, but rather lifts up the eyes of those who will believe to behold the meaning and purpose of the judgment they suffer. The oracle could have an appropriate setting in the terrible years after 733 when the cruel lash of the Assyrian had already made incurable wounds on the body of Israel.

[1.10] The prediction that the population of Israel would grow until it could not be counted is an assertion that the promise to the patriarchs would overcome even the decimation of judgment. 'The promise to the fathers becomes in the prophet's mouth a new eschatological word of salvation.'[a] A progeny so numerous as to be uncountable is a constant motif of the promise-formulations in Genesis

---

[a] H. W. Wolff, BK, p. 30.

(cf. 13.16; 15.5; 26.24; 28.14; etc.) and the specific comparison 'like the sand of the sea' appears in 32.12 and 22.17. For 'sons of Israel' as a name for the people of the northern kingdom, cf. 3.1, 4, 5 and 4.1. When the divine power of the promise of blessing begins to revive the very existence of the people, it will be apparent that the time of wrath and ruin under the broken covenant is over. The dreadful purpose of Hosea's 'you are not my people' (1.9; 2.23) will have been fulfilled. In its place another better sentence will be legitimate as the title to mark Israel's identity: 'sons of the living God'. The expression is unique in the Old Testament. 'The living God' as an epithet for Yahweh appears only in Josh. 3.10; Pss. 42.2; 84.2. The name (*'ēl ḥay*) may derive from the old oath formula 'as Yahweh lives' (*ḥay YHWH*) and could certainly have been in use by the eighth century. If the passage were a composition of Hosea's disciples in dependence on 1.9, one would expect the alternate name to be 'my people' (*'ammi*). Hosea, who in 11.1 calls Israel the 'son of Yahweh', may well be the creator of the expression 'sons of the living God'. Implicit in the new name is the recognition that the miraculous increase of the population is due to the vitality-giving presence of the true God in whom alone are the sources of life.[a] The unnamed 'place' where the names will be reversed must be Jezreel. It is in Jezreel that disaster comes, disclosing Yahweh's rejection of Israel and its kingship (1.4f.). Appropriately, it will be a great victory at Jezreel (see comment on v. 11) which will manifest Yahweh's resumption of his relation to Israel. The triumph will itself name Israel 'sons of the living God' for it will reveal the renewal of his choice of them.

[1.11] Verse 11 outlines the events which will make up the 'day of Jezreel'. The three separate acts are successive movements in one process, which is best understood as military in character. The old 'all-Israel' ideal of the tribal league lies behind the hope for the future reunion of Israel and Judah. When the two congregate in assembly as one people, the history of discord and warfare belonging to the time of the kings (cf. 5.8ff., 14) will be transcended. There is an implicit polemic against the king in the selection of a chief (*rō'š*) to represent and effect their unity. *Rō'š* as title for leader of the tribes appears only in the non-royal office of Num. 14.4 and Judg. 11.8f. where it is used in a context in which Israel proposes to pick a leader in a military situation. It is a quite neutral term, saying nothing with respect to the

---

[a] Cf. A. R. Johnson, *The Vitality of the Individual in the Thought of Ancient Israel*, 1949, pp. 105ff.

traditional offices that had figured in the history of Israel. The riddle in the picture lies in the sentence 'they shall go up from the land'. In Hosea 'the land' is consistently the territory of Canaan, the good earth given to Israel by Yahweh (cf. 2.21f.; 4.3), and could hardly denote a place of exile from which Israel shall return, as in Ezek. 37.21ff. The locution might mean 'grow up' as plants and be a play on the name 'Jezreel'; in the time when 'God sows' Israel into the land again (as in 2.23) they will grow up like flourishing plants (note 14.5ff.) and fill the land (so most recently Rudolph in KAT). Or the '$\bar{a}l\bar{a}$ min-$h\bar{a}$' $\bar{a}re\d{s}$ could mean 'gain ascendancy over the land'.[a] In this context the last is the more likely. The picture is military in flavour, and such a construction leads directly to the final triumphant shout: 'Yea, great is the day of Jezreel!' The best analogy for understanding 'day of Jezreel' is the similar phrase, 'day of Midian', in Isa. 9.4 where the glorious victory of Judg. 7.15–25 is invoked to show what the coming overthrow of Judah's enemies will be like. The day of Jezreel is the day when Israel will regain the promised land in a decisive battle against those who have occupied it (the Assyrians by 733 had brought most of the territory under their imperial administration) as a counterpart to the end of the kingdom in the valley of Jezreel (1.4f.). One might have expected the expression 'day of Yahweh', but in the contemporary piety of Israel, the conception was too beclouded with cultic associations (cf. 9.5) and corrupted by popular nationalistic hopes[b] to be useful in this oracle.

This, then, is the fascinating picture held up before the eyes of expiring Israel to lead their vision beyond the débâcle which their own failure had created. Beyond judgment, the promise to the fathers shall once again work in the body of the people to multiply them with a vitality which demonstrates that they are sons of the God who lives! As one people with one head they shall again possess the land. It is not said in so many words that Yahweh will be the one who is active in all this. But the events are so patently a resumption of the old normative history of Israel's beginnings in which Yahweh was the one at work as to leave no doubt. What once was through him, will be again. The narrative concentrates on the events themselves because in them Yahweh is manifest. To anticipate them in faith is in fact to await the personal act of Israel's God in the midst of his people.

[a] Cf. *KB*, p. 705, 4, and JPS *Torah* (A New Translation . . . according to the Massoretic Text: First Section), 1962, on Ex. 1.10.
[b] See J. L. Mays, *Amos* (OTL), 1969, pp. 103f., on Amos 5.18–20.

[2.1] The imperatives of the attached verse call upon Israel to reverse the symbolic names of judgment ('Unpitied' in 1.6 and 'Not-my-people' in 1.9) so that they became confessions that salvation will occur. In the light of what will happen on the day of Jezreel, the beleaguered folk can call one another (note the plural 'sisters' and 'brothers') the people of Yahweh to whom he will show his compassion. The eschatological renewal (2.23) must be anticipated in the very speech of the people who are to know one another in terms of what they yet shall be.

4. YAHWEH AND HIS WIFE: 2.2–15 (Heb. 2.4–17)

2 ²'Accuse your mother! Make complaint
    that she is not my wife,
    and I am not her husband.
  Let her remove her harlot's marks from her face
    and her signs of adultery from between her breasts.
 ³Otherwise I will strip her naked,
    and leave her as she was at birth;
  I will make her like the wilderness,
    change her to arid land
    and slay her with thirst.
 ⁴On her children I will have no pity,
    because they are children of harlotry.
 ⁵For their mother has played the harlot;
    she who conceived them has disgraced herself.
  Yea, she said, "I will go
    after my lovers,
  who give me my food and water,
    my wool and my flax,
    my oil and my drink."

 ⁶Therefore, behold, I will bar her ᵃ way with a thorn-hedge,
    cast up a stone wall before her,
    that she may not find her paths.
 ⁷She shall chase after her lovers
    and not catch them,
    seek and not find them.
  She shall say:
  "I will go return
    to my first husband,
  for I was better off then than now."

    ᵃ Reading with G; MT has 'your (sing.) way'.

⁸But she does not acknowledge
   that it is I who gave her
   the grain and the wine and the oil,
and lavished silver upon her,
   and gold which they made into Baal.
⁹Therefore I will take back my grain at its time
   and my wine in its season.
I will snatch away my wool and my flax,
   given to cover her nakedness.
¹⁰Now I will expose her shame
   in the sight of her lovers,
   and no one shall snatch her from my hand.
¹¹I will halt her merry-making,
   her feasts, her new moons, her sabbaths,
   and all her festal assemblies.
¹²I will ravage her vines and fig trees
   of which she said,
"These are my harlot's fee
   that my lovers gave to me."
I will turn them into a forest,
   and wild beasts shall devour them.
¹³I will call her to account for the feast days of the Baals
   on which she burned offerings to them,
decked herself with rings and ornaments,
   and went after her lovers.
But me she has forgotten!'
   a saying of Yahweh.

¹⁴'Therefore, behold I will entice her,
   take her into the wilderness,
   and speak wooing words to her.
¹⁵I will give to her her vineyards from there,
   and the valley of Achor as a door of hope.
She shall answer there as in the days of her youth,
   as in the time when she went up from the land of Egypt.'

At the very beginning of this rather long speech a husband appears
as plaintiff against his wife, and thereby two dominant features of
the piece are established. It is composed as an allegory with individual characters representing the situation of Yahweh with his people.
The style of the speech has been drawn from the court so that the
words are heard as those of a man engaged in legal proceedings. The
entire sequence is cast as an allegory about a husband, his wife, their
children, and the illicit lovers of the wife and mother. The husband
(vv. 2, 7) stands for Yahweh; the wife represents the corporate people
Israel, who at times are spoken of as though they were the land (v. 3);

the children have an even more fluid role, being individual Israelites over against the corporate nation (v. 2) and yet identified with the national guilt (v. 4); the lovers (vv. 5, 7, 10) are the Baals (v. 13), the gods of Canaan. The passage begins in the form of a legal proceeding by a husband against his adulterous wife. The children are invited to enter the litigation in hope of reforming their mother. It becomes apparent at once that the proceeding is held, not for the sake of divorce, but reconciliation. The fact that the 'husband' always speaks about the wife as though to a third party, and never directly to her, is part of the legal style; the court is being addressed. Along the way the style is used as clothing for indictments of guilt and announcements of punishment in the more usual prophetic fashion. Yahweh begins as plaintiff and shifts to judge. The daring freedom with which Hosea portrays Yahweh as a wronged husband who seeks to recover his wife must be related to the divine command to use his own marriage as a prophetic symbolism of God's dilemma in the face of Israel's 'harlotry' (1.2–9). The life-setting from which the details of the allegory's drama derive is the Canaanized cult of Israel; line by line the purpose and practices of the fertility religion of the Baals is presupposed. The speech must have been delivered in the earliest phase of Hosea's ministry during the final years of Jeroboam II. Abundant prosperity (vv. 5, 8) and a confident cult (vv. 11, 13) point to prosperous, untroubled times.

The style, form and subject of 2.2–15 set the speech apart from its literary context. It obviously does not continue the salvation oracle in 1.10–2.1; the temporal formula and direct address of 2.16 mark the opening of a new oral unit. But was this long, stylistically coherent sequence an original oral unit itself? The internal evidence is ambiguous. The entire sequence is held together by the dependence of the repeated pronoun 'her' on its antecedent 'mother' which appears at the beginning (v. 2). 'Mother' occurs once more in v. 5, but in this instance 'their mother' depends on 'her children' in v. 4 which in turn points back to v. 2. Any division of the sequence into smaller units creates fragments which presuppose the very context from which they are separated. Yet, within the progress of the whole there is a repeated circular movement from Israel's sin to Yahweh's proposed action which raises a question whether 2.2–15 is a rhetorical unit. Three times over, the 'therefore' used in prophetic oracles to introduce an announcement of punishment appears (vv. 6, 9, 14); normally, 'therefore' plus a prediction of what Yahweh will do concludes an oracular unit. The oracle formula at the end of v. 13 is not necessarily concluding; it is also used as an internal formula. The 'therefore' sections (vv. 6f., 9–13, 14f.) do not set forth a coherent sequence of events that follow one another logically. A more rational order of Yahweh's acts is created by placing vv. 6f. after v. 13, an expedient often adopted. The movement of thought would then proceed from outright punishment (vv. 9–13) to an action which marks a change of heart in Israel (vv. 6f.) and then to the climax of Yahweh's winning the people back (vv. 14f.). This rearrangement brings together vv. 5 and 8 with their common list of the produce of the land. But v. 7 with its 'Then she will say, "I will go . . ."' would then be separated from its counterpart in v. 5: 'For she said, "I will go. . . ."' Nor is the problem of the original unity answered by massing all the 'therefore' sections at the end. The best explanation of this ambiguity of structure is the assumption that Hosea or a disciple took oracles in which he had employed the same allegory and had drawn on the same background for the form of his language and wove them into this now inseparable fabric to fashion a kerygmatic unity (H. W. Wolff).

[2] The speech opens with imperatives which summon children to bring a complaint against their mother. The father speaks. Strife and division have broken out in a family – and the family is the household of God! Since there is no preparation for the roles introduced, the speech seems to presuppose that the prophetic symbolism used in 1.2–9 is widely known. The children are the individual members of Israel, which is represented by the mother as a corporate person; the individual and collective ways of thinking are juxtaposed to create flexibility in the allegory. 'Accuse' (*rib b-*; Jer. 25.31; Judg. 6.32; Gen. 31.36) means to attack with protests, raise complaints, a speaking which calls one to account as was done by the plaintiff in the informal legal situations in the village courts.[a] The specific complaint (*rib* as noun) is cited: 'she is not my wife and I am not her husband.' This sentence has been identified as a declaration of divorce,[b] but corroborating evidence for the identification from Old Testament times in Israel is lacking. In the context a declaration of divorce as the basis or purpose of the trial would make little sense; the purpose of the

[a] Among others see B. Gemser, 'The *Rib-* or Controversy-Pattern in Hebrew Mentality', in *Wisdom in Israel and the Ancient Near East*: Essays presented to H. H. Rowley (VTS III), 1955, p. 129; J. Harvey, 'Le "*Rib*-Pattern"', *Bibl.* 43, 1962, pp. 172ff.

[b] E.g. R. de Vaux, *Ancient Israel*, ET, 1961, p. 35.

proceedings is to regain the wife (cf. the following jussive, 'Let her remove . . .', and vv. 7, 14f.), who according to the complaint is not fulfilling her duties as wife and has taken lovers in the husband's place.[a] The complaint corresponds in form to the declaration that the Israel-Yahweh covenant was broken (1.9) and shows that the marriage represents the covenant. The use of marriage as an analogy for the covenant provides a concentrated emphasis on the personal dimension, on the relation itself, which transcends the cultic and legal. This husband is not preoccupied with his legal rights to separation or the punishment of his guilty wife. He wants her back. He demands that the wife strip from herself the embellishments of her unfaithfulness as a sign that she forswears her desertion. Let her take off her 'harlot-marks' and 'adultery-signs'. 'Harlot-marks' and 'adultery-signs' (abstract plurals in Hebrew) are probably pejorative names for jewelry worn in the Baal cult (cf. v. 13). The wife's adultery is in fact the cult of Baal. The wife can put it away from her, if she only will!

[3] The appeal for reform is followed by dire warning. If the wife will not strip away her adultery, then Yahweh will punish her in a way befitting her crime (Ezek. 16.36ff.; Nahum 3.5ff.). Now the plaintiff becomes the one who punishes, for in the legal speech as the prophets employ it, Yahweh plays all the roles. Clothing the wife was the legal duty of the husband (Ex. 21.10). If the woman persists, Yahweh will withdraw his support. Since the wool and flax of the land came from him (v. 9), he can by removing them leave Israel exposed. Ezekiel in his expansive allegory of Yahweh and the maid Israel (Ezek. 16) develops the themes of nakedness at birth, clothing by Yahweh, and exposure to shame because of sin. 'To be stripped like a prostitute' is a theme which appears in the treaty-curse tradition of the Ancient Near East; the threat may have overtones of punishment for covenant breaking.[b] In the second line the wife is now the land (cf. 4.1) and her stripping is the drought that renders it infertile, bare, dead. Again the Canaanite cult is in the background, for in it the land was considered the female to be fertilized by the rain of Baal. Yahweh's drought exposes the vanity of the whole religion.

[4] The children who were party to the conviction of their mother

[a] See the discussion by Rudolph, KAT, p. 65.
[b] See D. R. Hillers, *Treaty-Curses and the Old Testament Prophets* (BO 16), 1964, pp. 58ff.

are now declared to be involved in her guilt. The shift may be due to the plastic possibilities of the imagery or hint that a now invisible seam in the garment of this speech has been crossed, or reflect the assumption that the children fail to respond to the father's summons to join him in the trial. Children of harlotry (cf. 1.2) means the status of offspring born of a harlot, as v. 5 clearly implies. In acting shamefully their mother conceived them. When corporate Israel turned to Baal, the Israelites became children of that union, and no longer the son of Yahweh (11.1). The warning that Yahweh will not pity them is a statement of the motif in Hosea's daughter's symbolical name (1.6), and yet one more clue to how much chs. 1 and 2 are woven of the same fabric.

[5] Now the guilt of the mother is finally stated in bold terms; she has played the harlot and disgraced herself. Her very words are quoted and put in evidence as testimony to her crime. The implication of the quoted resolution 'I will go . . .' is that Israel's turn to the Baal cult (cf. Deut. 4.3) is blatant, bold and wilful. What a whore is this Israel! She does not wait for customers like the ordinary prostitute, but pursues her lovers anxiously. The 'lovers' are the Baals (v. 13), the Canaanite gods of the fertility cult. The word 'lovers' appears only in Hosea, Jeremiah and Ezekiel; the latter two clearly adopt it from Hosea and always use it in the same way as a term for substitutes for Yahweh. The term picks up and plays on the sexual aspect of Canaanite ritual (see the commentary on 4.13f.). The agricultural focus of the Baal cult emerges in their description as givers of the land's produce, which is categorized in three pairs: food and water (basic nourishment), wool and flax (materials for clothing), and oil and drink (the pleasant luxuries of the good life). The basic motivation for Israel's adoption of the Baal cult is anxiety to obtain from the land what was needed to sustain life and make it pleasant. The guilt is not in the desire nor is the problem that Israel is materialistic. The emphasis of guilt is on the 'ones who gave' – that Israel thought the Baals were the source of what she needed (cf. v. 8).

[6] 'Therefore' leads into the first of the three announcements by Yahweh concerning the measures he will take against his wife's adultery. In the present form of the material, the action described is a direct response to the conduct of Israel in v. 5. With what grace the husband will act, even in his severity! It is not the death penalty, but the end of the wife's sin that is proclaimed. Israel will be shut up by a woven hedge of thorns, blocked from the way she goes with a wall of

piled-up stones – as though she were a wandering animal that must be kept at home and out of the fields by fences. Cf. the metaphors for Israel in 8.9; 4.16; Jer. 2.23–25. The way and paths represent figuratively the possibility of maintaining the Baal cult. The idea is not that Israel will literally be barred from the shrines, but rather will find their ritual brings no result (cf. vv. 11ff.).

[7] Pursuing her lovers and seeking them depicts a people become frantic in their ritual because the expected result does not appear. 'Pursue' (Piel of *rdp*) means an avid determined chase. 'Seek' is a technical term for shrine visitation in 5.6, 15, where it is said that the same futility will overtake the cult devoted to Yahweh; the similarity may be a clue to the syncretistic religious situation in which Yahweh was called Baal (2.16) and worshipped with Canaanite ritual. The failure to make 'personal' contact with the deity is simply the absence of his agricultural gifts. When devotion to the Baals becomes fruitless, the people will reverse their earlier commitment (v. 5). When they have lost what they once had, like the prodigal son they will take a second thought. Life with their former husband (the covenant with Yahweh) was better than being a harlot to Baal. Everything for the people turns around the good things of the land. But Yahweh does not boggle at using this earthy material concern to bring the people back to him. Just as he gave the good things of the land as the blessing of the covenant, he will remove them for the sake of restoring the relation with Israel. With Yahweh it is the people's personal relation to him that is the sole concern. 'Return' means to enter once again into the original relation to Yahweh, the prophetic sense of what we call repentance. In the divine husband's dealing with his 'wife' he rises above his legal rights (Deut. 24.1ff.). He could give her a bill of divorce and forget her. He could execute her as an adulteress. But instead he seeks only a reconciliation. The connection of God's act in vv. 6f. with the further development in vv. 14f. and with the symbolic action of the prophet in ch. 3 is apparent.

[8] Verse 8 resumes the description of the wife's sin which the actions of Yahweh iterated in vv. 9–13 are concerned to correct. The opening 'But she does not acknowledge that it was I . . .' is echoed in the climactic anguish of 'But me she forgot' at the end of v. 13. The charge that Israel does not acknowledge that Yahweh is the giver of grain, wine, and oil shows that Hosea speaks from within a tradition which had always attributed the good things of the land to Yahweh. The ancient ritual of first-fruits recounted in Deut. 26 is an early

testimony to that theology. In the ceremony, Yahweh is hailed repeatedly as the *giver* of the land and its produce (Deut. 26.1, 2, 3, 9, 10, 11). The worshipper concludes with the presentation sentence: 'Behold, now I present the ground's first-fruit which you, Yahweh, have *given* me.' In the recitation of the worshipper, the gift of the land is connected directly with the history of saving events (Deut. 26.5–9). The blessings of agricultural life are viewed as the continuation of Yahweh's action in history on Israel's behalf. It is from this theology that the profound conflict between the 'lovers who gave' and 'Yahweh who gives' derives. Israel's turning to the Baals as the source of the land's produce was not merely a matter of divided loyalty. It was a denial of the whole Yahwist theology and the frustration of the contemporaneity of Yahweh's ongoing history with his people – a failure to acknowledge Yahweh himself. The trilogy of 'grain, and wine and oil' is a traditional and stereotyped formula for the land's bounty. In the poem of Keret,[a] 'sweet rain' from Baal is anticipated because grain, wine, and oil have dwindled; and in Deut. 7.13; 11.14; etc., the trilogy is the gift of Yahweh as covenant blessing. The abundance of silver is a sign of the economic prosperity in the time of Jeroboam II when trade flourished to the profit of the urban classes (cf. Amos 8.4ff.; 6.4ff.). 'Which they made into Baal' contains two surprises in the context: the third-person plural verb departing from the consistent third feminine singular, and the singular Baal in contrast to Hosea's usual plural (2.13, 17). Making images from precious metal is mentioned in 8.4 and 13.2, which may have influenced a glossator who added the relative clause (so BK). Neither silver nor gold is again mentioned in the depriving action of Yahweh in the rest of the saying.

[9] 'Therefore' introduces the second announcement of Yahweh's decision concerning his response to Israel's failure. Yahweh will assault Israel's worship of the Baals with deprivations which destroy the relation root and branch (9–13). Grain and wine point back to v. 8, wool and flax to v. 5. The repeated possessives (*my* grain . . . *my* oil . . ., etc.) iterate a vehement polemic against the basic assumption of Baal worship. The harvest seasons, which reached a climax in a festival, would bring no grapes or olives. Though no specific instrument of deprivation is mentioned, drought is probably in view (v. 3). It was the duty of a husband to clothe his wife; the wool and flax of Canaan were Yahweh's provision for his wife's decency. [10] Stripped

[a] *ANET*, p. 148.

and left naked (v. 3) the wife will stand exposed to public gaze, seen as a woman whose husband shames her in her folly. Her lovers will stand by helpless, unable to give to their mistress the very things which she sought from them. Yahweh's power over nature is total and in its grasp it will appear in whose hand Israel has actually been all along.

[11] The religious festivals of Israel were the crucial scandal because it was in their celebration that the people sought the Baals, i.e., in the language of the allegory, the wife chased her lovers. Hosea looks on their festive mirth with disgust, for this merriment had the sound of the tittering revelry of stolen love. *Feast* (*ḥag*) is the term for the three annual pilgrimage festivals which were co-ordinated with the periods of the agricultural year (Ex. 23.14–17; 34.18–23). *New moon* (*ḥōdeš*) was celebrated at the beginning of the lunar month and in its early form may have included fertility rites.[a] *Sabbath* was the weekly rest from labour (Ex. 23.12; 34.21); in Amos 8.5 it is also mentioned with New Moon as a feast celebrated in Jeroboam's Israel.[b] Yahweh will cancel this entire cultic calendar! Seasonal, monthly, and weekly celebrations will end, every festal assembly (*mō'ēd*). Long before the eighth century all these festivals and days had been established as times to worship Yahweh. But Hosea reckons them as 'feast days of the Baals' (v. 13). The possessive 'her' repeated after each festival emphasizes that they now belonged, not to Yahweh, but to Israel in her own mad pursuit of the gods of fertility. Note the same device of emphasis in Amos 5.21–23. Whether the pagan quality of the northern kingdom's celebration of these festivals lay in an outright worship of the Canaanite gods, or manifested itself in a syncretism in which Yahweh was called Baal (v. 16), was worshipped with fertility rites, and was more and more conceived as Baal – the cult was none the less a forgetting of Yahweh. In it HE was not known.

[12] The harlot's fee (*'etnā*; elsewhere in OT *'etnan*) is a gift to a prostitute in return for her service. The use of such a fee to pay vows to the deity was forbidden in the Yahweh cult (Deut. 23.18) in line with its strict exclusion of any sexual motif or ritual. Because the Israelites think the grapes and figs are a result of the fertility rites in the shrines, Hosea, with a quotation put in Israel's mouth, discloses how the prohibited thing has become the very goal of cult (cf. 9.1; Micah 1.7; Ezek. 16.30ff.). Since the ritual was overtly sexual in

[a] See H.-J. Kraus, *Worship in Israel*, 1966, pp. 76ff.
[b] See J. L. Mays, *Amos*, 1969, *ad loc.*

conception, some such thing might have been said at the shrines. What Yahweh gave as his blessing under covenant, expecting only thanksgiving and confession in return, Israel thought it necessary to purchase through a ritual of sympathetic magic. Under the influence of Canaanite myth, Israel could think of Baal as giving grapes and figs, but when they are denied and the gardens abandoned as useless to grow up in thickets and become lairs for wild beasts – who then is at work? The deprivations are the characteristic work of Yahweh's wrath (cf. Isa. 5.5; 7.23ff.; 32.12f.; Amos 4.9).

[13] The cult of Baal is Israel's harlotry. 'Reckon with' (*pāqad 'al . . .*) is 'a specific way in which God reacts to guilt that presupposes a relationship of responsibility' (4.9; 8.13; 9.7, 9; 12.2; BK, p. 48). Feast-days (literally 'days of . . .'; cf. 'day of Yahweh' in 9.5) of the Baals includes all the cultic celebrations listed in v. 11. What Israel did in the cult is outlined in v. 13b. To burn offerings (Piel of *qṭr*) refers to the sacrifice consumed by fire and sent up in smoke to the deity (4.13; 11.2 in parallel to *zbḥ*). The rings for nose and ear and other 'ornamentation' (the word occurs only here) had cultic significance of some symbolic function (Gen. 35.4; Ex. 32.2); here the cultic and allegorical blend as the harlot dresses up to follow her lovers, perhaps an allusion to ritual processions in which the people follow a cult object around and into the shrine. The explanation for Hosea's use of the plural, Baals, is disputed; the plural appears also in 2.17 and 11.2. It corresponds in 2.2–15 to the plural 'lovers', but a multiplicity of lovers is not required by the allegory, so it must derive from the cultic situation in Israel as Hosea saw it. In the OT the proper name Baal is used with a variety of epithets to identify the deity worshipped at a particular shrine: Baal of Peor (Num. 25.3), Baal Berith (Judg. 8.33), the Baal of Samaria (I Kings 16.32), Baal of Carmel (I Kings 18.19ff.), Baal of Hermon (Judg. 3.3). What is known of the god Baal from the texts of Ugarit[a] precludes the conclusion that all these names stand for local deities, limited to the sphere of the region which their shrine served. They were all manifestations and representations of the one high god. But Hosea, watching Israel go to the many shrines, would have thought of them as individual. The concluding 'But me she has forgotten!' mingles anger and anguish, accusation and appeal; it summarizes in a word the guilt of Israel and the problem of Yahweh. In Hosea's vocabulary 'forget' is the opposite of 'know= acknowledge'; it means the betrayal of

[a] See J. Gray, 'Baal', *IDB* I, pp. 328f.

Yahweh's relation to Israel established in his saving history (14.4–6) and his instruction (4.6), no longer paying attention to Yahweh as he was revealed. And this particular way of putting the problem between Yahweh and Israel opens on vv. 14f. in which Yahweh seeks to capture the attention of his people. For other instances of the oracle formula, 'a saying of Yahweh', (ne'ūm YHWH) cf. 2.16, 21; 11.1.

[14] For the third time 'therefore . . .' introduces the announcement of what Yahweh will do in response to Israel's desertion; this time he promises to assume himself the responsibility for the reconciliation of his faithless wife. Not only will he strip from her the imagined benefits of her harlotry (vv. 9–13) and disrupt her pursuit of her lovers, so that she begins to take thought of her first husband (vv. 6f.); he himself will do what is necessary to restore the original relationship. There is no logical line of continuity between the three sections which allows for the reconstruction of a clear programme of what was to happen. Each is a refraction of Hosea's message of God's love, related to the other only through the middle term of his knowledge that God would not let this people go. Yet this third announcement fulfils and completes the other two and brings to consummation the pleading with which the sequence opened (v. 2). The language is daring. The allegory continues as Yahweh becomes a husband who sets out to win back the love of a woman he has lost. 'Entice' means to persuade irresistibly, to overwhelm the resistance and will of another. The verb is used for the seduction of a virgin (Ex. 22.16) and for the divine constraint which holds a prophet powerless (Jer. 20.7). Like a lover who plots to be alone with his beloved, Yahweh will take the woman into the wilderness. 'Wilderness' is more than a place; it is a time and situation in which the pristine relation between God and people was untarnished and Israel depended utterly on Yahweh (cf. 13.4f.). Hosea is not the advocate of a nomadic ideal with a simple nostalgia for life away from the agricultural civilization of Palestine. As a place, the wilderness is bare and threatening (v. 3) but as an epoch in the history of God and Israel it represents a point of new beginning (cf. Jer. 2.1–3). In the wilderness Yahweh will 'make love' to Israel; the expression is literally 'speak to her heart', and we can feel its proper context in the speech of courtship by looking at its use in the talk of a man to a woman whose love he seeks (Gen. 34.3; Ruth 2.13; Judg. 19.3). Measured against Yahwism's studied aversion for speaking of God in any sexual terms, the picture is astonishing. Yet precisely at this point the allegory is not to be taken lightly. For it is

in this daring kind of portrayal that the passion of God becomes visible – a passion that does not hesitate at any condescension or hold back from any act for the sake of the beloved elect.

[15] The rendezvous in the wilderness is to be kept as the first movement in a recapitulation of the old normative salvation-history. The land is not forsaken, but taken away so that Israel may receive it once again as the gift of Yahweh and in its possession know the giver. 'Her vineyards' are those that once belonged to her and will again be hers as the wife of Yahweh. 'From there' indicates the directional orientation of the drama, Israel coming again from the wilderness on the east into the promised land. As though he were a bridegroom bringing his bride to her new home, Yahweh will make the 'Emek Achor a door of hope, an entry into a life of promise, a future unlimited by the painful past. The valley-plain of Achor (Josh. 7.24, 26; 15.7) is the modern el-Buqe'ah leading up from the Jordan plain south-west of Jericho.[a] The name probably appealed to Hosea because of its meaning: 'Valley of trouble'; it gave him the opportunity for a word-play on a name: 'the Valley of trouble is made the door of hope' – a favourite device of the prophet (cf. 1.4–9; 2.16, 22). Israel's response is described only after the saving gifts and acts of Yahweh, because this move from the wife's side is the consummation of the entire sequence. 'Answer' transcends the verbal to incorporate all the dimensions that go into personal rapport. She will succumb to Yahweh's wooing. The harmony of the first days of her history with him will reappear. Once again she will be a fresh, chaste 'girl', the Exodus behind, the land of promise beckoning, and Yahweh by her side. The original time will become the final time. Israel had worshipped the Baals to renew nature; but she shall find her true salvation in the God who shall renew her saving history.

5. THE DAY OF RESTORATION: 2.16–23 (Heb. 2.18–25)

2 16'It will come about in that day,' a saying of Yahweh,
    'that you will call (me) "my husband"';
    you will call me "my Baal" no more.
17I will take the names of the Baals from her mouth,
    and they will be invoked by their name no more.

[a] F. M. Cross and J. T. Milik, 'Explorations in the Judean Buqē'ah', *BASOR* 142, 1956, pp. 5–17.

[18]I will make a covenant for them, in that day, with the beasts of the
field,
and with the birds of the heavens and the crawling-things of the
earth.
Bow and sword and (weapons of) war[a]
I will break from the land,
and give them rest in security.
[19]I will betroth you to me forever.
I will betroth you to me with righteousness
and justice and devotion and compassion.
[20]I will betroth you to me with faithfulness
so that you shall know Yahweh.'
[21]'It will come about in that day
that I will answer,' a saying of Yahweh.
'I will answer the heavens,
and they will answer the land;
[22]the land will answer the grain and must and oil;
and they will answer Jezreel.
[23]I will sow her for myself in the land;
I will have pity on Unpitied;
I will say to Not-my-people "You are my people",
and he will say "My God".'

In these verses the prophet as spokesman for Yahweh recounts
what will take place in the time of salvation. By promise (where
Israel is addressed in the second person) and announcement (where
Israel is referred to in the third person) the portrayal of Yahweh's
historical relationship with Israel is extended beyond that crucial
turning point when the apostasy of the people is healed by the divine
chastisement (2.7, 15; 3.5). The themes and metaphors formulated
in ch. 1 and in 2.2–15 reappear: the allegory of Israel as wife and
Yahweh as husband, the analogy of covenant and marriage, the
problem of the Baals, the fertility of the land, and the symbolic
names of the children. The material appears to be a collection of sayings rather than one continuous unit of speech. There is a successive
transition from one subject and metaphor to another: the end of any
relation to the Baals (vv. 16f.), peace with nature and safety from
enemies (v. 18), the betrothal of God and his bride (vv. 19f.), revival
of the land's fertility (vv. 21f.), reversal of the symbolic names of
judgment (v. 23). The material is punctuated three times by the
eschatological formula 'it will occur in that day' (vv. 16, 18, 21), and

[a] 'War' (*milḥāmā*) stands by metonymy for 'weapons of war'; perhaps also in
1.7; cf. M. Dahood, *Psalms II, 51–100*, 1968, p. 218.

twice with the oracle formula 'a saying of Yahweh' (vv. 16, 21). There is a rapid change in the personal pronouns referring to Israel: 'you' (second fem. sing.) in v. 16, 'her' in v. 17, 'them' in v. 18, 'you' again in vv. 19f., and 'her' in v. 23. The Septuagint is somewhat more consistent in the pronouns in its text, but this is probably the result of a smoothing out to achieve continuity in translation. In Hosea the shift of pronouns cannot be taken as a sure guide to the composite character of material, but the frequency of the change here is remarkable. The section seems to be a closely knit collection of salvation prophecies gathered and ordered because they all have connections with the themes of chs. 1–2 and placed at the end of 2.2–15 to furnish a complete picture of the way in which Yahweh will lead Israel from her sin through judgment to a new beginning. The skilful way in which the material is ordered to accomplish this purpose suggests that the work was done by a contemporary disciple of Hosea, if not by the prophet himself. The inner connection of the material in every verse with the rest of Hosea's prophecy leaves no reasonable basis for doubting that the sayings are his. The historical setting can be determined only within approximate limits. Verse 23 presupposes the family history of ch. 1, so at least five years have elapsed since the beginning of Hosea's public activity. Such messages would be more credible after the undisturbed peace of the reign of Jeroboam II had been replaced by the following years of political instability and national decay. Verse 18 could take its point of departure from the calamity of the successful campaign by the Assyrians through Israel's heartland in 733. But if 2.6f., 14f. are closely connected in time with the rest of 2.2–13, then one does not have to come too far down in the development of Hosea's message to locate a possible setting for such material.

[16] In the time of renewal Israel will neither confuse Yahweh with Baal nor turn to the deities of Canaan. 'In that day' is a formula used to designate the time when Yahweh acts decisively in judgment or salvation; it probably refers to 'the day of Yahweh' which was anticipated in the eschatological piety of the northern kingdom, as we know from Amos 5.18–20. The formula appears in Hosea only in this collection of material (vv. 16, 18, 21) and in the fragmentary oracle of judgment (1.5) inserted in the narrative of ch. 1. The formula 'a saying of Yahweh' is also concentrated here (vv. 13, 16, 21); it appears elsewhere only in 11.11. Both formulae may be contributions of the redactor who arranged the material in chs. 1–3 (so

HAT and BK). Verses 16 and 17 are held together by a common theme, but are separated by a shift in the pronoun used for Israel and by a distinction in the problems with which each deals. Israel is first (16) directly addressed as 'you' (fem. sing.) and then referred to as 'her' (17). Verse 16 is concerned with the use of Baal as an epithet for Yahweh, v. 17 with the cultic service of other gods besides Yahweh. The juxtaposition is the work of the collector. Together the verses announce the total solution of the problem of 'Baal' in the time of salvation. Verse 16 takes up the drama of Yahweh and Israel as husband and wife at the time when judgment has brought the wife to the resolution to return to 'my former husband' (2.7), and at the point when Israel answers Yahweh as in the days of her youth (2.15). The wife will show her change of heart by calling Yahweh *'iš*, instead of *ba'al*. The two Hebrew words are used in a subtle play on meaning which cannot be reproduced directly in English, since both can mean 'husband'. *'iš* is the man who as husband is partner and counterpart of the woman (*'iššā*); cf. particularly Gen. 2.23; 3.6, 16. *Ba'al* comes from a verb which means 'to own' and 'have rights over', and tends to emphasize the husband's legal rights as possessor of the woman (cf. such legal texts as Ex. 21.3, 22; Deut. 22.22; 24.4). The first is the more intimate, personal and total term; it points to the full and unqualified way in which Israel will give herself to Yahweh as to a man who loves, and not merely to a husband to whom she is bound by legal commitment. But Baal is also the name of the primary deity in the fertility cult of Canaan; in the context of Hosea's prophecy a cultic and confessional dimension is certainly involved in the use of the word. The saying clearly presupposes that in Israel Yahweh was called 'Baal'. That the name was in common use among the Israelites in the late eighth century is demonstrated by the ostraca from Samaria which contain theophoric names using both Baal and Yahweh.[a] Whether Baal was employed as an epithet for Yahweh in the sense of 'owner, lord', or as the name of the Caananite deity, is uncertain. Probably both occurred. Where Yahweh was called Baal, a constant and dangerous erosion of the distinctive understanding of Yahweh set in. He was thought of and dealt with cultically more and more as though he were a Baal (cf. 5.6). The exclusion of the epithet Baal in favour of *'iši* represents Israel's return from being 'mistress' to Baal to 'the marriage bond' of covenant.

[a] Cf. *ANET*, p. 321; and W. F. Albright, *Archaeology and the Religion of Israel*, 1956, pp. 160f.

[17] Verse 17 presupposes the outright worship of the gods of Canaan as described in 2.13 and 4.11–14. The plural 'Baals' is Hosea's collective term for the gods of the land. On the plural see the comment on 2.13. To invoke (Niphal of *zkr*) a deity by name was to summon the god in ritual language, to use his name to represent and ensure his presence and participation in the purpose of the ritual.[a] In one of the expansions of the Covenant Code the crucial words of this text appear: 'The *name* of other gods, you shall not *invoke* (Hiphil of *zkr*); it (i.e. the name) shall not be heard from your *mouth*' (Ex. 23.13).[b] Yahweh himself will act so as to bring Israel to the fulfilment of the covenant requirement. The way in which he will remove the names of the Baals is probably to be understood in relation to his disruptive action depicted in 2.6–7, 9–13, where he brings the cult of the Baals to an end by frustrating its purpose. Again, the judgment of Yahweh is a work of creating the situation in which true confession is both possible and inevitable.

[18] Around the reconciled people, Yahweh will create an environment of peace, the manifestation of his blessing. The change in pronouns ('them') and the shift to another subject indicate that the third strand in the tapestry of the composition is reached. The creation of peace affects two spheres. First, Yahweh will make a covenant with all living creatures for the sake of Israel. The particular locution (*kārat bᵉrīt*) appears in 12.1 and 10.4, where covenant means an international 'treaty' made between Israel and another nation. In effect, this *bᵉrīt* is like Ezekiel's 'covenant of peace' (Ezek. 34.25); its reality and substance is the establishment of a relation of harmony between the partners. For a parallel to the procedure in which a third party establishes a treaty between two others, see the Mari letter in which a servant of Zimrilim reports that he has made a covenant of peace between two warring tribes.[c] All living creatures are encompassed in the three spheres of their distinctive habitat (Gen. 1.30; cf. field, sky and sea in 4.3). The covenant reverses the role of the beasts as the instrument of judgment (2.12). Second, Yahweh will eliminate all threat and harm of war so that Israel can live in her land in confidence. Just as he 'broke the bow' of Israel (1.5) in punishment, he will banish all weapons of war which threaten Israel. 'Land' means the place of Israel's residence (1.2; 4.1, 3; 9.3; 10.1), not the whole earth; the

[a] Cf. B. S. Childs, *Memory and Tradition in Israel* (SBT 37), 1962, p. 16.
[b] Cf. M. Noth, *Exodus*, ET (OTL), 1962, *ad loc.*
[c] *ANET*, p. 482.

peace in view is a local affair concerned with Israel, and not the world-wide peace of Isa. 2.1–4. This picture of peace established by Yahweh's action is constructed out of motifs drawn from the traditional stock of blessings and curses used to enforce covenant-treaty arrangements in the ancient Near East.[a] The same motifs appear in Lev. 26 where the blessings and curses that enforce the Yahweh covenant with Israel are listed (cf. vv. 6 for blessing and 22, 25 for curses). The peace is the blessing of the re-established covenant (cf. Ezek. 34.25–28). But the wonder of the time of renewal lies in the fact that Israel does not receive the blessing as a reward for the obedience required in Lev. 26, but as a gift of grace and as a sign that Yahweh himself has brought them again into the covenant.

[19–20] In 19f. the metaphorical situation changes again. Now Yahweh is a man speaking directly to the woman whom he intends to marry; Israel is addressed directly as the woman whom he has chosen with feminine second person singular pronouns. This promise consists of three elements: the finality of the marriage, the bride-price, and the fulfilment of the purpose of the marriage. The thematic verb translated 'betroth' is 'ēraś, which involves more than the sometimes tentative and preliminary matter of becoming engaged in our society. In the customary practice of marriage in Israel 'ēraś is the final step in concluding a marriage and includes the payment by the man of the bride-price which binds the arrangement and commits all concerned; it is the public legal act upon which the validity of the marriage rests so far as society is concerned.[b] Nothing remains but the actual cohabitation. In Deut. 22.23f. a *virgin* that is betrothed ('ēraś) to a man is considered to be already his wife for legal purposes (cf. also Deut. 20.7; Ex. 22.16f.; I Sam. 18.25). In II Sam. 3.14 David says in claiming Michal: 'Give me Michal my wife whom I *betrothed to me* with a hundred foreskins of the Philistines'; the idiom is precisely the same as our text, and shows the finality of the betrothal act. 'Forever' emphasizes the permanency of the commitment; it has the ring of 'as long as we both shall live' in the contemporary marriage service. Whereas the old marriage (i.e., covenant) was violated by Israel and revoked by Yahweh (1.2, 9; 2.2), this future one will endure. Unlike the old conditional covenant of Sinai, the new covenant will be un-

[a] For parallels to both wild beasts and war in treaties from outside Israel, cf. D. R. Hillers, *Treaty-Curses and the Old Testament Prophets* (BO 16), 1964, pp. 54–56, 60.

[b] H. J. Boecker, *Redeformen des Rechtslebens im Alten Testament* (WMANT 14), 1964, pp. 170ff.

conditional. The possibility of such a relationship, in which Yahweh takes upon himself by promise the responsibility for maintaining the covenant, lies in the fivefold list of righteousness, justice, devotion, compassion, and faithfulness. These five concepts are cited in the text as the bride-price with which Yahweh will establish the marriage, and therefore represent attitudes and actions of God. The analogy is not perfect because there is no father to receive the payment. But the analogy does hold in so far as the attitudes and acts of God are what satisfy all the requirements of the marriage-covenant and lead to its consummation. All five of the concepts denote a conduct which is appropriate to a relationship; their function is to describe the normative quality of living in the variety of relations which society provides. In the Old Testament they have been appropriated as the vocabulary in which one speaks of life in the covenant relation between Yahweh and Israel. 'Righteousness' (*ṣedeq*) is used here as in 10.12 to mean the saving help of Yahweh for Israel (cf. Judg. 5.11; Micah 6.5; Jer. 23.6); it is an act whose quality of rightness lies in the fact that it vindicates a relation, Yahweh's election of Israel.[a] 'Justice' (*mišpāṭ*) is the order of rights and claims which belong to a given relation, and also the action to maintain a person in those rights.[b] 'Devotion' (*ḥesed*) is conduct which favours another in accord with the obligations of recognized relationship, especially a covenant.[c] Yahweh's 'compassion' (*raḥªmīm*), which he withdrew in the announcement of the name of Hosea's daughter (1.6), will again be given to Israel; it is active sympathy toward one who stands in a relation of dependence or need. Faithfulness ('*emūnā*) is emphasized by repetition of the verb and its final position; it is the divine reliability and consistency of purpose and character with which Yahweh deals with Israel (cf. 4.1). These concepts represent, on the one hand, what Yahweh had a right to expect from Israel as his covenant people (cf. 4.1; 10.4, 12); on the other hand, they sum up what Israel could look for from its covenant Lord. But Yahweh commits himself to give them as the price of wedding Israel, although the old covenant is broken and finished. It is the promise of a great and unexpected grace. The reality of the concepts will find expression in such actions as those described in 2.6f., 14f., 17; 11.8f.; 14.4–6 where Yahweh overcomes and heals the

---

[a] Cf. W. Eichrodt, *Theology of the Old Testament* I, ET, 1961, pp. 239ff.; G. von Rad, *Theology of the Old Testament* I, ET, 1962, pp. 370ff.
[b] Cf. the commentary on 10.4; and W. Eichrodt, *op. cit.*, pp. 239ff.
[c] Cf. the commentary on 4.1; and N. Glueck, *Ḥesed in the Bible*, 1967.

faithlessness of Israel and renews the old history of the Exodus and wilderness for the sake of restoring his people. As a result of Yahweh's action Israel will 'know' Yahweh. The new salvation-history will reach its consummation. The responsibility of Israel in covenant is no longer presented as a requirement; it has become a promise of the eschatological time. The language of the sentence of consummation lends itself to a construction in terms of the marriage metaphor; 'to know' is one of the biblical terms for the sexual act (Gen. 4.1; 24.16; 38.26). Has Hosea gone so far as to assimilate even the *hieros gamos* to his eschatological drama? Probably not. In the context of the thematic and crucial use which Hosea makes of 'knowledge of God', the expression is best interpreted in terms of its theological meaning. 'To know God/Yahweh' is Hosea's inclusive term for what is expected of Israel as the covenant people. It means the whole response of Israel to the acts and words of Yahweh so that the people is defined in its total life by what Yahweh reveals of himself. (See the discussion of the 'knowledge of God' in the commentary on 4.1.) This portrayal through the metaphor of marriage of Yahweh's new covenant with Israel in which God takes upon himself the responsibility for its integrity and permanence is the forerunner of Jeremiah's new covenant (Jer. 31.31ff.) and the first proclamation of the Church as the eschatological bride of Christ (Eph. 5.23ff.).

[21–22] The eschatological formula 'in that day' introduces yet another motif to describe the time of salvation: Yahweh will initiate the process by which the blessings of a fertile land come again to his people. In this literary complex vv. 21f. have a logical relation to v. 20 in that the action of Yahweh in giving Israel the produce of the land is a means of knowing him (2.8; 13.4–6). The two verses are formulated as an 'oracle of a hearing' in which a priest or prophet announces that an appeal to the deity has been heard and will be answered. The emphatic 'I will answer' presupposes an intercession (I Sam. 7.9; I Kings 18.37; Micah 3.4; Ps. 3.4, etc.); in the immediate context the presupposition points to the response of Israel after trust in the Baals is broken by Yahweh's judgment (2.7, 15, 16). 'Answer' is an action word including the sense of responding to one in need with help (14.9; Isa. 41.17; 49.8). Yahweh's gracious response sets in motion a chain reaction which runs through all the stages in the fertility cycle: deity – heavens (rain) – land (soil) – grain, wine, oil (inclusive of crops, 2.8) – people. The fact that Yahweh's answer comes through these intervening mediators surely has polemical overtones against the fertility cult of Canaan. In its mythology the elements of the natural process were personalized and deified. Here Yahweh pre-empts the entire sphere of the fertility process; the cycle of seasons and the growth of crops is drawn into the covenant relation between Yahweh and Israel. Nature is de-mythologized and made an aspect of the covenant history. Jezreel must be meant as the name of the people since its use as the name of the valley (cf. 1.4f.) is excluded by the appearance of 'land' just before it in the series. But the etymology of the name, 'God sows', furnishes a motif for the entire saying: Israel's God is the source of fertility; and Jezreel takes on the sound of a confessional symbolic name which replaces the meaning of judgment attached to it as the ominous epithet for Hosea's first child.

[23] The final measure of v. 22 is connected with v. 23 because the same verb (zr') appears both in the name Jezreel (yizreʻeʼl) and in 'I will sow'. The pronoun 'her' however presupposes some antecedent such as Israel as wife or mother; and the subject shifts from the renewal of the land's fertility to the reconstitution of Israel's relation with Yahweh. Now the symbolic names of Hosea's children, given originally as a threefold message of Yahweh's judgment (1.4, 6, 9), are reversed and each in its own meaning becomes an announcement of the new covenant (cf. 2.1). The individual children of Hosea are no longer in view, only their names as the interpretation of Israel under judgment. In 1.4f. Jezreel was a place-name recalling the blood-bath which had happened in that city; now with a play on its etymology, it becomes a promise that 'God will sow' Israel into the land, as though he were the farmer and she the seed (cf. the use of zr' in agricultural metaphors in 8.7; 10.12). When God sows, the harvest is sure to be abundant. The people shall enjoy a fertility based on the promise of Yahweh (cf. 1.10; 14.5–7; Jer. 31.27). Once again Israel shall be nurtured and protected by the compassion of God which maintained her in the first fresh days of the wilderness (11.3f.; 'compassion' as a bride-price, 2.19). Yahweh will speak the sentence which designates Israel as his covenant partner: 'You are my people'; and the broken covenant (1.9) will be replaced by a new one. Israel in perfect accord will answer, 'My God!' The exchange is a dialogue between persons in which 'My God' rings forth as both confession and prayer, recognition and trust. And so the portrayal of the goal of Yahweh's coming history passes through judgment to a future which is the past made new, and reaches its climax with a covenant ceremony in which two simply devote themselves totally to each other.

6. THE WAY OF LOVE: 3.1–5

3 ¹Yahweh said to me again:ᵃ

'Go love a woman
    who is lovedᵇ by a paramour and commits adultery,
just as Yahweh loves the Israelites
    even while they turn to other gods
    and love raisin-cakes.'
²So I acquiredᶜ her for myself for fifteen silver (shekels) and
a homer and a lethech of barley. ³And I said to her:
'Many days you shall live as mine.
    You shall not play the harlot nor have a man.
    Even I will not goᵈ in to you.'
⁴For the Israelites shall live many days
    without king and without officer,
without sacrifice and without pillar,
    without ephod or teraphim.
⁵Afterwards the Israelites shall return
    and seek Yahweh their God (and David their king);
    and come in trembling awe to Yahweh and his goodness (at the
                         end of the days).

Once again Hosea hears the command of Yahweh, demanding that he make his own life the vehicle of the divine word to Israel. Once more he is to dramatize in his relation to a woman the way of Yahweh with Israel. He is bid to love an adulteress! Like 1.2–9 the material is in the form of a report of a prophetic symbolism. But here the report is written in the first person and must come from Hosea himself rather than from his disciples. The story is constructed from the three elements which make up the usual form of such a report: the divine command (v. 1), the execution of the typological act (vv. 2f.), and the interpretation of the symbolism (vv. 4f.). Within this basic structure there is a movement, a progressive unfolding in which the meaning of the symbolic act grows. Just how Hosea is to love the unfaithful wife and all that his action is to symbolize is not stated in the command which he receives. There is no anticipation of his possessing her and yet shutting her away from himself. When the

ᵃ 'Again' (*'ōd*) is best read as a modifier of the preceding verb, but it is possible that it is related to the following imperative: 'Go again, love . . .' (RSV).

ᵇ So MT with a passive participle; G's text ('loving evil') vocalizes MT differently and its active participle does offer a better parallelism to the following sentence.

ᶜ Opinion is divided whether the verb is *krh* II (*KB*, p. 454) or *nkr* (J. Gray, *The Legacy of Canaan*, 1957, p. 102. n. 4).

ᵈ Perhaps *lō' 'ēlēk* has been lost because of homoioteleuton.

final explication is given in vv. 4f., it depends on Hosea's unexpected act. The resolution in v. 5 is not anticipated at all by any specific element in the symbolism except in the unlimited intention of the initial command to love. Thus, the narrative is more complex than the form of the usual report of the prophetic symbolism (e.g. 1.2–9; Jer. 13.1–11; Ezek. 12.1–11; II Kings 13.15–19). The elements are not precise and self-contained; instead one hears an unfolding drama in which everything moves from the potential contained in the command to love. It is as though Hosea already knew what that word meant in this particular situation, and the explanation surely is the relation between what Hosea does and the portrayal of what Yahweh will do in the oracular poetry of 2.2–15. Attempts to reduce the narrative to precisely co-ordinated elements by removing v. 5 or vv. 4f. ignore this relationship. Without v. 4 the report has no real interpretation; the structure is incomplete. Without v. 5 Hosea's conception of the strategy of Yahweh's love is abridged. After all, there was no possibility of acting out the symbolism of Israel's return to the Lord; that lay with the woman; the profoundest typology of all appears precisely in the situation that Yahweh waits upon Israel in the time of her judgment just as Hosea waits upon the answer from his partner.

Who is the unnamed woman? Of what time in the life of Hosea does the report tell? Such questions about the biography of Hosea meet an oblique indifference in the material; it was not formed to assist in the quest for the historical Hosea. The narrative was fashioned to illumine one particular action as a form of proclamation; its connections with the rest of Hosea's life are ignored because the revelation of the divine intent did not require such elaboration. But in light of the meaning of the symbolism, who else could the woman be but Gomer! (see comment on 1.2f.). And when else could the act have been appropriate but after the events of ch. 1 had taken place? Of course the paucity of information about Hosea's career leaves us with many theoretical possibilities; any proposal on the problem is conjectural. When the question is raised, it can be answered only in terms of what seems the highest probability. The woman is not identified by name in the text; rather, she is identified in terms of her situation because that is what serves the need of the symbolism. The woman that Hosea must love is to be a wife who has given herself to the love of another and so is an adulteress. The command in v. 1 is a variation on 1.2; there the prophet was told *to go take* a wife, but here he is ordered *to go love* a wife, as though to imply that what was required was this personal commitment within a relationship already established. The symbolism is best served if the woman is Gomer; its point is that Yahweh's love will find a way with Israel even though this people has turned away from him to other gods. Just so, Hosea is to seek out a woman who has deserted him. The story of that desertion and how and under precisely what conditions Gomer lived when Hosea receives the divine command is unknown – the embarrassment of this reconstruction. But the same difficulty accompanies every proposal, and this one does the most justice to what is known. On the general problem of Hosea's marriage and the relation between chs. 1 and 3 see the comment on 1.2–9 and the literature cited there.

[1] 'And Yahweh said to me . . .' is a sentence with which the prophets often introduced the account of the peculiar experience in which their consciousness was concentrated on the other, the divine person (Amos 7.8, 15; 8.2; Isa. 7.3; 8.1; Jer. 3.6, etc.). It expresses all that is necessary from their point of view to explain what happened to them. What they experience is a situation in which the prophetic 'I' becomes the sphere and field for the expression of the divine 'I'. This pre-eminent reality obviates the need for any circumstantial explanations. Hosea does not tell how this occurrence fits into the fabric of his own life, or how he felt at the time, because what he does is not to be understood or interpreted in terms of him, but rather beheld and heard as the work of Yahweh's speaking, as a form of proclamation. This way of beginning precludes any understanding of the story which makes Hosea's own feelings the real point of departure. The flow in the symbolism does not move from Hosea's desire for a faithless woman to an intuition concerning the nature of God's feeling in a similar situation with Israel. Quite the other way. The astounding persistence of God's love in the face of betrayal creates the possibility and necessity for the prophet to articulate in his own life the way of God.

The command sets up an analogy between Hosea and the adulterous woman on the one side, and Yahweh and faithless Israel on the other. For the purposes of the analogy which underlies the symbolic act, the description of the woman's identity is not vague at all. She is said to have given herself in love to a companion (for *rēaʿ* meaning the desired sexual companion, cf. Jer. 3.1 and S. of S. 5.16), and in this situation to be committing adultery, violating marriage bonds. Precisely what lay behind this terse identification of the woman is impossible to say; the text furnishes no further clues. If the assumption

that the woman was Gomer be correct, she may have returned to her
life as a prostitute, perhaps this time as a common streetwalker; see
the discussion of 'woman of harlotry' in the comment on 1.2.

Hosea's interpretation of Yahweh's way with Israel as the way of a
husband with his wife furnishes the bridge of meaning from Gomer to
the Israelites. They too have left their husband for lovers, the Baals,
out of desire for their gifts of fertility and abundance (2.5, 13, 17;
11.2, etc.). 'Raisin-cakes' are sweetmeats made of pressed grapes, a
delicacy (S. of S. 2.5) distributed at cultic feasts (II Sam. 6.19).
Israel's love for such delicacies is put in parallel to 'turning to other
gods' because they mistakenly thought that the good things of the
fertile land were the gifts of the Baals (2.5, 8f.). 'Other gods' sounds
the theme of the decalogue's first word (Ex. 20.3), the commandment
of which all the others are refractions and interpretations. The issue
is the principle *par excellence* of Yahwism: exclusive allegiance to the
God of the covenant. Only when Israel's violation of their election is
clearly in view does the radical quality of Yahweh's announcement of
his love for Israel emerge as the incredible grace which is the subject
of the symbolism.

[2] To carry out the command Hosea had to pay a price. The reason
for the payment belongs to the woman's situation and can therefore
only be conjectured. If she were a prostitute then probably the price
was the fee for acquiring exclusive rights with her over a long period
of time (so Rudolph). Whether she had become the legal property of
another man in some way cannot be said for certain. The price was
fifteen shekels of silver and a homer and a lethech of barley. One
estimate of the Israelite shekel-weight puts it at 0.403 ounces, or
about the weight of an American half-dollar. The homer as a dry-
measure was of approximately 5.16 bushels in capacity; the lethech,
mentioned only here in the OT, is thought to have been one-half of a
homer.[a] Barley was the cheapest of the grains. Hosea carefully item-
izes the bill as though the amount were of real consequence; the
breakdown may suggest that he had some trouble in getting the
required sum together. Enough information about values is not available to estimate the worth of the price. A mature female slave was
valued at one time by the courts at thirty shekels (Ex. 21.32) and the
same value was set on the person of a woman in calculating the fulfilment of a vow (Lev. 27.4). Some such price is a likely guess in this

[a] On the above estimates cf. O. R. Sellers, 'Weights and Measures', *IDB* IV,
pp. 832ff.

instance and would fit the circumstances, if the woman was a slave or bound by vow at a shrine.

[3] Verses 3f. recapitulate the elements of v. 1. As part of his obedience to the divine command Hosea tells the acquired woman what she must do (v. 3) and what it means (v. 4). He could not enact his understanding of what the command to 'love' involved without drawing the woman into the enactment, so she in her turn must have an interpreted command. The necessity for this extension lay in Hosea's commission; he was to love this woman with a love that reflected Yahweh's love for Israel – a love that was both exclusively jealous and passionately generous, a love that closed the door on her sin and opened the door for her return to her husband. The woman must live in the prophet's house shut away from any opportunity to be a harlot, cut off from other men. Even he would not claim the conjugal rights of a husband, for what this stern imprisoning love seeks is not punishment, or mere possession, but the answer and response of the beloved. Just as Yahweh will bar the way to Israel's trysting with the gods of Canaan (2.6), Hosea keeps the woman apart from every man – and waits. 'Many days', an indefinite period, however long, he waits for the act that alone can complete the symbolism, the return of his love by the woman. He will not go in to her because more than anything he wants her to come to him. The pathos and power of God's love is embodied in these strange tactics (cf. 2.7, 14f.) – a love that imprisons to set free, destroys false love for the sake of true, punishes in order to redeem.

[4] The interpretation of Hosea's action is stated in strict parallelism to his own words to the woman in v. 3: 'The Israelites *shall live for many days* . . .' followed by a series of negatives which fix the circumstances of that interim. What goes on in Hosea's house is a prophecy of what will be done to the nation. What Israel will lack is itemized in a series of six things listed in related pairs. The first two, king and officer, represent the entire royal institution. Hosea viewed Israel's kings as a manifestation of their rebellion against Yahweh (5.1; 8.4, 10; 10.15; 13.10f.). The officer (*śar*) is a functionary of the king (7.3; 8.4, 10; 13.10) whose duties were often in the military service (5.10; 7.16). Sacrifice and pillar stand for Israel's public cult. Like Amos (Amos 5.21ff.; 4.4f.) Hosea rejected Israel's sacrifice, not just as unnecessary, but as an offence to Yahweh (6.6; 8.11, 13). The pillar (*maṣṣēbā*) was a standing stone erected in shrines. In the Canaanite cult it may have represented the male deity. It was for-

bidden by Deuteronomic law because of its pagan association, obviously a companion piece to the Asherah (Deut. 16.21f.). Ephod and teraphim are cultic objects, paired also in Judg. 17.5; 18.14, 17f. The exact meaning of ephod in many of its uses in the OT is not clear.[a] It is clear that it frequently was associated with the procedure of inquiring after the divine will. Teraphim is the name for images of a deity, often small and used in household shrines.[b] They could be used as a means of divination (Ezek. 21.21; Zech. 10.2). Perhaps as a pair ephod and teraphim represent Israel's ritual for getting a divine revelation apart from the tradition or the prophetic message. Israel, then, will be stripped of king, cult, and techniques for divination. This negative portrayal of Israel's situation is silent about causes and circumstances. Does it point to a deprived existence in their own land (2.6), or to life in the wilderness (2.14), or to exile (9.3; 11.5)? The description leaves the matter open, and concentrates on the removal of all that stood between Israel and the ancient and true relation to Yahweh.

[5] 'Afterwards'! In this one adverb is the sign that in the history which Yahweh makes there is hope. When his action fills and determines time, then time becomes pregnant with the birth of a new day and a new life. The deprivation of judgment opens the way to a second beginning. This 'afterwards' is a pivotal point in Hosea's 'eschatology' toward which the punishment of God always moves – the time of return (2.7), of the answer (2.15), of the 'my husband' (2.16), of the true confession (2.23). The turning point comes when the wife/people move toward Yahweh; their act is the wonderful event of the new time. And yet, it is not so much a matter of their working out their salvation, as accepting as grace the inexorable refusal of Yahweh to let them do aught else but move toward him. They would not seek him, if he had not already found them; their act is really an expression of his action. 'Return' (*šūb* used absolutely) is going back to the original relation to Yahweh; in Hosea it means leaving behind all that Canaan represented in the religion of Israel to take up the religious situation of the Exodus time. *Šūb* is a basic term in Hosea's theological vocabulary. Israel's guilt lies in their failure to return to Yahweh (11.5; 7.10); the prophet calls upon the people to return (12.6; 14.1f.), but Israel is driven by a spirit of harlotry, and *cannot* return (5.4); so Yahweh creates by his judgment the event of their *return* to him (2.7; 6.1; 14.7). The word is both demand and

[a] See R. de Vaux, *Ancient Israel*, 1961, pp. 349ff.
[b] See the picture in G. E. Wright, *Biblical Archaeology*, 1962, p. 44.

promise. *Seek* (*bqš*) is used as a synonym (cf. also 7.10; 5.15f.) for *šūb*.
It often means to approach a deity through cult (2.7) and is used in
this sense of the sacrifice Israel offers to Yahweh (5.6); but in this
text that sense is drastically modified because the usual cult is excluded.
In so far as cult is involved in the *return* and *seeking*, it can only be the
worship of the Yahweh of the salvation-history and the law (14.3).
Israel will seek 'Yahweh their God', Yahweh as he revealed himself
in the Exodus and in the wilderness; cf. the definitive definition of
this name from the covenant vocabulary in the formula of self-
identification: 'I am Yahweh your God from the land of Egypt'
(12.9; 13.4). Chastened and taught by Yahweh's wrath and having
experienced his power, the people will be free of all presumption and
arrogance; they will come in fear and trembling (*phd*, Micah 7.17)
to Yahweh. The *goodness* of Yahweh means his good gifts of grain, oil,
vineyards (2.8f., 15, 21f.; Jer. 31.12, 14); again they will receive the
bounty of the land from his hand. Both 'David their king' and 'at the
end of days' appear to be later additions to the text which overextend
the metrical quality of the measures. Cf. 'Yahweh their God and
David their king' in Jer. 30.9. Hosea's concentration on the conditions
of the wilderness makes this aspiration of Judahistic messianism
unlikely in his eschatology. 'At the end of days' is a stock phrase
probably added to note that this return belongs to the final period of
history, a perspective which suggests also a Judean redactor after
the eighth century (cf. Isa. 2.2; Micah 4.1; Jer. 23.20; etc.).

7. GOD'S CASE AGAINST THE LAND: 4.1-3

4 ¹Hear the word of Yahweh, O Israelites,
    for Yahweh has a complaint against the residents of the land,
  that there is no faithfulness, no devotion,
    and no knowledge of God in the land.
  ²Cursing and lying and killing
    and stealing and adultery proliferate in the land;[a]
  one bloody deed follows another.
  ³Therefore the land shall dry up,[b]
    and all its residents shall languish –
  including the beasts of the field and the birds of the sky;
    even the fish of the sea shall be taken away.

[a] 'In the land', missing in MT, appears in G and could have been lost through
homoioteleuton.
[b] Cf. '*bl* II, *KB*, p. 6.

This oracle stands at the beginning of the second major section of
the book, which in contrast to chs. 1–3 is wholly composed of an
arrangement of sayings. The collector must have found it an ideal
introduction to the sequence with its opening summons to the
Israelites to hear Yahweh's word and its comprehensive statement of
Israel's guilt and of the punishment to come upon the entire land with
all its creatures. In spite of its brevity the oracle is virtually a paradigm
of Hosea's message of judgment. The oracle begins with a proclamation formula (elsewhere in Hosea only in 5.1) which identifies the
words as Yahweh's message to Israel (v. 1a). The following sentence
(v. 1bα) defines the subject of the herald's proclamation; he is there
to make an announcement concerning the legal suit which Yahweh
has against the residents of the land. Appropriately the saying itself
is formulated in the idiom of speech in the court, an example of the
'court speech' in which the prophets on occasion clothed their
announcements of judgment.[a] Though the saying is introduced as the
'word of Yahweh', the saying never shifts to the style of the divine
speech; this may be due to the subject matter or more probably the
prophet reports the business of the divine court without resort to the
style. The prophet cites the complaint (*rīb*), the substance of Yahweh's
case, first in negatives using normative concepts for the conduct expected of Israel (v. 1bβ) and then positively (v. 2) by itemizing a
series of crimes against the divine law. The result is the most comprehensive picture possible of the sins of omission and commission, a
portrayal of a population living in flagrant contradiction of their
Lord. The announcement of punishment (v. 3) states the sentence of
the divine court. The source of the forms is legal procedure as
practised in Israel's court and their use has the effect of putting the
entire nation on trial,[b] but the dramatic and theological setting is
Yahweh's legal process against his people for breach of covenant.[c] In
the legal drama on which the saying is based Yahweh plays the role
of prosecutor (1bβ–2) and judge (v. 3).

[a] See C. Westermann, *Basic Forms of Prophetic Speech*, ET, 1967, pp. 199ff.
[b] See H. J. Boecker, *Redeformen des Rechtslebens im Alten Israel* (WMANT 14),
1964, pp. 152f.
[c] On this background to prophetic ideas and forms see, among others, H. B.
Huffmon, 'The Covenant Lawsuit in the Prophets', *JBL* 78, 1959, pp. 285–95; G. E.
Wright, 'The Lawsuit of God', in *Israel's Prophetic Heritage*, ed. B. W. Anderson,
1962, pp. 26–67; J. Harvey, 'Le "*Rib*-Pattern"', réquisitoire prophétique sur la
rupture de l'alliance', *Bibl.* 43, 1962, pp. 172–96; E. von Waldow, *Die Traditions-
geschichtliche Hintergrund der Prophetischen Gerichtsreden* (BZAW 85), 1963.

Whether the saying ends with v. 3, or continues in vv. 4ff. where the vocabulary and theme of Yahweh's *rīb* also continues, is a matter of disagreement. The problem turns around the interpretation of v. 3: are its Hebrew imperfect verbs to be understood as referring to the present or the future? Some prefer to interpret the verse as a description of the distress into which the land has already fallen and so to follow the oracle beyond v. 3.[a] The comment below adopts the other possibility of seeing in the verse a prediction of punishment and so the conclusion of the saying (Weiser, Wolff, Boecker).

[1] The prophet stands in Israel's midst as a herald sent by their divine Lord to announce the findings of the heavenly court against his subjects. The subject of the message is a legal suit which Yahweh as covenant Lord has brought against his people. For the locution 'to have a legal complaint against' (*rīb l- 'im-*) cf. 12.2 and Micah 6.2; for *rīb* in the technical sense of legal suit, cf. Ex. 23.2, 3, 6. Because the covenant was a relationship which had a content of legal requirements enforced by the punishment of curses, judicial process lent itself easily to the language in which the prophets spoke of covenant rupture between God and people. The suit is against 'the residents of the land'. In Hosea's vocabulary 'the land' plays a basic role in Yahweh's relation to Israel. It belongs to Yahweh (9.3); through it he gives his blessing under the covenant (2.8f.); at times the land is even used as the term for the people in their relation to Yahweh (1.2). The land with these overtones of meaning is thematic in the passage (twice in v. 1, in G's text in v. 2, and in v. 3). Yahweh's case is brought against people whose responsibility to him lies in the fact of their residence in the land and the history which brought them to its blessing.

The guilt of Israel on which Yahweh's suit is based is first depicted as sins of omission. In the land there is neither *faithfulness* nor *devotion* nor *knowledge* of God. Faithfulness and devotion are the active virtues which ought to be practised in the relationship of persons, and in the vocabulary of the Old Testament are used of the relationship of Israel to God or of one Israelite to another. Faithfulness (*'ᵉmet*, only here in Hosea) is a synonym of the faithfulness (*'ᵉmūnā*, 2.20) which God shows in the time of salvation. It is the firmness and the reliability of a man whose word is as good as his bond, who is consistent in his responsibility. Faithfulness is a frequent synonym of devotion (Gen. 24.49; 47.29; Josh. 2.14, etc.). Devotion (*ḥesed*) is a quality of the life

[a] See the case made by Rudolph in KAT, and the analysis by J. J. Jackson, 'Yahweh v. Cohen *et al.*', *Pittsburgh Perspective*, VII/4, 1966, pp. 28–32.

which God requires of Israel. No English word is a satisfactory equivalent for the Hebrew term; many have been proposed such as love, leal love, steadfast love, kindness, piety, religiosity, and devotion.[a] *Hesed* denotes the attitude and activity which founds and maintains a relation; the relation can be one given by birth or the social order, or created by arrangement. A man shows *hesed* when he is concerned and responsive to do in a given relation what another can rightfully expect according to the norms of that relationship. In Hosea the sphere of *hesed* is the covenant with Yahweh.[b]

The final position of 'knowledge of God' (*da'at 'elōhīm*) is a clue to its central importance as normative term in the prophecy of Hosea. 'Knowledge of God/Yahweh' is a pivotal and unique concern of his approach to Israel's situation. The expression 'knowledge of God' appears in 4.1 and 6.6, both times in an emphatic and final position in the sentence; 'knowledge' (*hadda'at*) used twice in 4.6 assumes the object 'God' and is the equivalent of the full term. The verbal formulation 'to know God' is found in 13.4 and 8.2. Yahweh is the object of the verb instead of God in 2.20; 5.4; 6.3. Twice in relevant texts 'to know' has as its object an act of Yahweh (2.8; 11.3). There is no discernible distinction between the formulations using God and Yahweh as the object of knowing; they are synonymous in Hosea. The lack of the knowledge of God is Israel's cardinal deficiency (4.2); it is what Yahweh demands rather than sacrifice (6.6); in spite of the people's claims and resolutions (6.3; 8.2) its reality is completely missing in their present life. Neither pious confession nor enthusiastic cult result in the knowledge of God. What is required is the knowledge that Yahweh as he was revealed in the Exodus is their only God (13.4), that his healing help saw them through the history of their beginnings (12.3), and that it is Yahweh who gives them the good things of the land (2.8). The knowledge of God is the peculiar responsibility of the priest, whose duty it was to pass on the instruction (*tōrā*) whose content is the acts and will of Yahweh (4.6). So 'to know God/Yahweh' is Hosea's formula for normative faith, the apprehension of Yahweh's history with Israel in the classical era before her life in Canaan, the revealing acts and words of those days – an apprehension so single and whole that it would define and condition the total life of the people. Therefore, 'to know Yahweh' is the goal of

[a] The last by A. R. Johnson, '*Hesed* and *Hasid*', in *Interpretationes ad Vetus Testamentum pertinentes Sigmundo Mowinckel missae*, 1955, pp. 100ff.

[b] See the classic study by N. Glueck, *Hesed in the Bible*, 1967, especially pp. 56ff.

God's eschatological acts by which he brings his people from their guilt through judgment to the new covenant (2.20). The knowledge of God is Israel's personal response to the salvation-history of election, and obedience to the requirements of the covenant.[a] The covenant orientation of know/knowledge in Hosea is supported by the use of 'know' in the vocabulary of ancient Near Eastern treaties where the verb has the sense of 'acknowledge, recognize' the authority of the suzerain.[b]

[2] The charge that Israel was not keeping the covenant is paired with a positive indictment citing specific deeds. In the Hebrew text five absolute infinitives (which emphasize the bare act of the verb) itemize the dimension of Israel's guilt. These five crimes are not simply breaches of general morality; they are acts prohibited by the normative tradition of Israel which summarizes the will of Yahweh under the covenant. The last three are literally equivalent to prohibitions of the decalogue (Ex. 20.2–17; Deut. 5.6–21). The first and second are references to actions covered by the ten words and forbidden in other series of the legal tradition, as the texts cited below with each crime show. A similar series is used in Jeremiah's temple sermon (Jer. 7.9 – 'Will you steal, murder, commit adultery, swear falsely . . .?') in precisely the same way. *Cursing* is not sheer profanity but an imprecation or malediction invoking a divinely caused misfortune on another. Where such a curse was uttered for evil or selfish purposes it would violate the prohibition of invoking Yahweh's name for vain reasons (Ex. 20.7). *Lying* was a particular problem in Israel in judicial procedure (Ex. 20.16; 23.1, 7) and, as the business economy of Israel developed, in trade (Deut. 25.13–16). On *murder* cf. Ex. 20.13. *Stealing* is prohibited by Ex. 20.15; 21.16; in the latter text the crime is classified as one punishable by death. On *adultery* cf. Ex. 20.14; Lev. 20.10. This series points to the moral-social character of faithfulness, devotion and the knowledge of God; evidence for their lack appears in the crimes of men against men. So there is no essential distinction between the positive and negative indictment. In the covenant structure the relation of Israel to God is articulated in the *tōrā* which orders the relation of men as covenant partners. Social

---

[a] See H. W. Wolff, '"Wissen um Gott" bei Hosea als Urform von Theologie', *EvTh* 15, 1953, pp. 533ff., and the literature cited there; J. L. McKenzie, 'Knowledge of God in Hosea', *JBL* 74, 1955, pp. 22–27.
[b] H. B. Huffmon, 'The Treaty Background of Hebrew Yāda‘', *BASOR* 181, 1966, pp. 31–37.

ethics and theological orthodoxy are inextricably interdependent. An Israelite was faithless to God in acting against the rights of his brother. And in maintaining the fabric of the social order an Israelite was showing faithfulness, devotion and the knowledge of God. The proliferation of such deeds shows that the northern state had already sunk to the level of a chaotic society which had no recognizable relation to the divine law. They had become like the Judah which Jeremiah would describe a century later, a nation that combined vigorous piety and heedless disobedience. Social violence had become the content of their life; as Hosea eloquently puts it, no moment was left free of their crime as one bloody deed followed another. The accusation, then, is a sweeping assertion that Israel has completely broken the terms of the Yahweh covenant and is punishable by the curses which enforced its integrity.

[3] In the normal oracle-form 'therefore' introduces the announcement of Yahweh's coming punishment. Verse 3 could be read in the present as Hosea's description of a contemporary situation for which the crimes of Israel are responsible. But the description really outruns the limits of a drought or any other empirical situation; it portrays a loss of vitality by land and population that affects every creature, even the fish. The catastrophe is not merely a drought, though partially pictured by drought-vocabulary, but a terrible diminution of life-forces which tends to a total absence of life. It is the effect of the divine curse and in this case for breach of covenant. See the juxtaposition of covenant breaking and such disaster in Isa. 24.4ff.; 33.8–9. The land is polluted by the crime of its inhabitants and will share the curse. No creature will escape. When the people of God break covenant, the whole creation suffers the consequences of their sin (Gen. 8.21; cf. Rom. 8.19ff.).

8. GOD'S CASE AGAINST THE PRIESTS: 4.4–10

4 ⁴Yea!ᵃ Let no man bring complaint,
　　and let no man reprove.
　　ᵇMy complaint is against you,ᵇ O priest.

ᵃ For 'ak as an emphatic particle at the beginning of a sentence cf. Hos. 12.8 and KB, p. 42, 2.
ᵇ⁻ᵇ Reading 'immᵉkā rībī for MT ('your people are like those bringing complaint against the priest'); cf. BH's list of the other most widely discussed conjectures.

⁵ᵃYou shall stumble by day,ᵃ
    and the prophet also shall stumble with you by night,
I will destroyᵇ your mother,ᶜ
⁶ as my people are destroyedᵇ
    for want of the knowledge.
Since you have rejected the knowledge,
    I have rejected you as my priest.
You have forgotten the instruction of your God,
    so I in turn will forget your sons.
⁷The more they increased the more they sinned against me;
    I will change their honour to disgrace.
⁸They eat the sin of my people;
    they lust after their iniquity.
⁹What happens to people will happen to priest!
    I will visit his ways upon him,
    and bring back his deeds to him.
¹⁰They shall eat and not be satisfied;
    they have played the harlot, but shall not increase.
For they have deserted Yahweh to practise [11]ᵈ harlotry!

The collector has placed vv. 4–10 after vv. 1–3 with good reason.
The theme of Yahweh's *rib* (v. 1) is repeated in v. 4; 'the knowledge'
whose lack is the responsibility of the priests (v. 6) is the 'knowledge of
God' mentioned in v. 1b. It could well be that both sayings were
spoken in the same situation, perhaps after a protest by a priest at the
severity of 4.1–3 (so Wolff). What sets vv. 4–10 apart as a separate
saying within the literary context is its addressee; it deals with the
priesthood while vv. 1–3 concerns the residents of the land and vv.
11–14 are concerned with the cultic community. Once again Yahweh
speaks as one who brings a complaint (*rib*) as if he were engaged in
legal process against the addressee (see the comment on 4.1–3). This
time complaint and sentence are announced against the priesthood.
The elements of complaint and sentence are not separated into sequen-
tial sections but introduced in an alternating contrapuntal style. As a
feature of this alternation the prophet uses a repetition of motifs by
which the failure of the priest and the judgment of Yahweh are made
to correspond: complaint (v. 4), stumble (v. 5), destroy (vv. 5f.),
reject (v. 5), forget (v. 5), increase (vv. 8 and 10), eat (vv. 8 and 10).

   ᵃ *wᵉkāšaltāh yōm* for *wᵉkāšaltā hayyōm; hayyōm* means 'today'.
   ᵇ Cf. *dāmāh* III in *HAL*, p. 216.
   ᶜ So MT; Rudolph revocalizes *'immᵉkā* as *'ummeykā* ('your clan/family'),
probably an improvement.
   ᵈ Adding the first word of v. 11 to complete the sentence.

The theological principle upon which this correspondence is based is stated precisely in v. 9. The saying opens using second person singular pronouns for 'the priest' (vv. 4-6), then shifts to the third person plural indicating the corporate nature of the office (vv. 7f., 10), with v. 9 using the third person singular. The shift from direct address probably goes with the double role of Yahweh who as plaintiff and judge makes complaint to the accused and speaks of him to the court. The setting for the saying would probably be the great national sanctuary at Bethel at the time of one of the agricultural festivals. It probably belongs to the early period of Hosea's career. It continues the emphases of chs. 1-3, and reflects the practice of a confident cultic establishment, undisturbed by the calamities of the later phases of his career.

[4] The divine saying seems to begin *in mediis rebus*. The opening emphatic exclamation and the indefinite jussives suggest that Hosea answers an official protest against his announcement of judgment. The indefinite jussives are comprehensive and meant to put a stop to all argument. 'Bring complaint' and 'reprove' belong to the legal vocabulary. 'Complain' (*rîb*, cf. 2.2) means to enter an accusation, to speak as one who seeks the settlement of a grievance against another; 'reprove' (Amos 5.10) is the correcting, rebuking speech of those who hear a complaint and seek to set the case right. Let no one accuse the prophet or seek to correct him, especially the priest, because Yahweh has a suit (*rîb* as in 4.1) against him in particular. In the following verses the priest is clearly the addressee of this message from Yahweh, a fact which favours the emendation suggested (p. 65 n. *b*). The narrative of the encounter between Amos and the priest of Bethel (Amos 7.10-17) is a likely guide in reconstructing the context of this passage. When Amos announces the coming destruction of Israel's shrines and the death of the king, the priest Amaziah orders Amos to stop prophesying and to leave; Amos answers with an oracle against the priest and his wife and children. Here we have only the answering oracle addressed first to the priest, and along with him to his guild-associates (vv. 17f.). In the ministry of the word of Yahweh the prophet comes into conflict with the authority of established religion. The priest is not by office a plenipotentiary of God into whose hands has been given some divine right over the person and will of Yahweh. He too is under the judgment of God and subject to his word. He most of all, as the oracle goes on to make clear!

[5] The interpretation of v. 5 is encumbered by uncertainties about

tense and text. The verb 'stumble' could be translated as present (ATD) or future (RSV, BK, HAT); that is, it could be a description of the current failure of the priest or an announcement of his imminent judgment. Usage of the verb (5.5; 14.1) favours the latter. When the verdict of Yahweh's suit against the priest is executed, he will stumble and fall even in the clear light of day. The prophet shall also share his fate. Since prophet is paired with priest, the reference is to that type of *nābī'* having a recognized function within the official cult and so sharing the corruption of the cult. He is the cult prophet who always preached salvation; these men are best known as the bitter opponents of Jeremiah in Jerusalem.[a] The prophet is not mentioned again in the following verses, and every other reference to the prophet in Hosea is highly approving (6.5; 9.7f.; 12.10, 13). Except for this one sentence, neither Amos nor Hosea seem to know of prophets who oppose their message in the shrines of the northern kingdom. The isolated character of this reference has brought 5aβ under severe suspicion; some (e.g. Wolff) attribute the sentence to the Judean redactor of the book, and others reconstruct the text to eliminate any mention of a prophet (see Rudolph's proposal: '. . . since by your fault my people have stumbled as though it were night', which does restore the correspondence of verbs characteristic of the saying as a whole). MT's 'your mother' (*'immekā*) is certainly possible; the judgment against the priest could include his family (cf. 'your sons' in v. 6; wife and children in Amos 7.17; mother of the king in Jer. 22.26). In 2.2ff. 'mother' is the symbolic role played by the nation; the symbolism could be continued here because the people are involved in the consequences of the priests' failure (cf. v. 6). But Rudolph's proposal to read 'your family' commends itself (p. 66 n. *c*). The collapse of the priest and the execution of his family are imminent; he is hardly in any situation to call Yahweh's messenger to account for he himself is among the guilty and already condemned.

[6] Yahweh announces the essential accusation of his suit against the priest and then, matching crime against punishment, he delivers his verdict. Verse 5b goes with v. 6a in a matching correspondence: Yahweh will destroy the family of the priest because his failure has destroyed Yahweh's people. The accusation has the sound of a lament in its mournful plaint over the plight of 'my people'. Israel was meant to be the elect, the covenant people, Yahweh's own, but

[a] On the conflict within prophetic circles, see J. Lindblom, *Prophecy in Ancient Israel*, 1962, pp. 210ff. and 202ff.

that identity has been destroyed in disobedience and faithlessness. The cause of that destruction is the lack of 'the knowledge' (cf. the culminating charge of Yahweh's *rīb* in 4.1 and the comment on 'the knowledge of God' in Hosea at that verse). 'The knowledge' is an abbreviated form of the expression 'the knowledge of God/Yahweh'. Its content is clearly indicated by the parallelism with *tōrā* in this verse and the list of crimes against the law in 4.2; 'knowledge' is learning and obeying the will of the covenant God in devotion and faithfulness; it is response to the unity of Yahweh's saving act and binding requirement such as is expressed in 'I am Yahweh your God who brought you up out of the land of Egypt, out of the house of bondage. You shall have no other gods before me . . .' (Ex. 20.2ff.). The lack of such knowledge had led to the loss of any reality in the role of being the covenant people. In Hosea's view of Israel's priesthood, the primary function of the office was to maintain and pass on the *tōrat ʾelōhēkā*, instruction concerning the covenant God. *Tōrā* means both the act of instruction and the content of what is passed on. This conception of priesthood reaches back to the cultic ideal of the tribal league when sacrificial ritual had not yet become the pre-emptive concern of priests (cf. 6.6) and the priest represented Yahweh to the people at the central shrine before his ark, proclaiming his salvation-history and announcing his will. [a] This conception was probably kept alive among the levitical circles in the north which had been excluded from the great state sanctuaries like Bethel; it finds its consummate expression in the book of Deuteronomy. [b] The priesthood of the official shrines of the northern state had demitted the very vocation given them by Yahweh in order to preside over a cult riddled with Canaanite practices (4.12–14) and a ritual which sought to deal with God through the manipulation of sacrifice (5.6; 8.11–13). It is not priesthood as an office, but priests who hold the office, that are rejected. Hosea has a very high view of priesthood; the *tōrā* of the covenant God has been given into the priests' charge. Their sin determines their punishment; what the priests have done to Yahweh, he will do to them. They reject his revelation; he rejects their priesthood. The father in office and the sons who would inherit the office (I Sam. 2.27ff.) are stripped of their ordination by the word of a lone prophet

[a] See R. de Vaux, *Ancient Israel*, 1961, pp. 353ff.; W. Eichrodt, *Theology of the Old Testament* I, 1961, pp. 395ff.

[b] See e.g. Deut. 31.9ff.; 33.8–10; cf. G. von Rad, *Studies in Deuteronomy*, ET (SBT 9), 1953, pp. 6off.

standing outside the organization of the official religion of the kingdom!

[7] In vv. 7f. the saying shifts from direct address to indirect description, referring to the priests with third person plural pronouns; the priesthood as a corporate group is now drawn into the judgment of Yahweh. The more numerous they had become the greater was the sum of their sin. Add another priest, and you add another sinner – the very opposite of what should have happened. The growth of the priesthood had become a yardstick for measuring the failure to carry out the vocation of Yahweh (*ḥāṭā' lᵉ*: 'sin against' in the sense of failing to reach a goal). The co-ordination of prosperity and growth with the proliferation of sin is a favourite theme of Hosea's (cf. 8.11; 10.1). Yahweh will change their honour (*kābōd*) to disgrace, shame (*qālōn*).

[8] The priests have changed the cult into a way for them to make a living instead of a way for Yahweh's elect people to live before him. The noun 'sin' picks up the verb of the previous verse and shows how the failure of the priests leads to and compounds the failure (*ḥaṭṭā't*) and iniquity ('*āwōn* – twisting and perverting a straight way) of 'my people'. Sin and iniquity are Hosea's favourite concepts for the guilt of Israel (in parallel in 8.13; 9.9; 13.12). What is meant by saying that the priests make a living (lit. 'eat') off the guilt of Israel is seen from texts like 8.11, 13; 5.6. The sacrifices offered on the many altars of the nation are sin in Yahweh's sight (cf. Amos 4.4f.); Yahweh rejects them because this cult of killing, burning, eating cattle has become the people's way of manipulating him, and has taken the place of devotion to him and knowledge of his revelation (6.6). Worship by sacrifice has become in fact rupture of the covenant. What Yahweh rejects, the people love and the priests encourage. Since the officiating priest received a portion of the sacrificed animal, they had a vested interest in a prolific cult. Their profit has become the true goal of their vocation, and they have turned the institution of worship into a service to the clergy. What do they care about the old orthodoxy of Israel as the people of Yahweh, when religion abounds and priests prosper? The bizarre result is a priest who officiates over sinning instead of nurturing true faith.

[9] With its singular 'priest' and third person singular pronouns, v. 9 interrupts the continuity of style between vv. 7f. and 10. Perhaps the reversion to 'the priest' of vv. 4 and 6 may be due to the proverbial character of the comparison, with the singular still holding the

corporate group in mind. The comparison reads literally: 'and it shall be like people like priest', an epigrammatic saying that is ambiguous in itself. In the context, however, the sense must be that the priest will suffer the same punishment as the people. The case of Yahweh against the land (4.1) includes the official leaders of religion. The rest of the verse in which Yahweh announces his decree of judgment is literally equivalent to 12.2 which introduces a statement of Yahweh's *rib* against Jacob. God will call him to account for the course of his life and bring back upon him the consequences of his acts. The punishment has the character of a strict, rational justice which brings the guilty face to face with the consequences which his sin has set in motion. The principle of correspondence underlies the entire formulation of the saying.

[10] The equivalence of God's justice appears in the two sentences which declare that the eating of the priests shall bring them only hunger and their harlotry result in barrenness. The punishment is formulated in the style of futility curses such as those listed in Deuteronomy as punishment for breaking the covenant (Deut. 28.30f., 38–40).[a] The sin of eating refers back to v. 8 and the greed of the priests to live on the profits of the sacrificial cult. The harlotry of the priests is both theological and literal. The priests participated in the ritual of the *hieros gamos*, the rites of sexual intercourse with a sacred prostitute for the purpose of invoking and assuring fertility for land and people (cf. the commentary on 4.14). But the purpose of the ritual will be frustrated for there will be no increase. The final sentence of the oracle gathers up all the charges against the priests in one final summary of the complaint: they have forsaken Yahweh to practise harlotry! Horrified amazement and sad recognition mingle in this juxtaposition of Yahweh and harlotry; one feels in it the vehemence of Jeremiah's astonishment at a people that change their gods (Jer. 2.9–13). The total incompatibility between Yahweh and harlotry is the fundamental theme in Hosea. The personal name of the covenant deity identifies the God of Israel's salvation-history whose *tōrā* expressly forbids the worship of other gods and the sexual commerce of Canaanite ritual; probably the style of direct address is changed just to achieve this emphasis. 'Harlotry' (cf. the commentary on 1.2) is Hosea's thematic word for the whole religion of syncretism and

[a] For other prophetic verdicts in the same style see 8.7; 9.12, 16; Micah 6.14–15; Amos 5.11 and the discussion in D. R. Hillers, *Treaty-Curses and the Old Testament Prophets* (BO 16), 1964, pp. 28ff.

apostasy observed for the sake of the land's fertility. Israel can no more be 'my people' and worship the Baals, than a wife can be married and be a prostitute. But in such a desertion the priests have been the chief conspirators – they whose duty it was more than any others to incarnate the 'marriage' of Yahweh and Israel.

9. GOD'S INDICTMENT OF THE CULT: 4.11–14

4 ¹¹Harlotry ᵃ and wine and must take away the mind!
¹²My people consults his piece of wood,
  and his staff interprets for him.
For a spirit of harlotry has brought confusion,
  and they have gone a-whoring away from their God.
¹³On the mountain tops they sacrifice
  and on the hills they burn offerings,
under oak and poplar
  and terebinth because its shade is pleasant.
Therefore your daughters play the harlot
  and your sons' wives commit adultery.
¹⁴I will not punish your daughters for playing harlot,
  or your sons' wives for committing adultery;
for they themselves go apart ᵇ with harlots
  and sacrifice with sacred prostitutes.
A people that does not understand shall be ruined.

The oracle begins and ends with proverbial sentences (vv. 11 and 14b), both of which share the theme of good judgment. Within the parenthesis set by these proverbs Yahweh speaks about the cultic practices of Israel. The effect is to categorize the cult as a loss of good sense (v. 11) which must lead inexorably to the ruin of Israel (14b). The insights of wisdom about the nature of life in general furnish a norm to uncover the folly and danger of the cult. The collector placed vv. 11–14 after vv. 4–10 because both deal with the cult and use 'harlotry' as a theme to denounce it.

The saying is a divine word; Yahweh speaks in the first person (vv. 12a, 14a; 'their God' in v. 12b is not an exception). Through

---

ᵃ Cf. note *d* on v. 10, p. 66 'Harlotry' is needed to complete the sentence in v. 10. and its presence in v. 11 is the basis for the use of this proverb to introduce vv. 12–14 whose theme is 'harlotry'. When the collector brought the two sayings together one of the words was lost.
ᵇ Reading a Niphal for MT's Piel.

most of the lines the people are spoken of in the third person plural or the corporate third person singular. In vv. 13c–14a this style is interrupted by two lines of direct address to the people, as Yahweh points to the consequences of the sexual cult which are already rife among them; this shift is characteristic of Hosea's style. The saying remains at the level of reproach throughout and never passes over to an announcement of punishment. Instead, there is a vehement catalogue of Israel's cultic practices recited as though accusation against the nation were bring brought before a court. The proverb in v. 15b rounds off the unit. Verses 16–19, in contrast to the divine-speech style of vv. 11–14, is a prophetic saying. The oracle, like the others in ch. 4, reflects the flourishing cult of the time of Jeroboam II.

[11] Verse 11 is a general observation about the way things work in life. Once a man turns to prostitutes and intoxicating drink for pleasure he loses his judgment. Harlots and wine take away a man's mind (the Hebrew word is heart, *lēb*, the seat of the will and under-standing in Hebrew psychology). The sentence was probably a popular Wisdom saying which the prophet selected because it mentioned harlotry and fitted his favourite characterization of Israel's cult. Israel's worship is harlotry! The proverb offers a way of showing that the kind of ritual practised in the shrines had robbed the people of their understanding. What is true of individual life applies to corporate existence.

[12] As a manifestation of the demented mind of Israel, Yahweh cites the techniques used among the people for communication with the deity. The terminology of 'consulting' (inquiring for an oracle) and 'interpreting' (*higgīd* with dream or riddle as object in Gen. 41.24; Judg. 14.21) clearly points to some kind of divination, though the exact technique referred to is uncertain. The piece of wood (Heb. *'ēṣ*, 'tree') could be an idol of wood (Jer. 10.3; Isa. 44.13ff.; Hab. 2.18f.), perhaps the Asherah beside the altar in Canaanite shrines (Deut. 16.21; Judg. 6.25ff.), or an oracle tree (Gen. 12.6; Judg. 9.37). The staff must refer to a technique of rhabdomancy in which a stick is thrown so as to learn the answer of the deity from the way it falls (cf. Ezek. 21.21f.). There is bitter irony in the contrast of pronouns: *my* people – *his* wood/staff. The chosen people who know Yahweh through history and covenant law resort to stupid practices because they have their own questions and anxieties. Moreover, the consulta-tion of another deity involved a formal recognition of and allegiance to the other god (cf. II Kings 1.16). How could the people of Yahweh

so completely have lost their mind? The explanation is that they are possessed by a 'spirit of harlotry' (5.4), a personal force whose effect upon them is to make them play the harlot. For analogous expressions, cf. 'spirit of confusion' (Isa. 19.14) and 'spirit of deep sleep' (Isa. 29.10), where the genitive indicates the effect of the spirit upon those on whom it falls. 'Spirit of harlotry' is another term for the intoxication of mind brought on by desire for the gifts of the Baals (v. 11); its source is the blandishments of these 'lovers' and it enters the mind of Israel through the mistaken folly of thinking that the land is the fief of the Baals. Israel is not free to decide and repent any longer, and it is this estimate of the people's condition which lies behind the programme of redemption set forth in chs. 2 and 3. On 'harlotry', Hosea's basic metaphor for the apostasy of Israel, see 1.2.

[13] 'Mountain tops' and 'hills' are the 'high places'[a] which were generally equipped with an altar, Massebah and Asherah, and a grove of trees. These are the shrines referred to in the stylized expression, 'on every high hill and under every green tree', in Jeremiah and the Deuteronomic literature (e.g. Deut. 12.2; Jer. 2.20; I Kings 14.23; II Kings 17.10). The high places had been old Canaanite shrines when Israel settled the land and their use opened the way for a continuation of the cultic practices of the old fertility religion. In such rural shrines, which usually contained no building, the shade of the grove would be the place where the portion of the sacrifice assigned to the worshippers was eaten. The sacrifices are not said to be offensive; the offence is where they occur and the relation they have to the sexual practices mentioned in v. 14. Indeed the concluding remark at the end of v. 13a about 'the pleasant shade' has a sarcastic ring and probably suggests in anticipation of v. 14 that the groves were used for more than sacrificial meals. The prostitution and adultery among the younger generation are a result of what their elders do at the shrine. Though v. 13b is introduced by 'therefore' and its verbs can be read as future, the sentence cannot be an announcement of punishment; the following statement in v. 14 precludes that interpretation. Apparently harlotry and adultery were perceptibly on the rise and the prophet brings the sexual disorder of society and the sexual focus of the cult together. The women are infected by the disease of harlotry contracted at worship; the spirit of harlotry spreads from cult to town and home. Whether the language of the text points to something other than general immorality is difficult to say; some

[a] *Bāmōt*; see R. de Vaux, *Ancient Israel*, 1961, pp. 284ff.

find an allusion to specifically cultic practices in which young women consecrate their wombs by giving up their virginity at the shrines and fathers have sexual intercourse with daughters-in-law before marriage to guarantee the fertility of the union.[a]

[14] Yahweh's reaction to the sexual promiscuity of Israel's women is astounding. Harlotry and adultery among those bound by marital contracts were judged severely by the stringent sexual ethic of Yahwism (Ex. 20.14; Deut. 22.13ff.); yet in spite of the guilt of these women Yahweh will withhold punishment. The guilt is not really theirs, but has its source in what their men do in the fertility cult. With the emphatic pronoun 'they themselves' 14b reverts to the descriptive style which was broken off after 13b. The sexual rites of the fertility cult, which gave a foundation of realism to Hosea's constant charge of 'harlotry', are tersely but plainly cited. The sacred prostitutes (qedēšōt) are professionals who served as cultic personnel at the shrines where fertility rites were practised. Sacrifice accompanied by ritual intercourse with them was meant to stimulate the sexual activity of the gods for the sake of the land's fertility. The custom of using both male and female sacred prostitutes was widespread in the ancient Near East.[b] The custom had been assimilated in Israel along with the syncretistic development of their cult under Canaanite influence (I Kings 14.24; 15.12; 22.46; II Kings 23.7) and was prohibited by the Deuteronomic Code (Deut. 23.17f.). Sacred prostitutes (in Heb. literally 'holy women') are not harlots; perhaps sexual orgies at the shrine had become so common that harlots were used as substitutes for cultic personnel. Nothing could be more inimical to Israel's role as Yahweh's covenant people than such a cultic use of sex; it meant a complete departure from the covenantal understanding of Yahweh as he had revealed himself, a sinking back into the morass of the common pagan conception of man and his relation to nature. This harlotry of the flesh was a far profounder harlotry of the spirit.

The final line (v. 14b) returns to the proverbial idiom. In style and vocabulary the line is a general Wisdom saying (cf. Prov. 10.8,

---

[a] See the discussion between L. Rost, 'Erwägungen zu Hosea 4.13f.', *Festschrift für A. Bertholet*, 1950, pp. 451–60; H. W. Wolff in BK, *ad loc.*; and W. Rudolph, 'Präparierte Jungfrauen?', *ZAW* 75, 1963, pp. 65–73.

[b] For Mesopotamia, see the Code of Hammurabi, sections 178–82, *ANET*, p. 174; also *ANET*, p. 427. For Ugarit see the texts associating *qdšm* with priests, cited by the glossary, 1664, in C. H. Gordon's *Ugaritic Manual*. See in general the classical texts cited in ICC, pp. 261f.; and W. F. Albright, *Archaeology and the Religion of Israel*, 1956, pp. 75ff., 158ff.

10). But this observation, which uttered independently would sound like a calm, dispassionate analysis of the way life works, in this context takes on the quality of a lament over inevitable doom. A saying of the wise becomes an announcement of doom. The proverb completes the logic of the oracle: harlotry takes away the mind (v. 11), the nation is caught up by a spirit of harlotry (vv. 12–14a), the resulting lack of understanding will lead to ruin (14b).

10. THE LITURGY OF THE LOST: 4.15–19

4   15Though you, O Israel, play the harlot,
     let Judah not incur such guilt.
  Do not enter Gilgal.
     Do not go up to Beth-awen.
     Do not swear 'As Yahweh lives . . .'
  16For like a balky cow
     Israel balks.
  Can Yahweh pasture them now
     like a lamb in a broad meadow?
  17Ephraim is a confederate of idols.
     [a]He has fallen in[a] [18] [b]with a crowd of drunkards.[b]
  They go on playing the harlot.
     [c]They go on loving[c] the disgrace of the shameless.[d]
  19A wind has wrapped them[e] in its wings,
     and they shall be ashamed because of their sacrifices.[f]

Both textual and literary problems encumber interpretation of these verses. The text of vv. 17f. is as difficult as any in the book, and one can be certain only that it is corrupt at several points. Any translation including the one above has to be made from a structure of conjectures. The literary problems add their complications. Verse 15 with its hortatory style and unexpected addressee (Judah) seems to be an orphan in the context; as a consequence it has been assigned by many to a Judean editor of Hosea's book. If the verse is reckoned authentic (see the discussion below), one is faced with the problem

[a–a] Reading MT's consonant's *hinnīaḥ-lō*, literally 'he has set himself'.
[b–b] See BH.
[c–c] Reading *'āhōb 'āhᵃbū* with most recent commentators.
[d] See *māgēn* II in *KB*; read *māginnīm*.
[e] MT has 'her'; read *'ōtām*.
[f] The fem. pl. of *zebaḥ* is probably dialectal; the versions have 'altars'.

whether to consider it a fragment or to connect it with vv. 11–14 or
16–19. Verse 16 with its reference to Yahweh in the third person
seems to be a prophetic saying rather than a divine word; v. 15 fits
this genre and vv. 17–19 continue the style of v. 16; perhaps this
justifies interpreting these verses in sequence. The metaphors and
themes of the sequence are characteristically Hoseanic. The general
subject of Israel's cult as harlotry, the central theme of vv. 4–10 and
11–14, continues. There are clear connections with the particular
emphases of the two foregoing passages. An irrational hardening of
mind has fallen on Israel. Drunkenness and sex dominate their
worship. They are captive to a spirit which drives them toward
their fall.

[15] With a threefold imperative the prophet warns against the cult
of the principal shrines of the North. Because of the reference to
Judah and the similarity between this exhortation and Amos 5.5,
many suspect that the verse is partially or entirely the work of a
Judean editor to give Hosea's words a relevance to a Judean congregation. But Hosea refers to Judah in other sayings addressed to an
Israelite audience (5.5, 10, 13f.; 6.4). And the similarity between this
verse and Amos' exhortation is not the literal copying to be expected
from an editor, but rather a free adaptation which may simply reflect
the influence of Amos' speech on his prophetic successor in the north.
Addressing the Israelites, Hosea delivers an exhortation for Judah in
high irony. Israel is hopeless, captive to a spirit of harlotry (v. 19).
Let Judah not fall in the same trap! Whether Judeans were inclined
to visit Gilgal and Bethel is beside the point. The exhortation to
Judah not to visit Israel's favourite shrines is simply bitter condemnation of their cult meant for the ears of those who did worship in
them.

Gilgal was an important Israelite sanctuary in the Jordan Valley 'on
the east border of Jericho' (Josh. 4.19), probably the mound called
Khirbet Mafjar. Hosea had a very low opinion of its role in Israel's
history (9.15) and of its cult (12.11). *Bēt-'āwen* ('house of evil') is a
scornful nickname for *Bēt-'ēl* ('house of god'), which Hosea seems to
have adapted (5.8; 10.5; 12.5?) from Amos' famous pun on the name of
the shrine (Amos 5.5). Bethel was the more important of the two
state shrines established by Jeroboam I (I Kings 12.28–32) and was
called by its priest 'the king's sanctuary' (Amos 7.13). Hosea's
prohibition would close the doors of the shrine where kingship began
(9.15) and which represents the official cult of the kingdom. It is not

only in local country shrines, but in the principal sanctuaries that worship has become a fouled source of Baalism. Hosea even goes so far as to prohibit the traditional oath taken on the life of Yahweh (Judg. 8.19; Ruth 3.13; I Sam. 14.39, etc.). In the mythological poetry about Baal from Ugarit, the cry

> 'Alive is the powerful Baal
> Existent the Prince, the Lord of Earth!'

is the greeting which interprets the return of the land's fertility in spring.[a] The formula calling upon the 'life of Yahweh' may have been used in a similar fashion in the fertility cult and given cause for Hosea's prohibition (so BK). Jeremiah reckons the oath-formula legitimate when it is sworn in truth (Jer. 4.2; 5.2).

[16] The cult of Israel's shrines is to be avoided because those who assemble in them are stubbornly committed to their folly. Like a balky cow which always bucks and plunges in the direction opposite to that in which she is pushed, Israel perversely resists every attempt of Yahweh to guide them. For a similar metaphor, cf. Jeremiah's 'untrained calf' (Jer. 31.18). Hardening of mind and spirit has set in. Yahweh can no longer shepherd his people, leading them to the pleasant and verdant places where pasture is abundant. Perhaps Hosea has in mind a cultic poem like Ps. 23 which celebrates Yahweh's shepherding care (so ATD).

[17] For the tribal name, Ephraim, as an alternate name for Israel, see 5.3, 5; 11.8. The covenant community with Yahweh at its centre is gone; Ephraim is now the confederate of idols. The nation gathers in worship about the calf-image (8.4f.; 13.2; 14.8), uses teraphim, inquires of wood for oracles (Asherah ? 4.12). [18] The next line ('He has fallen in with a crowd of drunkards') is a structure of conjectures. The reference to an alcoholic drink (*sābā'* – beer?) is fairly clear, and an allusion to the bacchanalian character of the fertility cult would not be inappropriate (cf. v. 11). Along with ritual drunkenness goes the sexual perversion of the fertility cult; the harlotry is the literal sexuality of the rites in which the holy prostitutes and occasional harlots play a part (14). Wine and women in the holy place! Worship has become an orgy!

[19] 'Wind' is a double entendre; the Hebrew word *rūaḥ* means

---

[a] *ANET*, p. 140.

both storm-wind and spirit. The metaphor is that of a stormy wind
which has caught the people in its currents ('wings') and drives and
buffets them helplessly in the direction in which it blows. The metaphor picks up the force of Hosea's 'spirit of harlotry' (4.12; 5.4)
which leads the people astray and blots out the knowledge of God
from their hearts. It is but one more image for the recalcitrant hard-
ness of heart which has come upon the people of Yahweh. But the
wind drives them toward a chasm of doom. Their sacrifices only prepare for their humiliation.

11. THE LEADERS HAVE LED ASTRAY: 5.1–2

5 ¹Hear this, you priests!
  Pay attention, O house of Israel!
  O house of the king, listen!
because the judgment applies to you.
For you have been a trap at Mizpah,
²   a net stretched over Tabor,
  a pit^a dug deep^b at Shittim.^a
But I am a chastiser for you^c all.

This brief oracle has been precisely composed in a structure of
balanced and corresponding parts. The opening proclamation formula (cf. 4.1) is extended by two additional imperatives so that a
summons to three specific groups as addressees is heard. In the next
poetic line there are three corresponding reproaches which are composed of three place names and three metaphors from the practice of
hunting. Each triplet is rounded off by a final sentence which stands
outside the sequence and completes its thought. The entire oracle is
in the style of a divine saying. This carefully constructed gem stands
on its own as an individual oral unit. With v. 3 the direct address is
dropped and the audience becomes the entire nation. Since the royal
house is addressed the oracle could have been spoken at Samaria,
though a setting at a shrine during an annual festival is as likely.

The threefold formula of introduction is itself part of the divine
saying. Its imperatives summon a specific audience to hear the follow-

---

^a Read *weśahat haśśiṭṭīm*; MT makes little sense.
^b Literally 'they dug deep' – a relative clause without *'aśer*.
^c MT 'for them all'; cf. G.

ing proclamation as a direct message from their sovereign. Three groups are named. The priests are the corps of clergy to whom the oracle in 4.4–10 is addressed. The house of the king is the royal family or more likely the entire court. 'House of Israel' does not fit into the sequence since the normal meaning of the expression is the entire nation inclusive of the royal and ecclesiastical establishment. The sentence in which it stands cannot be removed without destroying the symmetry of the structure. 'House of Israel' is either an abbreviated expression which here denotes the representatives of the people (Wolff) or the phrase must be emended to read 'elders of the house of Israel' (Rudolph). The acute problem which separates the exegetes and determines the interpretation of the entire oracle is the meaning of the explanatory sentence which rounds off the imperatives. Is it to be translated 'for justice is yours' or 'for the judgment is yours'? Does it remind the three groups named that justice is their responsibility (so Wolff, Robinson and Weiser), or does it assert that the following announcement of punishment applies to them (so Rudolph and Ward)? Texts like Micah 3.1 and the similarly formulated Deut. 1.17 support the first possibility. And it is true that, if justice (*hammišpāṭ*) is understood broadly as the right order of life, it was in various ways the responsibility of priests, royal administrators, and elders. In favour of the second interpretation is the difficulty of connecting the administration of justice with the misdeeds at Mizpah, Tabor, and Shittim. Granted, these crimes are described by to us enigmatic metaphors, but all that is known about these places is that they were the location of shrines. The collector who placed 5.1–2 in this context must have thought it dealt with cultic sin because ch. 4 and 5.3–7 are concerned with Hosea's favourite theme, the harlotry of Israel's cult.

Using three images from the techniques of hunting, Yahweh scornfully accuses his ministers of making a quarry of others instead of being their protectors and benefactors. The trap (*paḥ*) was a device made of two spring nets which when triggered came together to catch birds (cf. Amos 3.5). The net (*rešet*) was placed along paths or in the forest to entangle its quarry. The pit was a covered hole which gave way when an animal walked on it.[a] The offices of religion and government were established to save and protect the people, but these leaders have instead been like snares that catch and imprison.

The three place-names raise tantalizing problems. Mizpah, Tabor,

---

[a] See L. E. Toombs, 'Traps', *IDB* IV, pp. 287f.

and Shittim are each meant to call to mind some case or situation in which the responsible leaders perverted their office. Such cryptic allusions presuppose occurrences at these places which would make them meaningful to the contemporary Israelite. But our information is too sparse for us to be sure of their specific significance. Does Hosea refer to the Mizpah in Benjamin near its southern border with Judah, or to Mizpah in Gilead? The site of Benjamite Mizpah is contested; opinion is divided between Nabi Samwil and Tell en Nasbeh. It was an important centre for the tribes before the monarchy and probably contained a sanctuary; it was one of the places where Samuel functioned as a judge; and some texts associate it with the selection of Saul as king (Judg. 20.1-3; 21.1-8; I Sam. 7.5-6; 10.17-24). The other Mizpah was somewhere in the north of Gilead, but the exact location is unknown (Judg. 10.17; 11.11). The story of the covenant between Jacob and Laban in Gen. 31.43-55 suggests that it was also a holy place from ancient times.[a] Tabor, the famous mountain on the southeastern edge of the Valley of Jezreel, was also a place of worship and at one time a Baal of Tabor was worshipped there. The site also played a role in the tribal religion of the period of the judges (Deut. 33.19; Judg. 4.6, 12; Ps. 68).[b] The third place, [2] if the emendation (p. 79 n. a) is correct, is the Abel Shittim on the eastern edge of the plain at the mouth of the Jordan where 'Israel yoked himself to the Baal of Peor' (9.10; Num. 25.1ff.). One can only guess at what would link these three places in the mind of Hosea and his contemporaries. In the available tradition they have one thing in common: each contained a shrine which in all likelihood had close connections with the worship of Baal. Perhaps all were remembered by the prophet as places where Israel's leaders had led them into the snare of a pagan cult.

The leaders were especially accountable to Yahweh. Because they have betrayed their office he himself personally will be a discipline (*mūsār*) for all of them. The noun and its corresponding verb denote the training through instruction and punishment which parents provide for children (Prov. 1.8; 4.1; 13.1). Yahweh as covenant God exercises discipline through his mighty acts in history (Deut. 11.2f.), and chastises his people as a father chastises his son (cf. Hos. 11.1ff.). He will not tolerate their disobedience, but his punishment aims at correction for the sake of restoration (cf. Hosea's programme of redemption through judgment in 2.6f., 14f.; 3.3ff.).

[a] See J. Muilenburg, 'Mizpah', *IDB* III, pp. 407ff.
[b] See H.-J. Kraus, *Worship in Israel*, 1966, pp. 165-72.

12. THE PROPHET'S PRIESTLY WORD: 5.3–7

5 ³I myself know Ephraim,
    Israel is not hidden from me;
  that now Ephraim has played ᵃ harlot;
    Israel is defiled.
⁴Their deeds will not permit them ᵇ
    to return to their God,
  for a spirit of harlotry is in their midst,
    and Yahweh they do not know.
⁵The pride of Israel testifies against him;
    ᶜEphraim shall stumble ᵈ by his ᵈ guilt.
  (Judah also has stumbled with them)
⁶With their sheep and cattle they may go
    to seek Yahweh.
  But they will not find him;
    he has withdrawn from them.
⁷Yahweh they have betrayed,
    for they have borne bastards.
  Now the new moon shall devour them.

5.3–7 continues the consistent theme of the oracles in the first four chapters of the book – Israel's betrayal of Yahweh in the harlotrous cult. The oracle is a prophetic saying. It is Hosea who asserts so passionately that he knows the truth about Israel; at the beginning the saying has the tone of discussion-speech delivered in controversy with hearers who demur at his evaluation of the state of the nation. Verses 3f. delineate the prophet's estimate of Israel's plight; vv. 5f. describe how in the time of punishment all will learn what the prophet knows. The nation will stumble and fall for the cult will fail them. Verse 7 is a reprise combining accusation and announcement of disaster.

Because the oracle points to a flourishing cult in which the people are secure, and deals with the theme of religious harlotry so characteristic of Hosea's early period, the oracle may be assigned to the last years of Jeroboam II or soon after. It would have an appropriate setting in a cultic centre like Bethel.

ᵃ *hiznāh* with G; MT has 'you have played harlot'.
ᵇ 'them' has been lost in MT by haplography.
ᶜ Omitting 'and Israel' which is superfluous and destroys the alternation of Ephraim and Israel in the successive measures.
ᵈ MT's text has been changed to plural to adjust to the addition of 'Israel' as a second subject.

[3] The energetic way in which the speaker begins seems to pre-suppose some rebuttal by the audience of a foregoing indictment of the people. Cf. the commentary on 4.4 for a similar case. 'Let none demur at the divine accusation in pretended innocence, claiming that you have truly worshipped Yahweh all along. I, myself, God's prophet, know you all too well and nothing in your career is hidden.' Ephraim is a synonymous name for Israel, and not an indication that the nation exists only as a rump-state reduced virtually to the tribal territory of Ephraim by the invasion of Tiglath-pileser in 733 (so Alt, Weiser). Israel, the 'wife' of Yahweh by covenant, has become a harlot. By turning to the fertility cult of Baal (cf. 1.2; 4.11-14) and engaging in its sexual rites, the people have become unclean like an adulterous woman (cf. 6.10). Uncleanness disqualifies a person for access to God, makes one ineligible for participation in the cult. Both the sexual and the pagan nature of Israel's current cult contribute to their state of defilement. 'Everything that has to do with alien gods or their cultus is condemned as unclean, and debars from the cult of Yahweh.'[a] Hosea does not hesitate to presume to act in the place of the priests (Lev. 10.10) to disclose the real situation of Israel; it is not the work of the priesthood, but its abdication that he condemns (4.4-10).

[4] This uncleanness of Israel is a far more radical contamination than any cultic disqualification that can be corrected by ritual purifi-cation or atonement. Israel's defilement involves a paralysis of soul. They are held prisoner in the grip of the deeds of their past. These 'deeds' (4.9; 7.2; 9.15; 12.2) are the fateful blunders during Israel's history in the land (cf. 6.7ff.; 9.10ff.) which have shaped their character so totally that they are surrounded by these deeds like an insurmountable wall (7.2). A spirit of harlotry (cf. 4.12) is at work among the people; they are possessed by a charisma that comes from Baal and his cult. As a result they do not know Yahweh nor can they return to him. 'To know Yahweh' is Hosea's basic formula for the relationship which Israel ought to have to its God under the covenant (cf. the commentary on 4.1); it means being guided and determined by devotion to Yahweh's revelation of himself at the Exodus and in the wilderness, and by his will given through tōrā. Its lack can only be repaired by a 'return' (šūb) to Yahweh. But in Israel's tragic total depravity šūb is a human impossibility from which only Yahweh's action in judgment can rescue them (cf. 3.5). This radical description

[a] W. Eichrodt, *Theology of the Old Testament* I, 1961, p. 134.

of sin as deeds which enslave men in their consequences is very near to the Pauline portrayal of sin's incapacitating power (Rom. 6.15ff.).

'Testify against' (*'ānāh b-*) is legal terminology for introducing prejudicial evidence in a trial (cf. I Sam. 12.3; II Sam. 1.16; Micah 6.3). The 'pride of Israel' is not Yahweh, but the undisturbed confidence which Israel places in the cultic activity mentioned in the next verse (cf. Amos 6.8). For other texts in which one's own crimes are said to testify against a person, see Isa. 3.9; Jer. 14.7. The line is repeated in 7.10a. By holding persistently to the fertility cult in confidence that its ritual will bring blessing, Israel gives evidence against herself in her trial before Yahweh. Their punishment will come out of their sin; they shall stumble and fall through the guilt of the cult, for its failure will destroy them. In approaching Yahweh as though he were Baal, they cut themselves off from his blessings (14.1).

The reference to Judah is the work of a Judean editor. By adding a third measure to the line he testifies that Hosea's indictment applies equally to Judah in later times.

[6] Verse 6 discloses how Israel's fall will come. The cult will fail them. 'Seek' (*biqqēš*) is used here for the religious act of repairing to a shrine to solicit the help and answer of a deity through ritual, not as a synonym for an authentic returning to Yahweh as in 3.5; 5.15. In Hosea's eyes Israel's attempt to approach God through the sacrifice of sheep and cattle is tantamount to treating him as though he were a Baal to be placated and solicited through a pagan cult (cf. 4.8, 13). Note the antithesis which Amos formulates between 'seeking Yahweh' and 'seeking a shrine' in Amos 5.4f. But Yahweh is not available to this unclean people through their sacrificial cult. In a time of need they learn that he has become an absent God (cf. 5.15). The smoke of their offerings will stir no blessing or prosperity or protection from heaven.

[7] Verse 7 rounds out the speech with a reprise of accusation and prediction of punishment. The basic crime is betrayal. The evidence is the bastards (literally 'strange sons') born to the people. Hosea takes up again the imagery of the covenant as a marriage between God and people. Israel as wife and mother has gone after other gods, her lovers, and the people are children born of the harlotry of the fertility cult (cf. 2.4f.; Jer. 2.27). Under the order of the covenant with its rigid exclusiveness the worship of another deity was the ultimate betrayal. The last sentence clearly announces a punishment, but what the text means is obscure and proposed emendations are creatures of need.

MT says: '*ḥōdeš* ['new moon' or 'month'] will devour them.' By reading 'locust' (*ḥāsīl*) or 'destroyer' (*mašḥīt*) or other plausible subjects a reasonable sentence can be created. Or one can hold to MT and press some sense from the text as it stands. Rudolph suggests that the sense is: one single month will suffice for them and their fields to be devoured (KAT). In the midst of the uncertainty the final threat is clear. Israel has sought divine blessing for womb and field in the Canaanized cult; in the end people and crops will be consumed.

13. WAR AMONG BROTHERS IS SIN AND JUDGMENT: 5.8–6.6

5 8Sound the horn in Gibeah,
   the trumpet in Ramah!
Cry alarm in Beth-awen!
   Put Benjamin on guard![a]
9Ephraim shall be ravaged
   on the day of punishment.
Among the tribes of Israel
   I declare what is sure.

10The captains of Judah have become
   like those who remove the landmark.
Upon them I will pour out
   my wrath like water.
11Ephraim is oppressed,
   justice abused,
because he chose to go
   after an enemy.[b]
12But I am like pus[c] to Ephraim
   like caries to the house of Judah.

13When Ephraim saw his sickness,
   and Judah his wound,
Ephraim went to Assyria
   and sent to the great king.[d]
But he cannot heal you
   nor cure your wound.

[a] Read *haḥᵃrīdū*. MT's 'Behind you, O Benjamin' is not out of the question; perhaps it is itself a warning cry or a summons to battle (Rudolph).
[b] MT's *ṣāw* is a sound, not a word; cf. Isa. 28.10, 13. The emendation *ṣār* commends itself (Duhm, Rudolph).
[c] See *ʿāš* II, *KB*, p. 743; a better parallel to 'caries' than the usual 'moth', which is inappropriate as a pest for a human in any case.
[d] Reading *malkī rab*; cf. the Assyrian designation of the king as *šarru rabu*.

¹⁴For I am like a lion to Ephraim,
    like a young lion to the house of Judah.
I! I myself will rend and depart;
    I will drag away and none can deliver.

¹⁵I will go back to my place
    until they suffer for their guilt and seek my face;
    in their distress they shall look to me.

6 ¹Let us go back to Yahweh;
    for he has torn and he will heal us,
    he smote^a and he will bandage us.
²He will revive us after two days;
    on the third day he will raise us up
    that we may live in his presence.
³Let us know – let us pursue the knowledge of Yahweh.
    Like the dawn his going forth is fixed.
He shall come to us like rain,
    like spring showers that water the land.

⁴What shall I do with you, O Ephraim?
    What shall I do with you, O Judah?
Your devotion is like morning mist,
    like dew that soon disappears.
⁵Therefore I have fought^b (them) with the prophets,
    slain them with the words of my mouth;
    and so ^cmy decision like light^c goes forth,
⁶that I desire devotion, not sacrifice,
    the knowledge of God, rather than burnt offerings.

The cry of alarm in 5.8 marks a new situation and theme. In chs.
1–3 and 4.1–5.7 the setting was the quiet last years of the reign of
Jeroboam II, and the dominant concern of the oracles was the cultic
apostasy of Israel. Now suddenly the focus shifts to the political scene
with both Israel and Judah on the stage. It is now generally recognized that the events referred to in 5.8–14 belong to the history of
Syrian-Ephraimite war.^d It was throughout a venture of tragic folly
with grievous consequences for the brother nations of Judah and
Israel. In immediate danger of invasion by the Assyrian, Tiglath-

---

^a Read *wayyak*.

^b *ḥṣb*='hew (stones, a pit)' makes no sense; see Ugaritic *ḥṣb* || *mḫṣ*='smite, fight'.

^c–c Reading MT's consonants *mišpāṭī kā'ōr*; cf. GST.

^d Since the definitive study of A. Alt, 'Hosea 5.8–6.6. Ein Krieg und seine Folgen in prophetischen Beleuchtung', *Kleine Schriften* II, 1959, pp. 163ff.

pileser, Israel's king Pekah (737–732) joined forces with Rezin of Aram to face their common foe. These two allies were unsuccessful in persuading King Ahaz of Judah to join their coalition. Anxious for Judean assistance and fearful of an unaligned power on their southern borders, the two kings attacked Judah and invested Jerusalem. Ahaz appealed to Tiglath-pileser whose approach brought an end to the attack on Judah. In 733 Israel was overwhelmed, a large segment of the population was deported, and all her territory except for the central hill country of Ephraim and Benjamin was incorporated into the Assyrian provincial system. Pekah was assassinated by Hoshea (732–724) who assumed the throne of Israel and became a vassal of Tiglath-pileser to save what was left of the nation.[a] The references to contemporary events in 5.8–6.6 fit the situation in Israel during the time after the Assyrian attack had begun, just before and after 733. The sayings are addressed to both the northern and southern kingdoms, with the former called Ephraim throughout.

This long sequence of course does not represent one oral unit, as the shifts in style and form make clear; it is held together by its setting within the same complex of events. But, though different units of speech are present, they are interrelated by literary and thematic dependence as well as common setting. 5.8–9 is a prophetic saying in which Hosea appears as a watchman crying alarm in Benjamin about an attack from the south; the saying sets the historical scene. Verses 10–12 are a divine saying about the brother-nations and their guilt in the war; Judah's captains expropriate territory (v. 10) and Ephraim seeks help from a foe (v. 11). So Yahweh works through the suffering they create; their 'wound' is his work (v. 12). The divine saying in vv. 13–14 is yet another announcement of judgment at a somewhat later point. In v. 15 the interpretation of punishment is pushed further; it is a declaration by Yahweh that he will withdraw to await Israel's penitence. The song in 6.1–3 is a liturgical expression of the demanded penitence; the song continues the sequence, because it picks up and responds to elements of 5.11–14. The divine saying in 6.4–6 is an oracle answering the song. The collectors assembled this larger composition of related material because they knew or recognized its coherence. Under just what specific circumstances each saying was spoken and with what interval between them cannot be known.

[a] On the history of the period, see J. Bright, *A History of Israel*, 1959/1960, pp. 256f.; M. Noth, *The History of Israel*, 1960², pp. 257ff.

[5.8] With a cry for blast of horn and sound of trumpet, Hosea assumes the role of a watchman in a time of crisis. As part of the defence arrangements in Israel a guard would be posted when invasion threatened; it was his duty to see that the alarm by horn and outcry was spread throughout the land so that the populace could flee to fortified cities and towns for safety. By taking up the watchman's cry the prophet steps forth in the midst of military danger as a guard who sees the threat in a larger context than that of national politics and strategic defence. Because a prophet cries alarm, the crisis brings a confrontation with divine action. Jeremiah would later use the same dramatic device in warning Judah of danger from the north (Jer. 4.5f.; 6.1; see also Joel 2.1). The alarm is to be sounded in Benjamite territory on the southern edge of Israel's boundaries. If the order in which the places are named is significant, the movement of the invasion proceeds from the south to the north along the highway which ran from Jerusalem on the central ridge into Ephraimite country. Gibeah, Ramah, and Bethel ('Beth-aven' is a scornful nickname for Bethel; see 4.15) are set just a few miles apart in that order along the road across the centre of Benjamin. This locale is a clue to the best conjecture about the threat to which the prophet refers. All three towns belong to the territory allotted to the tribe of Benjamin under the amphictyonic system (Josh. 18.21ff.). After the schism between Israel and Judah, the southern kingdom had appropriated part of Benjamite territory, and Gibeah and Ramah had been fortified as part of Judah's military defences on the north (I Kings 15.16–22). When Pekah and Rezin pressed to the very walls of Jerusalem during the Syrian-Ephraimite war this territory would have been reclaimed (II Kings 16.5; Isa. 7.1ff.). But once the Assyrian approach had necessitated the withdrawal of the armies of Israel and Aram, Judah would have moved immediately to secure her northern defences again in the region of Benjamin. It is against such a counter-attack that the prophet warns.

[9] Though the alarm is to be sounded in Benjamite territory, Hosea appears to expect the crushing blow to fall on Ephraim in the very centre of Israel's hill country. Whether he thought that Judah would overrun Benjamin, or speaks of the Assyrian invasion, is not certain. Ephraim continues in the following verses to be Hosea's name for the northern state alongside of Judah for the southern kingdom. Ephraim's devastation will be her day of correction, her time to learn through the severe discipline of God's punishment about the error of

her policy. Among the extant oracles of Hosea there is none in which he speaks specifically of his attitude toward Pekah's strategy of alliance with Aram against Assyria and Judah, but it is easy to imagine that he regarded it with the same dismay which Isaiah expressed concerning the appeal of Ahaz to Tiglath-pileser for aid against Aram and Israel (Isa. 7.1ff.). Neither prophet had any patience with the frantic plots and conspiracies by which the reigning kings sought to save themselves. Hosea thought in terms of the covenant league, saw the divided north and south from an 'all-Israel' perspective. They were 'the tribes of Israel', a people whose real existence was to be found in the unity of a folk under Yahweh (cf. 1.11). In his view these ruinous wars against one another were a tragic manifestation of the sin of schism to which they had committed themselves under their kings. Now Ephraim must learn better through a searing chastisement. Verse 9b has the summary ring of a concluding line. What the prophet makes known is utterly certain, not just in the sense that it is true, but as well in the sense that the prophetic word has the power to fulfil itself. Because it is the articulation of the Lord of history, it is a word that makes history. The 'I' could be the first person of Yahweh or the prophet, though the character of the claim, which sounds like a disputation-word, makes the latter the more likely.

[10] This divine word forms a complete saying of judgment, containing in its two lines the full structure of indictment and sentence. The accusation is directed against the captains (*śārīm*) of Judah. As a prophet of Yahweh as covenant Lord, Hosea is messenger to all the tribes of Israel, even though they be separated into distinct political entities. The crime of Judah's captains is uncovered by a comparison; in a successful military venture they have become like those who remove the landmark. The context seems still to be the Syrian-Ephraimite war and its aftermath. The counter attack of Judah against which the prophet warned in vv. 8f. has taken place, and the military leaders of Judah have annexed Benjamite territory. This pressure of one state against another is measured in terms of an old moral principle known in the ancient Near East generally and incorporated in Israel's law and Wisdom norms. 'To remove the landmark' means the malicious obscuring of boundary lines to encroach on the fields of another. In Israel's tradition the boundary marks were sacred to Yahweh because they fixed the line of a man's holdings according to the allotment of the land as Yahweh's gift (Deut. 19.14); such a crime was forbidden in the old series of curses which enforced the covenant

order (Deut. 27.17) and occupied a prominent place in the list of sins against which the teachers of Wisdom warned (Prov. 22.28; 23.10; Job 24.2). Judah's military adventure is reduced to the dimensions of the guilty act of one covenant brother against another and put under the curse. Yahweh will pour out his wrath upon them. In Hosea the wrath of Yahweh is the passionate feeling of God against his people in their sin. The anthropomorphism is meant in all seriousness because in his dealings with Israel Yahweh reacts with a full range of emotional responses displaying his character as person in radical fulness (8.5; 13.11). Here wrath is spoken of as though it were an instrument of work as well as an attitude and feeling (cf. 11.9; 14.4). Like a torrent of water it will cascade down upon Judah's captains as the effective force of Yahweh's 'No' to what they have done. Though the judgment-word of two lines is complete, it now goes with vv. 11f. to make up an oracle concerning both Judah and Ephraim.

[11] Turning to Ephraim, the other division of God's people, the prophet raises a lament over the calamity which their political folly has brought upon them. The language of the lament assumes that Ephraim has already been struck a shattering blow. The circumstances of Ephraim's oppression are doubtless the invasion of Tiglath-pileser from the north. And in the second measure the prophet's eye seems to remain also on Judah's thrust from the south. The captains of Judah have shattered the order (mišpāṭ) of the covenant, the right of Benjamin to its allotted land. All this because Ephraim had turned to an enemy for an ally. Syria is undoubtedly in mind. How could Ephraim make common cause with this ancient foe against its brothers? Perhaps MT's ṣāw is a derisive term referring to Pekah's Aramean ally to whom he turned in resisting Assyria and in conspiring against Judah (BK). Ephraim's plight is pitiful; the prophet cannot stand aloof from the agony of his own folk. But as prophet he must uncover the roots of the tragedy in Ephraim's betrayal of her covenant brothers in the alliance with Aram.

[12] The response of Yahweh deals with the sins of both Ephraim (v. 11) and Judah (v. 10). Yahweh declares that he is already at work within this tragic complex of events. The metaphors used for the work of Yahweh are shockingly bold and abrasive, even for Hosea. God is putrefaction and bone rot in the body of both peoples. The comparisons are drawn to the extreme limit, but their boldness is meant to reveal how God in hiddenness is already at work, sapping away the

vitality of Ephraim and Judah through the very actions which they initiate and execute. The debilitating effects of their policy is not to be thought of as separate from the effect of his presence in their history.

[13] A blindness has fallen upon Ephraim and Judah. As national states, they 'see' only what is inescapably obvious – their tenuous predicament; but they do not perceive the theological dimension of what is happening to them. They can only recognize the danger to their very existence. 'Sickness' and 'wound' are images of military devastation by an enemy, the damage to the body politic (as in Isa. 1.5f.; Jer. 30.12f.). Already Israel has been reduced to a fractional vassal state by Tiglath-pileser. Judah was earlier invested by the armies of Israel and Aram, and now quivers in dread before the uncertainty of Assyrian policy. But nowhere in the crisis do the national leaders sense the presence of Yahweh; instead they seek some solution within the realm of international politics. Both states turned to their mortal foe in desperation and in doing so fell into the arms of the one appointed to be their executioner. 'Ephraim went to Assyria' probably refers to the submission of King Hoshea (c. 732) immediately after the assassination of Pekah (II Kings 17.3ff.) when he paid tribute to Assyria and became a vassal.[a] Earlier, about 738, Menahem had bought off the Assyrians with a vast tribute (II Kings 15.19f.).[b] Hosea's reference is so generally phrased that both could be covered, but the later incident is probably in focus because of the orientation of the entire sequence to the context of events after the Syrian-Ephraimite war. Since Ephraim and Judah are so regularly paired in alternating lines in this sequence, one expects Judah as the subject of 'sent to the king'. The appeal of Ahaz to Tiglath-pileser (II Kings 16.7ff.) would fit the reference perfectly, and one is tempted to insert Judah (or Jerusalem) in the measure as its subject. However, the measure could be no more than a parallel to the foregoing one, with the prophet concentrating for the moment on his immediate audience. That he may be doing so is suggested by the shift of style to direct address in the second-person pronouns of v. 13b. The prophet lays bare the vanity of seeking help and health by adjusting national politics to the might of Assyria. That is to deal with symptoms, not the disease. Yahweh, not the Assyrian, is the ultimate source of their wound (vv. 12, 14), and he alone can heal them.

[a] *ANET*, p. 284a.
[b] Cf. *ANET*, p. 283a.

[14] 'I am like a lion. . . .' Pronoun and metaphor combine in shocking urgency to insist that Yahweh is the primary factor in Israel's history. Accommodation to Assyria will bring no health to Ephraim and Judah *because* it is Yahweh whose wrath threatens them. The emphatic repetition of the pronoun 'I' at the beginning of v. 14b insistently demands that the hearers recognize the revelation of Yahweh in their crisis and see their predicament in terms of covenant relations, not international politics. Israel is under the power of its God Yahweh like the helpless prey of the hunting lion; when the king of beasts crouches over his kill, none dares assault him. The language of Hosea evokes by imagery what is actual and sensuously terrifying to his audience so as to create a feel for the actuality of Yahweh's wrath. The same theriomorphism is used again in 13.7. The threat of the lion hangs over both Ephraim and Judah; Yahweh stalks his entire covenant people. A judgment draws near that will outrun anything that would be expected. Every hope of escape is false, a failure to perceive that there is no way out but the one which Yahweh prepares through his wrath.

[15] Verse 15 stands apart from vv. 10–14 and 6.1–3; it does not continue directly the foregoing description of Yahweh's punishment nor does it belong to the following song. Yahweh's action is no longer the visitation of his wrath to destroy, but a strategy to bring his people back to him. Yet v. 15 is an indispensable transition. It prepares for the song of penitence by portraying Yahweh as the God who waits for the response of his people. And the song is clearly composed as a response to the judgment described in vv. 10–14 (see the comment on 6.1–3). What the announcement of Yahweh's withdrawal does in effect is to interpret Yahweh's wrath in such a way that the experience of punishment becomes an invitation to penitence. It introduces a constant theme of Hosea that God in his anger against his people's sin ultimately seeks their reconciliation. Whether v. 15 was spoken as part of vv. 10–14 or was separated from it by an interval of time cannot be said. However, it presupposes an audience that has heard the word of wrath. 'I will go . . .' is a catchword that echoes 'I will depart' in v. 14 (both *'ēlēk*). But the theriomorphism is dropped; Yahweh is not a lion dragging his prey to his lair. He will leave the scene and dwell in 'his own place'. The notion of the 'absent God' is a feature of Israel's laments which speak of the God who is not 'with us', does not hear, answer, help, save. The location of 'his place' is not specified in Hosea; the prophet could refer to Yahweh's mount or to

a heavenly palace. Amos 1.2 places Yahweh on Zion; for other references to a locale of Yahweh see Deut. 33.2; Judg. 5.4; Pss. 18.6; 46.4, etc. Just as the coming of Yahweh from his place meant aid for Israel against her foes (Judg. 5.4), his going away left the people in the hands of their enemy to suffer alone the ravages of history. The absence of God is qualified by a temporal limitation; its duration will be ended by an event in the soul of Israel when in the fire of their agony the people seek Yahweh and look to him. The event is designated by the verb '*šm* which in Hosea means either 'incur guilt' (13.1; 4.15) or 'suffer the consequences of guilt' (10.2; 13.16); the second meaning is appropriate here. Israel and Judah must experience their calamities as suffering for sin and discover in the experience that they have deserted their God. His desertion uncovers their sin. Out of such significant suffering they will seek him and turn eagerly to him. 'Seek' means a whole-hearted submission to Yahweh as Lord of Israel's history and life (cf. Amos' 'Seek me and not Bethel', 5.4) instead of merely cultic adoration (as in 5.6). 'Look to' (*šiḥar*) is a more intense verb, represents a direct personal turning to Yahweh out of the deep trouble that leaves one helpless apart from his help. (Pss. 63.1; 78.34; Isa. 26.9). Though the formulations and images vary, Hosea's conception of the character of God's eschatological action remains constant: to bring his people through judgment to that point at which they truly return to him (2.7, 14f.; 3.5).

[6.1–3] These three verses make up a distinct unit. It has long since been recognized that the piece is liturgical in form and is to be identified as a song of penitence.[a] Such songs were used in times of national crisis when the people were assembled for fasting, lament, petition, and sacrifice to avert the wrath of God.[b] The song is composed of two elements: a twofold summons to return to Yahweh and to acknowledge his lordship (vv. 1*a*, 3*a*), followed by assertions of confidence that Yahweh will save. The cohortatives of the first element could be sung by people or priest as an invitation to penitence; the assertions of confidence are regular features of the lament. The language of the song shows that it is not a random piece, but belongs precisely in its present literary context. It echoes the sayings in 5.10–15. Its penitence is the response for which Yahweh waits (v. 15). It

[a] H. Schmidt, 'Hosea 6.1–6', *Beiträge zur Religionsgeschichte und Archäologie Palästinas* (Festschrift for E. Sellin), 1927, pp. 111–26.
[b] See Gunkel-Begrich, *Einleitung in die Psalmen*, 1933, pp. 117ff.; S. Mowinckel, *The Psalms in Israel's Worship* I, ET, 1962, pp. 193ff.

recognizes the suffering of the nation as the punishment of Yahweh and even repeats the language of v. 13 ('rend, heal' in v. 1). The summons to return and to know Yahweh take up the two basic demands which Hosea makes upon Israel. Verse 4 assumes that both Ephraim and Judah are involved in the penitence as well as in the judgment of 5.10–14. And the divine saying which resumes in vv. 4–6 is a direct response to the song. How is the song to be understood in its context? The Septuagint added an introductory 'saying' at the end of 5.15 to indicate that the song is to be read as a continuation of the divine word in ch. 5; the translator understood it as prediction of what Israel would say when they turned to Yahweh in their trouble. He may have been guided by the formally similar case in 14.1–3. But the song cannot be an ideal model for the people's penitence spoken by Yahweh or recommended by the prophet. Verses 4–6 are a lamenting protest that the song and the response it represents come short of Yahweh's expectations. Nor can it be an ironic mimicry on Hosea's part of the shallow penitence which the people substitute for true repentance; the song incorporates too much of Hosea's own language and theology and responds precisely to his announcement that Yahweh's punishment sought only the response of his people. It must be a song which was composed in the situation for use in a liturgy of lament and penitence in response to his prophecy. The collectors of Hosea's material have placed it between 5.15 and 6.4–6 because the latter requires it to be understood. Evidence that such ceremonies were held during the Assyrian crisis appears elsewhere in Hosea. Ephraim sought God with herds and flocks (5.6), cried out in anguish that they 'knew Yahweh' (8.2). The song thus has a double character; its language is determined in part by its relation to Hosea's preaching, but its significance and intention depends on the cultic environment of Israel's Canaanized worship.[a]

[6.1] The summons to return (*šūb*) to Yahweh takes up a basic theme in the message of Hosea (2.7; 3.5); in his vocabulary *šūb* means leave off the Baalized practices current in religion and go back to the original relation to Yahweh of the wilderness period. But this call in the mouth of the nation's priests presumes that 'return' can be brought off by the mere resolve of their current religiosity. The act which this pseudo-summons has in mind is turning to the national God for help through the cultic devotion of sacrifice (5.6; 6.6). The shallowness of

---

[a] On the latter, see R. Hentschke, *Die Stellung der vorexilischen Schriftpropheten zum Kultus* (BZAW 75), 1957, pp. 89ff.

the summons is apparent in the self-centred reasons which undergird the call – they want to survive as they are. That Yahweh alone kills and makes alive, wounds and heals, was an old dictum of faith in Yahwism (Deut. 32.39), originally a way of saying that in effect Yahweh alone is God. But the ancient affirmation is twisted to link the acts of wounding and healing together as though they were an automatic sequence, an expected cycle of divine work on which the devotees of Yahweh could rely willy-nilly. There is no mention of the iniquity of the nation as in 14.1ff., no word of the change that must be wrought through judgment. 'When he is "worshipped" he will tend our wounds, for that is his business and nature.' [2] The call is issued in presumptuous confidence that Yahweh will be quick to respond. 'After two days' and 'on the third day' are synonymous expressions for a short period. In the cult of Adonis the Syrian god was believed to die and rise again on the third day. If there is any connection between the formulations of this verse and the mythology of the dying-rising deity, it is at most an allusion.[a] The people, not the deity, are the subject; nor are they portrayed as dead. Rather they are sorely wounded and Yahweh is expected to revive them by restoring their vitality and so saving them from death. There is no notion of a national resurrection as in Ezek. 37. According to the OT view, should the people die, they would be separated from Yahweh, absent from his presence, incapable of worshipping him and of satisfying him with their praise (Pss. 6.5; 30.9; 88.10–12). Yahweh would have no people to live before him as his peculiar possession. The song arrogantly assumes that Yahweh's purpose is fulfilled in their mere existence.

[3] The second summons employs Hosea's basic formula for what Yahweh requires of Israel (6.6; see the commentary on 4.1). In his theology 'to know Yahweh' means to acknowledge with heart and life the lordship of the God of the Exodus and covenant. But here Israel uses the formula in liturgy as a cry to Yahweh that they claim him by the act of worship (8.1f.). The strenuous intensity of this second exhortation expresses the desperation of the nation's need, their terrified frantic plan to undertake the 'knowledge of God' as an emergency measure. The following affirmations of trust are phrased in metaphors which compare God's availability to the repetitious events of nature. His going forth is like the dawn which is certain to

[a] See the discussion in F. Hvidberg, *Weeping and Laughter in the Old Testament* 1962, pp. 126ff.

break. 'His going forth' probably refers to Yahweh's procession from 'his place' to come to the aid of his people (see the commentary on 5.15 and the texts cited there). The free historical intervention of Yahweh as the God of Israel's holy warfare is transmuted into natural process. Here, and in the last two metaphors, Israel's God is brought within the frame of reference of the deities of Canaan whose activity was a function of weather and season. Rain is the peculiar provenance of Baal in Canaanite theology. As surely as the winter and spring rains return each year to revive the life of the land, so Yahweh's beneficent presence is sure to be manifested. Once Yahweh is thought of in this unhistorical impersonal fashion, the notions of 'return' and 'know God' lose their validity and power for reformation, because they have no focus on the saving history and covenant relation, and so can only stir the current religiosity of Israel.

[4–6] In vv. 4–6 Yahweh again takes up the word. See the comment on vv. 1–3 for a discussion of its relation to the immediate literary context. The divine saying opens with a dismayed lament over the transitory covenant loyalty of Israel and Judah (v. 4), explains that this lack of constancy has provoked the history of Yahweh's struggle with his people through the prophets (v. 5), and concludes with a declaration of Yahweh's will concerning the mode of Israel's relation to him (v. 6). Israel and Judah are addressed directly with a 'you' in v. 4; in vv. 5f., where the perspective turns to the past, the nations are spoken of in the third person. The divine saying stands where an oracle of salvation would be expected. Such oracles were anticipated by the laments offered to God in the cult; the congregation hoped for and usually received an affirmative answer to their appeal through a prophet.[a] But the answer received and delivered by Hosea is negative! The opening questions express a perplexed frustration at Israel's penitence. The metaphors in vv. 4f. oppose those in v. 3. The declaration in v. 6 implies directly that Israel's frantic turning to Yahweh was centred in sacrificial ritual. That was not what Yahweh waited for.

[4] Both Ephraim and Judah are addressed. As in 5.8–15, the prophet speaks to all 'the tribes of Israel' (5.9), the total constituency of the old tribal league as the members of the covenant people. It is of course unlikely that Hosea addresses an audience composed of people from north and south. But the word he had in the crisis was

[a] See S. Mowinckel, op. cit., Vol. II, 1962, pp. 58ff.; C. Westermann, The Praise of God in the Psalms, 1965, p. 61.

from the beginning for the whole people of God, so the anguished questions reach out for dialogue with all God's chosen. Without reserve God discloses the frustration caused by the inconstancy of his people. In the election of Israel Yahweh involved himself in the consequences of their acts. He is the true subject of Israel's history; but he is inextricably by his own free choice a part of the history of which Israel is subject. The history of Israel is the sphere of the struggle and dialogue between man and God – and here the dialogue is like that between husband and fickle wife, father and prodigal son. Yahweh concedes that Ephraim and Judah have brought forth a kind of devotion, but their devotion has the form without reality and power. Note the counter-demand for devotion (ḥesed) in v. 6. The loyalty of Israel in the covenant relation is evanescent, temporary, episodic. Like the morning fog and early dew, it seems to appear only to vanish. The metaphor discloses the temporary ardour of Israel's appeal to Yahweh in the song of vv. 1–3. The comparisons are touched with irony for they correspond to those in v. 3 where Israel said that Yahweh's coming to help is sure as the certain dawn and the fixed seasons of rain. He responds that Israel's ḥesed is as vaporous as the moisture of morning mist and dew.

[5] This treacherous unreality of devotion is nothing new. It is but one case of the very problem which has provoked Yahweh to send his prophets with ominous messages of divine wrath. Through the 'opposition prophets' Yahweh has waged war against his people precisely because their past has been a record of an all-too-fleeting ḥesed. The 'prophets' could be such figures as Elijah, Micaiah ben Imlah, Amos, and Isaiah. 'Words of my mouth' is a phrase which expresses the understanding of prophecy manifest in oracle-form of the divine word where Yahweh speaks directly in the first person (cf. Jer. 1.9; 15.19). The prophetic oracles are represented as death-dealing weapons, a dynamic activistic conception of the word of Yahweh. The oracles not only inform, but inaugurate and execute the judgment of which they tell. They are connected with the ominous power of the curse, perhaps because oracles of judgment often announced the enactment of the curses which enforced the covenant. In this struggle through the prophets against Israel's empty religiosity, the will of the covenant Lord has been set forth with the clarity of the sun whose rising dispels all darkness. Perhaps the metaphor 'like light' is again a response to the song and its comparison of Yahweh's coming to help to the certainty of the dawn. Israel clamours for help but ignores the

revelation through the prophets. Yahweh's judgment (*mišpāṭ*) is his decision concerning the order which ought to determine the relation of God and people in the covenant, formulated in the declaration in 6.

[6] The *mišpāṭ* is announced in the form of an instructional sentence. The good pleasure of Yahweh is the single point of reference for determining how the covenant is to be kept, because by its terms he is the exclusive Lord of Israel and alone has the right to fix the conditions of their existence. One does not turn to a suzerain for help while ignoring his desire. The principle of covenant order is formulated by contrasting terms from the vocabulary of personal relations to acts of cultic sacrifice. Devotion (*ḥesed*) is opposed to the sacrifice in which the worshippers participate by sharing a meal to establish community with the deity (*zebaḥ*). Knowledge of God is opposed to the burnt offering in which the whole animal is consumed as an act of adoration to the deity ('*ōlā*). On the meaning and significance of devotion and knowledge of God in Hosea, see the comment on 4.1. *Ḥesed* means the attitude and acts which loyally maintain and implement a given relationship, the covenant in Hosea's usage. The knowledge of God is the unqualified response to Yahweh as he was revealed in the Exodus and wilderness and the obedience which hears and obeys his instruction. It is, therefore, a knowing which becomes a state of being. Yahweh wants community with Israel through loyalty and love instead of sacrificial meals. He desires the service of faith and obedience, not the adulation of burning altars. In his election of Israel Yahweh had not meant to found one more religion of ritual by which men might manage the divine; he had intended to become absolute Lord of all life. In the eighth century, sacrifice was the essential religious act; Hosea's hearers probably could not conceive of religion apart from sacrifice. The declaration rejecting sacrifice must have sounded radical and nihilistic. But Hosea does not think of the principle as revolutionary. In I Sam. 15.22 a pronouncement quite similar in form and vocabulary is attributed to Samuel; this prophetic radicalism against the cult also appears in Amos 5.21ff.; Isa. 1.12–17; Micah 6.6–8; Pss. 51.16f.; 40.6. It is characteristic of the form of these declarations that they oppose normative terms understood as covenantal values to acts of sacrifice. The formulation is probably rooted in the long struggle between the Mosaic Yahwism of the amphictyonic league and the characteristic cult of Canaan. The struggle did not end in the Old Testament (Matt. 9.13; 12.7).

14. A GEOGRAPHY OF TREACHERY: 6.7–7.2

6 ⁷But in ᵃ Adam they broke covenant;
  there they betrayed me.
⁸Gilead is a city of evildoers,
  whose footprints ᵇ are bloody.
⁹Like a lurking ᶜ robber
  is the priestly guild.
They murder on the way to Shechem;
  yea, they have acted shamefully.
¹⁰In Israel's house I have seen a ghastly thing!
  There is Ephraim's harlotry,
  Israel is defiled.
¹¹Also, O Judah, for you a harvest is set.
  When I would change the fortunes of my people,
7   ¹when I would heal Israel,
  then is disclosed Ephraim's guilt,
  Samaria's evil deeds.
For they act in deceit;
  the thief enters;
  robbers roam outside.
²It never enters their mind
  that I remember all their evil.
Now their deeds surround them;
  they are before my face.

What is the covenant God to do with a people whose land can be described in terms of a geography of evil? When he would restore them, he confronts a nation surrounded by evil and empty of repentance. The oracle is a divine saying with Yahweh speaking in the first person throughout. Israel is referred to in the third person as if Yahweh were speaking of them to another party. There are two movements. 6.7–10 is a sort of miniature guidebook to the geography of sin in Israel; going from one place to another it catalogues the famous crimes of various localities as an indictment of the whole nation. Its interpretation is fraught with problems. The text is difficult, and, beyond that, the incidents which were infamous in Hosea's time are unknown. So the allusions remain enigmatic. 6.11b–7.2 is a lament

---

ᵃ *beʾādām* for MT's *keʾādām* ('like Adam/man'); see the comment.
ᵇ Reading *ʿiqbēhem dām*.
ᶜ Assuming that *ḥkh* ('wait') can mean 'wait with hostile intent'; on the unusual form see *BL*, p. 424.

over the impasse between Yahweh's willingness to restore his people
and their total identification with evil. The oracle continues some of
the themes of 5.8–6.6. The dilemma of Yahweh in 6.11b–7.1 is like
that of the frustrated questions in 6.4. 'Heal' (7.1) appears in 5.13;
6.1. The sins catalogued in 6.7–10 are intended as demonstration that
Israel lacks the devotion which Yahweh requires (6.6). In the present
text 6.7 opens with an adversative ('But they . . .') which does
connect it with the foregoing verse. But the saying is concerned only
with Ephraim; the pairing of Ephraim and Judah in the circumstances of the aftermath of the Syrian-Ephraimite war does not
continue. The adversative is probably the work of the collector who
has assembled the oracles in 6.7–7.16 as a documentation that Israel
lacks devotion.

[6.7] The first sin in this bill of indictment is a case of breach of
covenant. The particulars of the incident are hidden in MT's *ke'ādām*
which could mean 'like Adam' (a reference to an 'original covenant
rupture' in Eden), or 'like a man' (an allusion to human frailty in
keeping agreements). The emendation proposed (p. 99 n. *a*) is supported by the locative 'there' in the parallel measure, and by the thematic
use of place names in the following lines. A city named Adam is
mentioned only in Josh. 3.16, which locates it on the Jordan river
where the waters were cut off so that Israel could cross over. It is
probably to be identified with Tell ed-Damiyeh on the east bank some
thirty miles above the Jordan's mouth. Covenant (*berīt*) is the technical term for the form of the relationship established by Yahweh with
Israel through which he became their divine suzerain with the
obligation to protect and bless his subjects and the right to claim
their obedience.[a] Hosea does not speak specifically of the Sinai
covenant, but he says repeatedly that the Israel-Yahweh relation
began in the Exodus time (9.10; 11.1; 12.9; 13.4). The verb 'to
break' (*'ābar*), when it is used in the sense of transgressing, overstep-
ping, takes covenant or commandment as its object.[b] In 8.1 'to break
my covenant' is parallel to 'rebel against my instruction (*tōrā*)' and
Hosea emphasizes the central importance of the commandments of
Yahweh (4.1f., 6; 8.12). Apparently the incident at Adam involved
some breach of a specific requirement of the covenant. The second
measure interprets the crucial importance of the incident; any breach
of covenant is a betrayal of Yahweh, violates the integrity of the

[a] See G. Mendenhall, 'Covenant', in *IDB* I, pp. 714ff.
[b] See the texts listed in *BDB s.v.*, para. 1i, p. 717.

personal relation between God and people. In chs. 1–3 Hosea uses the image of marriage for the covenant in order to highlight the personal dimensions and values of the relation which are not explicit in 'covenant' when it is understood in a restricted legal sense. Since the theme 'breach of covenant' is introduced in the first line, it is doubtless the category to which the entire list of crimes belongs (ATD).

[8] The city of Gilead is next in the catalogue of sins. The name usually applies to the mountainous region in the north of Transjordan. There was a Jabesh-gilead in the Jordan valley on the Brook Cherith, and a Ramoth-gilead in the centre of the highlands of Gilead; probably the latter is meant, but what is known of its history is of no help in interpreting Hosea's enigmatic allusion (cf. 12.11). Nor does 'evildoers' tell us anything specific. The term ($p\bar{o}^{a}l\bar{e}$ '$\bar{a}wen$) is a favourite category in psalms of lament where '$\bar{a}wen$ means the threatening power of sorcery and curse exercised against those depending on Yahweh, and more generally the malicious intrigues and attacks of enemies.[a] It can be used of those who engage in political intrigue against the purposes of Yahweh (Isa. 31.2). Was Gilead a centre of revolt in one of the violent uprisings of the period? Fifty men of Gilead joined Pekah in the assassination of Pekahiah (II Kings 15.25). The deeds of Gilead's citizens left a trail of bloody footprints (cf. I Kings 2.5).

[9] Shechem is the third city named. The indictment is not drawn against the place or those who live there, but against an association of priests who murder those on the way to Shechem. This specific identification of priests raises the possibility that the indefinite 'they' in vv. 7f. might also point to them (cf. 4.4–10). Why would priests murder folk who were on the way to Shechem? It was one Israelite city against which Hosea directed no polemic. The ancient site had been a cultic centre associated with the Mosaic covenant tradition from the time of the conquest (Deut. 27; Josh. 8.30ff.; 24). Perhaps after the establishment of Jeroboam's state cult it continued to be a threatening competitor to the official shrines at Bethel and Dan, a hotbed of religious dissent against the state's cultic programme. Did the priests of the state cult go to the length of plotting for pilgrims to Shechem to be waylaid (BK)?

[10] The final item in the catalogue deals with the entire house of

[a] See S. Mowinckel, *The Psalms in Israel's Worship* II, 1962, additional note xxviii, pp. 250f.

Israel instead of a particular place. Its inclusiveness indicates that the specific charges in the foregoing lines were but illustrations of a guilt which belonged to the whole nation. Because particular place names are thematic in the sequence, and because the emphatic 'there' seems to call for another (cf. v. 7), it has been suspected that 'house of Israel' stands in the place of an original 'Bethel' (Wellhausen, ICC, ATD, HAT). The theme of 'harlotry' has a clear cultic setting in Hosea, so an indictment of Bethel would be appropriate (cf. 10.15; Amos 5.6). Yahweh cries out in astonished revulsion at what he sees. The 'ghastly thing' (Jer. 5.30; 18.13; 23.14) is Israel's apostasy, the cult of a foreign god which defiles and disqualifies for approach to Yahweh (see the comment on 5.3b). On 'harlotry' as Hosea's primary metaphor for Israel's sin, see the comment on 1.2. The emphases on Yahweh's 'seeing' Israel's sin prepares for 7.1f. where Yahweh laments the open presence of Israel's iniquity before his face.

[11a] Verse 11a is the contribution of a Judean editor who glosses the text to show that its radical accusations apply also to the southern kingdom in a later time. For other Judean expansions, see 1.7; 3.5; 4.15; 5.5. 'Harvest' is an eschatological metaphor for the final act of God in the progress of history (Joel 3.13; Jer. 51.33). Judah is not to forget that the tragedy of Israel has a prophetic meaning for them; they too face a time of reckoning!

[11b–7.1] In the midst of the environment portrayed by the catalogue of sins a divine lament breaks out. When his people turn to him with wailing about their suffering, what is the covenant God to do if their very appeal is a disclosure of their sin? No other can heal their wounds (5.13). No other can restore the goodness of life. The will of Yahweh to rescue and bless his people is undiminished; he is faithful to his promise in the covenant. In spite of their sin he looks on Israel as 'my people', the folk whom his election has raised up to be 'my son' (11.1). 'To change the fortune' (šūb šebūt) is a figure of speech (literally, 'turn the turning') which means a return to an original starting point, a *restitutio in integrum*. It may have a background in the festival of New Year as the term for the expected change when God would take away the barrenness of the land and bring back its fertility with the seasonal rains.[a] Generally in the OT the phrase is used in a historical rather than a natural frame of reference to speak of God's shift from the work of anger to the blessing of grace

[a] See Pss. 126 and 85, and Amos 9.14; cf. S. Mowinckel, *The Psalms in Israel's Worship* II, additional note xxvii, pp. 249f., and the literature cited there.

(e.g. Lam. 2.14; Job 42.10). Something of the way in which the popular cultic mind interpreted the shift is reflected in the song of 6.1–3 with its celebration of Yahweh's almost automatic change from punishment to help. But in Hosea's vocabulary the restitution is the restoration of the integrity of the covenant relation of the wilderness where the blessing of Yahweh is the sign of the devotion of his people. 'Heal' is one of Hosea's verbs for redemption (5.13; 6.1) and it too involves blessing in a restored covenant relation (cf. 14.4). The tragic truth about Israel which God has to face is the awful evidence of the catalogue of sins. Israel's frantic appeal and religious busyness is itself a disclosure of the nation's iniquity. They approach him as though he were some Canaanite deity to whom the quality of their lives is irrelevant, as though there were no covenant and no revelation in the past of what it means to be 'my people'. So their very religion is a deceitful act, a revelation of their evil. The priests who enter the temple and minister outside in its precincts are robbers and thieves (cf. 6.9; 4.8).

[2] What one line could better sum up the profound theological failure of Israel! – it never enters their mind that the real issue between them and their God is the evil of their lives. The erosion of Canaanite ways of religious thinking has erased any real understanding of Yahweh; the knowledge of him whom to choose is to choose the good of his will is gone. They do not remember the history of Yahweh's revelation, but he remembers the history of their sin. Now their deeds surround them like the wall of a prison; they have become what they have done (cf. 5.4). When they turn to Yahweh in worship and stand in his presence, he is ready to heal and restore. But when he looks upon them he must see the reality before him – the evil, the iniquity, the sin.

15. 'ALL THEIR KINGS HAVE FALLEN': 7.3–7

7 ³With their evil they gladden a king,
        with their lies officers.
    ⁴All of them are adulterers;
        they burn ᵃ like an oven
    whose baker ᵇ stops stirring (its fire)
        from the kneading of the dough till it is leavened.

ᵃ Cf. BH.
ᵇ Reading 'ōpēhū.

> [5]On their[a] king's day they weaken
>   the officers with the glow of wine,
>   [b]whose power draws the scorners.[b]
> [6]For they are kindled[c] like the oven,
>   their heart [d]burns in them.[d]
> All night their anger[e] is sleeping.
>   At morn it blazes like a flaming fire.
> [7]All of them are hot like the oven
>   and devour their rulers.
> All their kings have fallen
>   but none of them cry to me.

The political energy of Israel is a burning anger that is devouring the very monarchy in which it trusts. Kings are enthroned in Israel only to fall. Yet, through all this self-defeating history, it occurs to no one to appeal to the Lord who made them instead of the kings they make. The five verses are a divine saying (v. 7) in which Yahweh describes the political life of Israel as a creation of evil and an engine of wrath which rushes toward its own end with no appeal to him. The oracle remains at the level of accusation throughout and never moves to the announcement of judgment. Instead, the final line of v. 7 rings like a lament which implies a doom inherent in the nation's failure which works its own punishment. The saying is built around one of Hosea's characteristic metaphors. The image of the baker's oven (vv. 4, 6, 7) is used to bring to light the passionate wrath that drives Israel's political life. The descriptive role of the metaphor is sustained in an unusual way; the oven and its fire furnish a shifting sequence of analogies to depict the assassination of a king. The historical basis of the saying is the tragic instability of the monarchy in Israel.[f] By 733 there had been a rash of revolutions; within the previous twelve years four kings had been victims of assassination as the political leaders (the 'they' in the saying) sought frantically to find national salvation by changing kings. Zechariah, Shallum ben Gadi, Pekahiah and Pekah were sacrificed in the vain quest. The particular occasion of the oracle is probably the assassination of Pekah in favour of Hoshea (II Kings 15.30) to rid the nation of the incubus of his anti-Assyrian policy. The Hebrew text of vv. 4–6 is in such bad repair that an

[a] Read *malkām* because of context.
[b-b] The sense is obscure; see the comment.
[c] Reading *qādᵉḥū*; cf. G.
[d-d] Reading *bōᶜēr bām*.
[e] cf. BH.
[f] See J. Bright, *A History of Israel*, 1959/1960, pp. 253f.

interpretation can be based at best on conjectures about its meaning. Details must remain uncertain though the general movement of thought is discernible.

[3] The first line sets the tone for the following verses. The conspirators give the king and his court officials joy by their evil and treachery! The prophet speaks as though the celebrations held at the coronation of a new king were before his eyes. The new occupant of the throne assumes power in the midst of festive joy and self-satisfaction at his success. But the prophet sees that this joy has been created by evil. The singular 'king' suggests that Hosea describes some particular one of the many throne-changes in Israel's recent history, probably the coronation of Hoshea ben Elah in 733. Behind Hoshea's rise to power lay the will to murder and the plotting of deceitful treachery as the assassination of Pekah was arranged. Undoubtedly some of the conspirators had sworn allegiance to the king they betrayed. A king should rejoice in justice and righteousness, but here is one whose joy is the fruit of violent evil. With the installation of such a king Yahweh has nothing to do; indeed his inauguration is an act of rebellion against him (8.4).

[4] 'Adultery', in contrast to 'harlotry', is usually used by Hosea for literal sexual unfaithfulness (4.13f.; 3.1). Here the term is used, as in Jer. 9.2 (cf. 23.10), for those whose acts are evil and treacherous, betraying Yahweh in political life as he is betrayed in cultic worship ('harlotry'). 'All of them' gathers up king, court officials, and conspirators as a band of adulterers who transgress the order of their relation to Yahweh with their evil and lies. Hosea's preferred way of characterizing events and people is the use of metaphor. The image of the bake-oven is employed as a device to narrate the course of the conspiracy. The oven (tannūr) was a round structure made of burnt clay. It had a floor of packed earth or stone; its walls curved inward in dome shape. A fire was built inside the oven; when the fire had burned down, flat cakes of dough were spread around the walls, the aperture was closed, and the dough left to bake. The reference to the 'baker' indicates that the comparison is drawn from a commercial or royal installation, perhaps the bakery of the king in Samaria. The term of comparison for the conspirators is actually the fire, not the oven. At first they are like an oven with smouldering ashes. The baker does not bother to stir up the embers and add fuel; he is busy with kneading flour into dough and must wait overnight for the leaven to work. Just so the conspirators. Their evil plot is already a burning

fire in their hearts. But the time is not ripe. They first elaborate their plans and wait for the opportune moment.

Verse 5 seems to describe the stratagem by which the palace revolt is accomplished. When all is ready the conspirators arrange for the officials of the present king to be drunk. While they are intoxicated and the king is defenceless, they strike. The assassination of Elah by Zimri in 876 was carried off while the court was drunk (I Kings 16.8–14) and the strategy may well have been used on other occasions. The 'day of their king' would seem to mean the coronation day of the candidate in whose behalf the conspirators acted. Did assassination and enthronement occur on the same day? It might have in the midst of the political chaos in 733. Hoshea's kingship after all was a creature of the nation's desperation over the failure of Pekah's anti-Assyrian policy. The third measure of v. 5 is obscure. Literally it reads: 'his hand draws scorners', which may be a comment about wine to the effect that it has power to attract the loud-mouthed who are vulnerable to its appeal. Others take it to mean that 'he [the king?] made common cause with the rebels' (ATD, cf. RSV).

[6] When the plot breaks into the open, the hot passion of the conspirators is like the oven fire which is stirred and fed at morning until the flames leap out of the oven door. If the sequence of words in MT's text are rearranged, the first line can be translated: 'When they draw near in their ambush/their heart is like the oven.' The sense is essentially the same.

[7] In v. 7 the oracle reaches its climax. The accusation against Israel's political life is summarized in an inclusive statement which repeats the metaphor of the oven. The entire tragic history of the monarchy is subsumed under the particular incident just described. And the divine reaction to what has happened is offered in a final cry. 'All of them are . . . like an oven' is a reprise of vv. 4–6. The inner dynamics of the entire political history of the northern kingdom has been a fiery anger. Israelite statecraft was driven by a passion that inevitably destroyed its own achievements. *Their* rulers . . . *their* kings have fallen prey to *their* consuming wrath. The prophet sees that the genius of Israel has been their attempt at autonomy. In spite of the state's public religion they had always sought a nation which possessed its own security and justification – and, when a king did not bring about the consummation of this dream, the passion which created him became the wrath that destroyed him. Like every revolutionary state that has no faith in anything beyond itself, Israel

was burning up in its own anger. And Israel had no such faith. In twelve years four kings dead! Was not this sign and summons enough to look beyond themselves? But none of them cried out to Yahweh, seeing in his rule and power the security and prosperity which in their pride they avidly sought to create themselves. The national ego had blotted out any consciousness of their dependence on the divine 'I'.

16. EPHRAIM AMONG THE NATIONS: 7.8–12

7 ⁸Ephraim! among the nations
    he mixes himself.
Ephraim! he is a cake
    that has not been turned.
⁹Foreigners have devoured his strength,
    but he does not know it.
Yes, grey hair shinesᵃ on him,
    but he does not know it.
¹⁰The pride of Israel testifies against him;
    they have not returned to Yahweh their God,
    nor sought him in all this.
¹¹Ephraim has become like a dove,
    easily fooled, without a mind.
To Egypt they've called,
    to Assyria they've gone.
¹²As they go I will spread
    my net upon them.
Like a bird of the sky I will bring them down.
    I will chastiseᵇ them ᶜaccording to the report of their evil.

In the final years of its national existence, Israel's political life was a succession of frantic experiments with coalitions and alliances in search for survival. The particular theme of these lines is the international policy of the dying nation (see also 5.8–13 and 8.7–10). Ephraim has lost all sense of the identity created by the election of Yahweh. The nation is being swallowed up in history's melting pot, following a half-baked policy. They are old; their death is near – and they don't even know it. They flutter from one alliance to another like a silly dove, darting about to escape the net of history's dangers.

ᵃ Cf. *zrq* II, *KB*, p. 269; the meaning is not certain; *HAL* has 'creep in' (p. 272).
ᵇ Vocalizing MT's consonants *ᵃyassᵉrēm*; cf. the versions.
ᶜ⁻ᶜ MT: 'according to the report to their congregation', which in the context has no sense; reading *lᵉrāʿātām* for *laʿᵃdātām* in dependence on G is only a conjecture.

But the net is in the hand of Yahweh. It never occurs to them to turn to him, and he will let them turn to no other. The common theme runs through all five verses, but the sequence is easily divided in two parts. The lament over Ephraim's condition in vv. 8–9 is rounded off by the accusation in v. 10 that in spite of their woeful situation they do not return to their God. Verses 11f. are a divine saying composed of indictment and verdict. The metaphor of the silly dove, stated in 11a, is broadened in v. 12 where Yahweh appears as a fowler. The oracle could have been delivered in Samaria to members of the court during the early years of King Hoshea.·

[8] Hosea uses the tribal name Ephraim repeatedly to refer to the northern kingdom, perhaps to personalize its identity. The name is called out twice as an emphatic vocative, separate from the rest of the sentence, as if to hold the name itself up to scorn. Each of the two lines uses an image from the culinary realm. 'To mix' is a verb from the vocabulary of preparing cakes; usage in the Old Testament is confined to technical language describing preparation of offerings (Lev. 7; Num. 28), but the background here is certainly the cooking of daily secular life. Ephraim is as involved with other nations as oil stirred in with flour! The image gathers up in one visual picture the whole story of Israel's international policy and the succession of coalitions with Aram, Egypt, and Assyria. Where a people seek to maintain themselves by identifying their interests with those of others, they end by losing themselves in the process (cf. 8.8). The second image pictures Ephraim as an unturned cake, 'half-baked', burned on one side and undone on the other. The cake ('ūgā) is the round, flat pat of dough that was laid on the coals or pressed on the sides of the oven. 'Oven' is the structural metaphor in the preceding passage (7.3–7) and there could be a connection in time and situation between the two sayings. What the metaphor means precisely can hardly be determined. A half-baked bread cake was unsatisfactory, useless – perhaps only a remark of mournful derision at a people who never fulfilled their destiny.

[9] Two parallel lines ending in identical refrain-like measures depict Israel as a man in the last stages of life – strength drained away, hoary with advanced age. The 'foreigners' are more likely to be such erstwhile allies as Arameans and Egyptians than Assyrians. The ravages of the latter could hardly be said to be unknown. Rather, the strength of the nation is consumed by aliens who involve Ephraim in their schemes and use them for their own ends. Everywhere in the

body politic are the marks of a dying nation. Weak and greyed, the
people totter toward death – and they act as though they are unaware
of what is happening to them.

[10] Verse 10a repeats 5.5a. In v. 10bc the subject shifts from singular to plural, and the description of Israel's failure to respond to
Yahweh seems to be an anti-climax after the refrain ('but he does not
know it') of v. 9. For such reasons, the originality of the verse, at
least in this textual setting, has been questioned with good reason. In
its present location the verse brings the lament of vv. 8f. to a climax
with an accusation that Israel's folly and decay is a substitute for a
return to Yahweh. Israel's pride blinds him to his weakness and he
staggers on the way he has chosen, wilfully confident of finding his own
solutions to his problem. What he does in his pride is evidence against
him in the court which Yahweh convenes (see the commentary on
5.5a). Turning back to the original relation to Yahweh as it existed
in the wilderness period is the constant centre of Hosea's eschatology
and the goal of Yahweh's judgment. The failure of God's people to
respond to his chastisements was used by Amos (4.6–12) as a refrain
of indictment against Israel a few decades earlier.

During the career of Hosea the international policy of Israel swung
back and forth between Assyria and Egypt like a pendulum. Menahem was quick to submit to Tiglath-pileser at the cost of a vast
tribute (II Kings 15.19f.). Pekah joined the coalition formed to
resist Assyria's power (II Kings 15.37); possibly the allies hoped for
Egyptian aid. Hoshea came to the throne in a shift back to Menahem's
policy of submission to Assyria, but later appealed to Egypt (II Kings
17.4) and revolted. Using one of his ready metaphors, Hosea compares the nation to a silly dove that is easily deceived. The way the
comparison is stated in v. 11 and extended in v. 12 suggests that the
dove is thought of as a bird with such little sense as to be trapped
easily. To the prophet's eye, Israel is all too easily deceived into
thinking that in first Egypt and then Assyria lies her help. But the
people's fluttering from one to the other is lack of sense, for their real
crisis is not caused by the great powers. Appealing to them is like
sending for a physician who cannot heal (5.13). Once again Hosea
terms the failure to recognize dependence on Yahweh as a basic
stupidity (5.11, 13).

[12] The metaphor continues in the announcement of Yahweh's
coming act of judgment. The divine Lord stands with a fowler's net
(cf. 5.1) in his hand waiting to snare the dove in its passage to and fro

between the great powers. In their very search for help they fly into the real danger that threatens them. Turning to the nations to find their way through history is desertion of Yahweh who alone makes the history which Israel lives out as his people. The final measure is obscure. MT reads 'I will chastise (?) them according to the report of (to?) their congregation.' Even when the last word is emended (with an uncertain dependence on G) little is gained. HAT, revising the entire line to continue the metaphor, translates: 'I will hem them in on account of their evil.' ATD, emending only the first word, renders: 'I will catch them when I hear their flock.'

17. NO HELP FOR THE REBELS: 7.13–16

7 ¹³Woe to them, for they have strayed from me.
   Devastation to them, for they have rebelled against me.
I would redeem them, but they!
   – they speak lies about me.
¹⁴They have not appealed to me with their heart,
   for they wail upon their beds.
For the sake of corn and must they gash themselves;ᵃ
   they are rebelliousᵃ against me.
¹⁵It was I whoᵃ strengthened their arms,
   but against me they plot evil.
¹⁶They return to what is useless,ᵇ
   they are like a treacherous bow.
Their captains shall fall by the sword
   on account of their insolent tongue.
This shall be their derision
   in the land of Egypt.

The divine saying begins with a cry of woe, accuses the nation of rebellion against Yahweh (vv. 13–16a), and concludes with an announcement of punishment (v. 16bc). The theme of the accusation is the incredible treachery of Israel against the God who has been their strength in the past and would even now redeem them. The dimension of Israel's guilt is intensified by contrasts between the way and will of Yahweh and that of the nation (vv. 13cd, 15). After the general indictment of rebellion (v. 13) the accusation focuses first on Israel's

ᵃ Cf. BH.
ᵇ The text (*lō' 'āl*) is corrupt. Perhaps *l'lō' yō'īl* ('to what does not profit'; cf. Jer. 2.8, 11). Others suggest *l'ba'al* ('to Baal').

Canaanized cult (v. 14) and then on their search for help among other nations (vv. 15, 16a). The oracle fits best in the circumstances of Hoshea's reign.

[13] A woe-saying is spoken over those who are doomed or dead. It is not an invocation of disaster, but rather a statement of sorrow and warning that the consequences of some act or situation are impending and inevitable. In prophetic speech it becomes a dirge for those under the sentence of Yahweh's judgment. The 'woe' is provoked by the 'devastation' which Yahweh has decreed against his people who have fled from him to another, 'and so rebelled against his lordship. 'Rebel' (*pāša'*) as a sin-word presupposes a structure of authority under which Israel exists; the verb is used for political revolt against a king (I Kings 12.19). In 8.1 its object is the instruction (*tōrā*) of Yahweh. Israel has broken away from the servant-vassal role bestowed on them in the covenant, and thereby invited the punishment which a suzerain must execute to maintain his role. Devastation is not the will of the divine suzerain. For his part he would deliver his servants; the covenantal system was meant to be a system of security under his reign. But the divine will to redeem is frustrated by the treachery of his subjects (6.11b–7.1; 6.4; 11.2; 13.14). Because of Israel's sin, the old covenant can bring only judgment; redemption must come beyond the present covenant after judgment has created the possibility of a new relationship. 'Redeem' (*pādā*) is a term of commercial law for reclaiming or ransoming of an obligated person or thing by payment. In Ex. 15.13 the verb was put in service as an interpretative term for Yahweh's deliverance in the Exodus from Egypt (also Deut. 7.8; 9.26) and Hosea uses it for a similar intervention in Israel's historical plight (13.14).The God of the Exodus is unchanged in his will, but because of Israel's lies there will be no 'exodus' from the Assyrian danger. The 'lies' are the false notions of Yahweh expressed in Israel's approach to him through the ritual of a Canaanized cult, as described in the next verse.

[14] The Assyrian campaign in 734/3 undoubtedly left the land stripped of its crops and the renewal of harvest became a desperate matter (8.7). In their plight the Israelites raised the lament for help (*zā'aq*) to Yahweh (8.2). But the ritual by which they appealed was taken from the fertility rites of Canaan and dealt with Yahweh as though he were Baal. 'With their heart' is not a phrase of earnestness or sincerity; heart in Hosea is the mind, the responsible intelligence (4.4; 7.11). Israel cried out to Yahweh in stupidity, forgetting the

conditions of the covenant and trying to manipulate him as a nature
god whose amoral function is to produce corn and new wine (2.5, 8f.).
There is some evidence that ritual wailing was performed in prostra-
tion (II Sam. 12.16; Ps. 4.4) and was practised in fertility rites
(S. of S. 3.1; Isa. 57.8). The prophets of Baal in the contest on Mount
Carmel lacerated themselves as they entreated Baal to come as the
god of the thunder-storm and so end the drought (I Kings 18.28);
ritual gashing in mourning for the dead was prohibited in Israel
because of its Canaanite connections (Deut. 14.1; Lev. 19.28). The
Israelite thought of Yahweh as absent (dead?) like Baal and tried by
the laments that summoned Baal to gain his help with crops. So their
very appeal was stubborn contumacious rebellion against the person
of Yahweh.

[15] Again the action of Yahweh in his salvation-history is set over
against the practice of Israel's religion. In Israel's past the power to
cope with the threats and problems of national life had come from
Yahweh (11.1–4; 13.4f.). The people's strength had been his action.
But now in their time of greatest danger they seek strength through
alliances with Egypt and Assyria, and so disdain the revelation of
Yahweh in their normative history. Every treaty with another power
is a plot against their sovereign Lord. To Yahweh's good that sought
their salvation, they return the evil of seeking their own desires in
their own way. The contradiction lays bare the fundamental sin of
Israel – the rupture of the relation between the persons of God and
people, the loss of the knowledge of God.

[16] The tribulations of Israel were a divine call to return to
Yahweh (5.15; 7.7, 10), but instead they turn to things that are of no
help (cf. p. 110 n. *b* on the text). The mention of captains and the metaphor of the bow strengthen the suggestion that Israel's policy of
seeking military help from Assyria and Egypt (7.11) is included with
cultic perversion in the evil which Israel devises against their God
(BK). Not to Yahweh, who is the one who gives them strength, but to
Baal and the nations they turn! Using another of his many metaphors,
Hosea compares them to a treacherous bow, one that is warped so
that its arrows do not reach their target (cf. Ps. 78.57). Now they are
useless in the hands of Yahweh and helpless before the danger that
threatens them. In the last two lines the oracle moves to Yahweh's
announcement of the punishment which will befall the leaders who
take the nation's destiny into their own arrogant hands. The captains
themselves shall fall by the sword (cf. the commentary on Amos

7.17; 9.1, 4, 10). The captains have been the architects of the royal assassinations in the search for an alignment of security. Their death will bring derision from the Egyptians whose help they alternately sought and spurned.

18. OF GODS AND GOVERNMENTS: 8.1–14

8 ¹To your mouth the trumpet!
    One like the eagle is over Yahweh's house,
  because they have broken my covenant,
    and against my instruction they have rebelled.
²To me they appeal:
    'My God! We* know you!'
³Israel has rejected good.
    An enemy shall pursue him.

⁴They themselves made kings, but I had nothing to do with it;
    they made officials, but I did not authorize it.
  With their silver and gold they made
    idols for themselves (so that it might be cut off).ᵇ
⁵Your bull, O Samaria, is rejected;ᶜ
    my anger burns against them.
  How long will they be incapable of innocence?
⁶ For what has Israel to do with it?ᵈ
  An artisan made it!
    A god it is not!
  Yea, splintersᵉ shall become
    Samaria's bull.

⁷When they sow the wind,
    they reap the storm.
  Grain without head
    yields no bread.
  Were it to yield,
    strangers would swallow it up.

ᵃ Omitting 'Israel' with GS.

ᵇ The final clause seems to leave the thought sequence; see the comment.

ᶜ MT's 'he has rejected' (zānaḥ) does not correspond to the next line; revocalize as zānûaḥ, for which there is some versional support.

ᵈ Following MT's punctuation, and with Nyberg vocalizing mîyiśrāʾ ēl as mayyiśrāʾ ēl=mā-yiśrāʾ ēl.

ᵉ So KB for šĕbābîm, found only here. W. F. Albright suggests 'flames' (Archaeology and the Religion of Israel, p. 220, n. 109).

[8]Israel has been swallowed up.
  Now they are among the nations
  like a useless vessel.
[9]For they have gone up to Assyria;
  a wild ass off to himself,
  Ephraim gives[a] gifts of love.
[10]Even though they give[a] (love-gifts) among the nations,
  now I will gather them.
They shall shortly writhe[b]
  because of the burden of the king of princes.

[11]When Ephraim multiplied altars to atone for sin,[c]
  they became for him altars for sinning.
[12]Though I write for him a multitude[d] of my instructions,[e]
  they are considered as an alien thing.
[13f]Sacrifice they love, so they sacrifice;[f]
  flesh (they love), so they eat;
  but Yahweh does not accept them.
Now he will remember their iniquity
  and punish their sin.
  They shall return to Egypt.

[14]Israel forgot his maker
  and built palaces.
Judah multiplied
  fortified cities.
I will send fire on his cities
  and it will devour her strongholds.

Chapter 8 opens a new sequence of oracles. The initial summons
to sound the alarm (v. 1) recalls the beginning of the sequence concerning the Syrian-Ephraimite war in 5.8–6.6. Here too a foe is at
hand and the danger clearly comes from Assyria. The details of the
situation reflected in the oracles are not sufficiently specific to establish
the exact date, but clues in the text point to the years immediately
after 733. The first oracle (vv. 1–3) not only sets the scene but also
serves as an overtone by summarizing the sin and punishment of

  [a] With Wellhausen reading $yitt^e n\bar{u}$ where MT has a form of the verb $t\bar{a}n\bar{a}$
('hire'?, *BDB*, p. 1071).
  [b] Reading $w^e y\bar{a}hil\bar{u}$ with Wolff, Rudolph.
  [c] Revocalizing MT to read $l^e hatt\bar{e}$' with Rudolph.
  [d] Q^{e}rē.
  [e] Plural with G Aleph; MT is sing.
  [f] MT's $habh\bar{a}bay$ is a puzzle. The translation is based on a reconstructed text:
$zebah$ '$\bar{a}h^a b\bar{u}$ $w^e yizb^e h\bar{u}$ (Duhm, Marti, Wolff). Rudolph identifies a substantive
$habh\bar{a}b$ ('voracious greed') and holds closely to MT.

Israel in the briefest and yet most comprehensive fashion possible. The rest of the chapter is a tightly knit sequence of sayings arranged to spell out the correctness of the indictment with one example after another. Verse 4 is a reproach against man-made governments and gods. Verses 5f. denounce a specific case of the latter, the bull of Samaria. The proverbial sentences in v. 7 could go with either vv. 5f. or the following saying (vv. 8–10) which deals with Israel's international policies. Verses 11–13 return to the theme of the cult. The collector has added a floating saying (v. 14) from an earlier time at the end. Whether he or Hosea created the composition is difficult to say. Somewhat the same technique is used in 6.7–7.16 where a more loosely related series of sayings illustrate the lack of devotion charged in 6.4, 6. But here the entire sequence has a common immediate background and is more tightly woven.

[1–3] A terse excited call for the alarm to be sounded at the presence of an eagle-like foe opens the divine saying (v. 1a), and it concludes with the reiteration of the threat as an announcement of punishment (v. 3b). The crisis is the onset of judgment, because in spite of its frantic appeals to Yahweh (v. 2), Israel is estranged from Yahweh. In vv. 1b and 3a the sin of the nation is cited in the most elemental and comprehensive terms.

[1] The call for a trumpet blast to warn of an approaching enemy was used in 5.8 at the beginning of the oracles delivered during the crisis following the Syrian-Ephraimite war. Now the 'enemy' is undoubtedly Assyria, but once again the crisis is interpreted as an event in Yahweh's dealings with Israel because the divine 'I' sounds the alarm. The command is addressed to one person (in contrast to 5.8); the pronoun 'your' is singular, but the addressee is not identified. Was the prophet himself the addressee (Rudolph)? Or does the prophet speak to some commander of Israel's army (Wolff), or to the nation as a corporate person? The eagle is a large bird of prey, perhaps the griffon-vulture,[a] celebrated for its swiftness in swooping on its quarry (Job 9.26); it was used in metaphors to depict the ominously rapid approach of an enemy (Hab. 1.8; Jer. 4.13; 48.40; Lam. 4.19; Deut. 28.49). 'The house of Yahweh' is Hosea's phrase for the land as God's gift to Israel of a place to live (cf. 9.15, 8; 2.8). The use of 'house' with a proper name to designate places was a formulation current in the general speech of the ancient Near East; note Tiglath-pileser's 'House of Omri' as a name for Israel,[b] and place names

[a] *IDB* IV, p. 794.   [b] *ANET*, p. 284a.

beginning with Beth- (e.g. Beth-Haran, Beth-Anath, etc.). An indictment against Israel could hardly be drawn in more comprehensive terms than this accusation of breach of covenant and rebellion against instruction. On the significance of 'covenant' in Hosea, see the commentary on 'broke the covenant' in 6.7. Covenant (*berît*) is the term for the formal structure of the relationship instituted by Yahweh's election of Israel. Because of the term's provenance in the political practice of international alliances, it casts Israel in the role of a vassal or servant under the suzerainty of Yahweh, who assumes responsibility for their security and establishes the claims of his lordship over them. Instruction (*tōrā*, in parallel with *berît*) represents the policy which the Lord has promulgated as the covenant's stipulation. The singular term stands for the total body of tradition about the will of Yahweh which the priests should pass on (see the comment on '*tōrā* of your God' in 4.6). Hosea thinks primarily in terms of a decalogic formula (4.2) and knows of a written tradition of instruction (8.13). The possessive 'my' qualifying covenant and instruction raises the accusation to the level of rebellion against the person of Yahweh himself (7.13).

[2] 'To *me* they appeal' is an outraged aside which plays on the possessives of the previous line: '*My* covenant and *my* instruction they break – and lament in their trouble to *me*!' In their distress after the Assyrian invasion of 733, Israel wails in ritual lamentation to Yahweh for food and protection (7.14), whimpering to the sovereign whose lordship they reject. The quotation with which Hosea epitomizes the lament of Israel contains two elements, both authentic and proper enough as forms of speech to Yahweh. They call him 'my God', an appellation which lays hold on the election and claims its blessing in trust (2.23; Pss. 18.2; 22.1; 63.1, etc.). In the confessional sentence, 'We know you', the worshippers take up a primary motif of Hosea's prophetic speech, perhaps in response to his sayings (cf. commentary on 'knowledge of God' in 4.1), and claim to express in their lives the revelation of Yahweh. They break the covenant and say 'my God', rebel against the *tōrā* and say, 'We know you'!

[3] With the simple value-word 'good' Hosea comprehends the normative significance of covenant and instruction for Israel. See Amos' use of 'good' as a surrogate for Yahweh (5.14f.) and Micah's 'good' (Micah 6.8) which sums up the requirements of Yahweh. Possibly the term is even broader in Hosea and includes the goodness of life under the covenant (3.5; 2.8). In her rebellion Israel has written

her own sentence. When good is rejected, what is left but evil – the evil of an enemy pursuing them to their doom? The foe is not named, though Assyria stands at the door; the enemy is the rod of God, the instrument of his punishment.

[4] The sentences of accusation in v. 4 deal with the double theme of king and cult. They are not a direct continuation of the announcement of judgment in vv. 1–3, which is a well-rounded unit in itself. But the opening 'they' presupposes 'house of Yahweh' (v. 1) and 'Israel' as its antecedents. The two lines show how in the sphere of royalty and ritual Israel has rejected the good (v. 3), and were probably placed after vv. 1–3 to mark out clearly these two themes which are dealt with by the following units in the sequence. The first line puts Hosea's evaluation of Israel's monarchy. The succession of royal governments in Israel were the independent work of men thinking of kingship as an institution whose management was their prerogative. By deceit and murder one king had displaced another without any appeal to Yahweh (7.1–3). Sovereignty over Israel belonged to him and in the older charismatic conception of kingship the king was Yahweh's elect and regent.[a] But neither by gift of charisma nor by prophetic designation had Yahweh acted in the selection of any of the recent kings or court officials. The rejection is not of kingship *per se*, but of its development as a focus of power independent of Yahweh. For that reason, judgment will create an interlude when Israel lives without king and official (3.4; 7.10b).

Making and using idols was common in the syncretistic religion of Israel in the eighth century (4.17; 13.2; 14.8). The practice was strictly forbidden in the covenant norms (Ex. 20.3–6, 23; 34.17; Lev. 19.4). Besides the bull images in Bethel and Dan, figurines and plaques of various deities designed for use in private rites were abundant.[b] Since silver and gold were the materials used for the idols mentioned here, Hosea probably has the bull image in mind (cf. vv. 5f.). The statement that 'they *made* idols *for themselves*' is a typically prophetic way of scornfully disclosing the folly of such images (v. 6; Isa. 44.9ff.; 46.5ff.), and puts idol and king on the same level of guilt – both are made by Israel, the work of their rebellion against Yahweh. Since it was Jeroboam I who introduced the bull images into Israel's cult, Hosea had good historical reasons to combine idolatry and kingship in this double indictment. The final enigmatic clause (to what does

[a] W. Eichrodt, *Theology of the Old Testament* I, 1961, pp. 439ff.
[b] J. Gray, 'Idols' and 'Idolatry', *IDB* II, pp. 673ff.

the singular subject refer?) seems to be a gloss reminding the reader of the inevitable judgment on all who turn to idols (Lev. 20.3; Deut. 4.3; Ezek. 14.7f.).

[5–6] Verses 5f. are concerned with the particular theme of Samaria's bull image. The general subject of idols is raised in the second line of the rebuke in v. 4; this oracle announces Yahweh's attitude and coming action against the most famous of the images in Israel. The opening verb 'reject' picks up the thematic word of 3a. The divine saying opens in the style of direct address ('*your* bull'), as does 1a, but shifts immediately to references to Israel in the third person plural.

[5] Samaria refers to the residents of the capital city (7.1; 10.5) rather than to the place itself. It is doubtful whether a bull image was ever set up in Samaria, though some find in this text a hint that such a cult object did exist in a sanctuary in Samaria.[a] The temple and altar for Baal built by Ahab in his capital (I Kings 16.32) were destroyed by Jehu and the sacred site was used as a latrine to desecrate it (II Kings 10.25–27). Jeroboam I had set up bull images in Bethel and Dan when he founded his two state sanctuaries (I Kings 12.26–33); the bull in question is the one in Bethel, Dan having fallen into the hands of the Assyrians in 733. The bull was not meant to be an idol, but rather a pedestal or throne for the invisible deity, similar to the Ark.[b] But 8.6 protests that the Israelites had come to regard it as the deity. Probably contemporary Israelites thought of it as serving the function generally attributed to images in the cult of the surrounding cultures; it was the way in which the deity was near to the worshipper to reveal and help.[c] Though the image had been set up to serve the Yahweh cult, the bull was associated with the mythology and cult of Canaan as a representation of Baal and El.[d] Confusion was bound to result in syncretism and idolatry. The response of Yahweh to those who own the bull is exactly the same as it was in the case of the image made at Sinai (Ex. 32.10f.); turning to other gods invites the burning anger of Yahweh (cf. Num. 25.3; Deut. 11.17; Josh. 23.18), against those who break his covenantal instruction (Ex. 20.3f.). 'How long . . .' is an interrogatory exclamation used repeatedly in

[a] E.g. H.-J. Kraus, *Worship in Israel*, 1966, p. 152.
[b] W. F. Albright, *From the Stone Age to Christianity*, 1957, pp. 298ff.; see the representations of a deity standing on a bull or lion in J. Pritchard, *ANEP*, pp. 163ff. and 177ff.
[c] G. von Rad, *Theology of the Old Testament* I, 1962, pp. 213f.
[d] J. Gray, *The Heritage of Canaan*, pp. 117f., 109ff.

songs of lament (cf. Pss. 4.2; 6.3; 13.1f., etc.). The question which it introduces is rhetorical; the line is really a cry of anguish and sorrow over Israel's inability to live in innocence, free of the deeds that disqualify for relation to God (often 'innocence of hands', Ps. 26.6; 73.13; Gen. 20.5). What can Israel, the people of Yahweh, possibly need with an idol! In this juxtaposition of lament and burning wrath the God of Hosea discloses the suffering in which the election of Israel has involved him. His anger is not bitter hatred; it is the passion of purpose that will not surrender in spite of frustration and rejection.

[6] The blunt assertions of the first line of v. 6 are scornful and abusive. How can a deity be manufactured in an artisan's shop! This analysis of the ridiculous folly of an idol focuses on the one fact that it is the creation of a human being, which made it an impossibly futile figure to those who knew Yahweh by experience and tradition as the maker of history (Isa. 8.2, 20; 40.18–20; 44.9ff.). The protest that the bull is no god implies that the Israelites had come to see the image itself as divine. It was incredible to Hosea that they should have faith in what they had made and could control. Their reverence will be shown up for superstition in the fate to come upon their image. This thing carved of wood and covered with gold will be riven into splinters!

[7] In v. 7 there are two Wisdom sayings with a threat of judgment added to enforce the point of the second. The sayings could well have been current proverbs which Hosea quotes to illuminate the folly of Israel's conduct. Note his use of proverbs in 4.11 and 14b to establish the danger of the cult. Like all proverbs, each sentence is complete in itself, and it is impossible to tell whether the general principle of the sayings applies to Israel's folly in seeking help from 'Samaria's calf' (vv. 5f.) or to Israel's futile international policy (vv. 8–10). The last measure of v. 7 and the first of v. 8 are connected by the catchword 'swallow up'; but the juxtaposition is probably the result of the collector's art. The first saying is a formulation of the principle that there is a direct correspondence between what a man does and what happens to him later. Life is controlled by a rational power which inexorably works out the consequences of a man's act and visits those consequences upon him. 'Deed is seed, which is multiplied in harvest' (BK), a 'law' repeated often in biblical literature (Prov. 11.18; 22.8; Job 4.8; Gal. 6.7; II Cor. 9.6; Matt. 13.24ff.). In Wisdom 'wind' stands for the illusive and elusive, for what amounts to nothing (Eccles. 1.14, 17; Prov. 11.29; Job 7.7). In worshipping the calf and

turning to other nations, Israel sows the seed of futility and so shall reap the harvest of destruction. The second saying is set in rhyme, a somewhat rare device in Hebrew poetry. 'Grain without growth (*semah*) yields no meal (*qemah*).' What fails in the beginning can hardly succeed at the end. This saying applies to the same folly in Israel's life as the first. They have called on the cult for fertility and turned to allies for security, but to no avail. Now can they expect better of such conduct in the future? Hosea nails the point down with an added prediction of judgment. Even if their present crop did yield grain, they would not harvest it, for strangers would swallow it up. The enemy sent by Yahweh (v. 3) guarantees the truth of the Wisdom principle!

[8–10] The divine saying in vv. 8–10 is an oracle against Israel's current international policy. Once more the prophet takes up the theme of Israel among the nations (cf. 5.13f.; 7.8–12). Beginning with a lament over Israel's uselessness to Yahweh as one more nation immersed in the alliances of international struggle (v. 8), the message points to the specific act of autonomy and shame of which Israel is guilty (v. 9), and announces the punishment which Yahweh has decreed (v. 10).

[8] The oracle begins with a lament over the present plight of Israel. Already their peculiar identity has been dissolved in the currents of historical expediency. They are mixed in with the peoples (7.8), no more than another nation fighting the losing battle for survival. That would be sad enough in itself, but its significance for their relation to Yahweh is even more tragic. Israel was chosen from among all the tribes of earth (Amos 3.2) to be Yahweh's peculiar treasure (Ex. 19.5). Now that particularity has been swallowed up and the nation is a worthless vessel no longer giving pleasure or service to its owner (cf. the same figure of speech in Jer. 22.28; 48.38). After the Assyrian invasion of 733, Galilee and Gilead were separated from the Israelite kingdom and made into Assyrian provinces. The vessel was already broken and the judgment already begun.

[9] Hoshea, Israel's last king, was quick to submit to Assyria and resume payment of tribute after he murdered Pekah. It was his only chance to preserve the throne that he had seized by violence. Like his predecessor, Menahem, he 'went up to Assyria' instead of looking to Yahweh (cf. 7.8–12). The wild ass lived in herds, but as a species it was noted for wariness of men and civilization (Job 39.5–8). The comparison is with Ephraim, not Assyria; 'wild ass' (*pere'*) and

'Ephraim' (*'eprayim*) have common consonants and the juxtaposition
may involve a play on the words. Its point is Ephraim's wilful stub-
bornness in not remaining in the company of Yahweh. In the third
measure of the verse Hosea clearly shifts to the metaphor of the harlot
to describe Israel's conduct, though uncertainty about the text makes
interpretation tenuous (cf. notes on the text). Israel is portrayed as a
harlot so little sought and so frantic for love that she gives away her
favours as gifts. Hosea usually employs the metaphor of harlotry for
Israel's cultic dealings with other gods; here it is applied to the
nation's dependence on Assyria. 'Gifts of love' could be a scornful
allusion to the tribute of ten talents of gold and one thousand (?) of
silver which Tiglath-pileser reports as his booty from Hoshea.[a]

In v. 10 Yahweh announces the measures he will take against an
Israel that gives itself to 'the nations' in hope of help. Their 'gifts of
love' will not buy them security because it is Yahweh's action that
really threatens them. 'Gather' (*qibbēṣ*) is a rather opaque verb for
describing the divine judgment. Perhaps it is appropriate because of
the context – Israel casts her lot with the nations and mingles with
them; Yahweh will counteract their movement with a gathering for
judgment (cf. Zeph. 3.8; Joel 3.2). Some emend and read 'disperse'
or 'scatter' (cf. BH) which would suggest an exile. The terrible
shepherd who will gather this people will be the ruler of Assyria, for
whom 'king of princes' is a title. The tribute which he will exact from
them will make them writhe in anguish, and the ultimate folly of
seeking help from Assyria will be disclosed when the Assyrian king
turns out to be Yahweh's executioner.

[11–13] Once again Yahweh addresses himself to the subject of
Israel's cult. The specific subject is altar and sacrifice. The oracle is a
rounded announcement of judgment with reproach (vv. 11–13a) and
punishment (v. 13b). Israel's burgeoning cultic establishment is in
fact the institutionalization of sin (v. 11). While building many altars,
the people shun the law of Yahweh (v. 12). Sacrifice and ritual feast-
ing is their true love (v. 13a). The time has come ('now!') for the
execution of the verdict of the divine judge who will punish them by
letting them regress to Egypt (v. 13b). Yahweh speaks in the first
person until the third measure of v. 13 where the style is pulled into
the third person by the use of a priestly declaratory sentence. The
flourishing cult need not be a sign that the oracle belongs to the time
of Jeroboam II (ATD); the expansion of cultic sites belongs to the

[a] *ANET*, p. 284a.

past, but the ritual continues at those left to Israel after 733. The message fits in the context of the rest of the material in ch. 8.

[11] An altar marked a holy place, a shrine where a deity was thought to be available for worship and communion; it was an instrument of commerce with the god. Building altars was a pious act. Had not the fathers done so (Gen. 12.7; 33.20; 35.7)? Altars meant sacrifice and sacrifice atoned for whatever sins were committed. As Israel prospered in the land, more and more altars were erected (10.1). Religion got its proportionate share of the nation's prosperity, probably because the cult was imagined to be the machine which produced such abundance. Ephraim had an impeccable record in the cause of sanctuary extension. Yet Yahweh sends no commendation by the prophet. His startling word is that the many altars built to deal with *sin* have become a place to *sin*. As Israel now uses them, altars come between Yahweh and his people instead of bringing them to encounter. Sacrifice has become an end in itself (v. 13a; see Amos 4.4f.) and has displaced attention to the will of their Lord (v. 12). The sacrificial cult was practised according to the ways of Canaan and was an occasion for depravity and evil (4.13f.). Just as the expansion of the priesthood meant increase of iniquity, the multiplication of altars brought the proliferation of sin. The cult resulted in the very opposite of its pious purpose!

[12] Against Israel's *multiplication* (*hirbā*) of altars Yahweh sets the *multitude* (*rubbē*) of his instructions (*tōrā*). Perhaps the line suggests that tables of Yahweh's covenant will were prepared for the many shrines (cf. Ex. 32.15f.). The statement clearly assumes that Hosea knew a written form of *tōrā*. What its precise content was can only be guessed from clues like 4.2 with its reflection of the Decalogue. In Hosea's view *tōrā* was an inseparable feature of covenant (8.1) and the special responsibility of the priest (4.6). According to the old cultic tradition of the tribal league, it should play a central role in the cult of Yahweh.[a] In the state and local shrines of the northern kingdom, its place had been pre-empted by sacrifice, if it ever was used at all. Israel treats the instructions of Yahweh as though they were alien, the will of a strange god, and so reverses the order of Yahweh's relation to them. It was the strange god and his cult that should be excluded (Deut. 32.16), but now Israel treats Yahweh's laws as something strange!

[a] G. von Rad, *Theology of the Old Testament* I, 1962, pp. 190ff. and the literature cited.

[13] Though the text of the first measure is corrupt, the general sense is suggested by the parallelism of the second. It is not Yahweh that the people love and trust, but the practice of sacrifice itself. The ritual has become an expression of Israel's ego, because their avidity for sacrifice manifests no more than their own pleasure and pretence. Behind this delight in sacrifice is the confident theory that by its ritual killing and eating, their solidarity with the deity is reconstituted and their welfare guaranteed. The sacrifice referred to in the text is the *zebaḥ*, the most common of the offerings in the pre-exilic cultus; part of the slain animal was burnt on the altar and the rest eaten in a meal of communion (cf. Lev. 3; 7.11–18). Hosea declares that for all their sacrifices to establish solidarity with God, Yahweh does not accept them. The style and vocabulary of the sentence (v. 13c) is like the formal priestly declaration by which sacrifice was evaluated.[a] The prophet usurps the office of the priest and announces that their approach to Yahweh is rejected. The second line contains the announcement of Yahweh's judgment (it is quoted [?] in Jer. 14.10). 'To remember (*zākar*) one's sin/iniquity' is an idiom rooted in Israel's legal life; it has a strong forensic flavour.[b] This is the action which Yahweh, the judge, will take, refusing to overlook the iniquity of Israel. The 'formula' of the judge's decision appears also in 9.9. On 'iniquity // sin' see 4.8. The concrete punishment is disclosed in the final measure: 'they shall return to Egypt'. What this 'return to Egypt' means as a form of punishment is clarified by 9.3 and 11.5, where the expression is used in parallel with the threat of Assyria. When Assyria falls upon the remnant of Israel in Hoshea's kingdom, the populace will either have to submit to Assyrian deportation or flee as refugees to Egypt. In this fate there is the slash of irony, for in the return to Egypt the whole salvation-history is reversed (11.1; 13.4) and Israel will be once again where she was before Yahweh found her.

[14] Verse 14 is a brief but complete announcement of judgment with indictment (v. 14a) and verdict (v. 14b). Because the text begins with a consecutive verb, concerns both Judah and Israel, calls Yahweh the 'maker' of Israel (cf. Deutero-Isaiah 51.13; 44.2), and corresponds in part to the verdict formula in Amos' oracles against the nations (cf. 14b and Amos 1.4, 7, 10, 12, etc.), many conclude that

[a] See G. von Rad, *op. cit.*, p. 261; Lev. 1.3; 19.5; II Sam. 24.23; Jer. 14.12; Amos 5.22; Ezek. 20.40f.
[b] B. S. Childs, *Memory and Tradition in Israel*, 1962, p. 32; cf. 7.2; 9.9.

the verse is a later addition to the Hosea material. The question is not subject to confident argument. Hosea addresses Israel and Judah in 5.8–6.6. The similarity to Amos probably depends on the fact that the line in question is a stereotyped formula (see the commentary on Amos 1–2). The idea of Yahweh as Israel's maker appears nowhere else in Hosea, but its conception is not impossible for him. The building activity would not have occurred in the time in which the rest of ch. 8 is set; Israel's situation was by then too desperate. Probably the oracle was a floating piece which the redactor thought would bring 8.1–13 to a good conclusion. Hosea describes Israel's faithlessness to Yahweh several times as a 'forgetting' (2.13; 4.6; 13.6). Instead of remembering that their existence is the work of Yahweh, the people have tried to found their security on buildings which they could construct. 'Palaces' (*hēkal*) may be either royal residences or temples. The multiplication of fortified cities belongs to the expansion of a defence system against the threat of an enemy, a manifestation that Judah looks to her own strength for deliverance. Cities and strongholds are doomed to destruction by the fire of Yahweh, a theologoumenon for Yahweh's destructive wrath.

19. FROM MIRTH TO MOURNING: 9.1–6

9 ¹Rejoice not, O Israel;
        ᵃexult not like the nations.
    For you have gone a-whoring away from your God;
        you have loved a harlot's fee
        on every threshing floor of grain.
    ²Threshing floor and (oil) press shall not feed them;
        new wine shall fail them.ᵃ
    ³They shall not dwell in Yahweh's land;
        Ephraim shall return to Egypt;
        in Assyria they shall eat unclean (food).
    ⁴They shall not pour out wine to Yahweh;
        nor shall they bringᵇ their sacrifices to him.
    (It shall be) like mourner's food to them;
        all who eat it will defile themselves.
    For their bread is for their own hunger;
        it may not come into the house of Yahweh.

ᵃ Cf. BH.
ᵇ On ʿrb in this context, see G. R. Driver in *Studies in Old Testament Prophecy*, ed. H. H. Rowley, 1950, p. 64.

5What will you do on the festival day,
    on the day for the feast of Yahweh?
6For behold, when they have gone because of destruction,
    Egypt shall gather them,
    Memphis shall bury them.
The thing of desire shall become their downfall;[a]
    weeds shall inherit them,
    thorns (grow) in their tents.

While the autumn festival of Sukkoth is in progress, Hosea steps
forth and commands that its celebration cease. He calls the service a
liturgy of harlotry conducted by those who love the harvest so much
that they have deserted Yahweh. This festival will be their last! They
will be carried away into the uncleanness of foreign lands where the
cult of Yahweh is impossible. When the time for the next feast of
Yahweh comes around, this sanctuary will lie silent and abandoned.
Instead of worshippers, weeds! The speech is a prophetic saying at
times in direct dialogue with the audience (v. 5). It opens with
imperatives to arrest the attention of the celebrants, followed by the
charge that they are apostates (v. 1). The rest of the sequence describes the way in which the observance of Sukkoth will be brought to
an end (vv. 2–6). In vv. 1, 5 where he particularly seeks the response
of his audience Hosea uses direct address; elsewhere he speaks about
his audience in the third person as he describes their future. The scene
is obviously one of the many shrines in Israel; Bethel is a likely possibility. Since a normal celebration is in progress, there must have been
no immediate visible danger to the nation; the time is the breathing
space in the years after the crisis of 733.

[1] Rejoicing and merry celebration were a feature of the autumn
festival that was held when the harvest had been gathered. The seven-
day observance of Tabernacles or Booths was called the 'festival of
Yahweh' (cf. v. 5 and Judg. 21.19–21; Deut. 16.13–15; Lev. 23.39–
43). The festival was Canaanite in origin and had been adopted by
Israel after they settled in the land.[b] Though the celebration in progress is a Yahweh festival (vv. 4 and 5), Hosea sees it as the expression
of Israel's apostasy. In their exultation they are 'like the peoples'; the
term has the sense of 'pagan'. By the character of their worship they
have sunk to the level of the nations around them. The harvest whose

---

[a] On this understanding of kesep, see G. R. Driver, WO 1954, p. 26; and the
discussion by Rudolph.
[b] S. Mowinckel, The Psalms in Israel's Worship I, 1962, pp. 130ff.

bounty they celebrate is received as the result of the fertility cult in which they dealt with Yahweh as though he were Baal whose bounty for the land is bought by the favours of their cultic service. By worshipping Baal, or Yahweh as though he were Baal, Israel has broken the covenant's 'marriage' bonds and become a harlot. On 'harlotry' as Hosea's term for Israel's cultic unfaithfulness, cf. the comment on 1.2. 'Harlot's fee' (Deut. 23.18; cf. Ezek. 16.31ff.) in the prophet's metaphorical speech represents the grapes, fruit, and grain which Israel considers a gift of her lovers, the Baals (2.12). The broad, flat threshing floor, frequently located near the city gate, was used for public and cultic assemblies (II Sam. 24.18; I Kings 22.10), and presumably it was the location for part of the harvest festivities. Israel's true love was the grain. And since the people had set their heart on harvest and dealt with God primarily for its sake, no matter whether they thought of themselves as Yahwists, their worship was a fertility cult.

[2] Threshing floor and (oil) press are the natural focus of the harvest festival (Deut. 16.13). The press was used to extract oil from olives as well as juice from grapes;[a] since new wine is mentioned in the second measure, the trilogy of grain, oil, and wine is in mind (cf. 2.8). Obviously at a harvest festival, the results of the year's crops were already in hand. The prediction that the worshippers will not get to enjoy the harvest expects the bounty to become the booty of the enemy when the population is deported (v. 3).

[3] The phrase 'Yahweh's land' expresses the theological significance of the territory of Canaan in Israel's relation to its God. The land is regarded as the peculiar property and sphere of the God Yahweh, and Hosea can call it also the 'house of Yahweh' (8.1; 9.15). 'Yahweh's land' is a polemical formulation aimed at the cult and theology of Baal, worshipped as the owner of the land and dispenser of its gifts. Yahweh alone has that role. 'The land is mine; for you are strangers and sojourners with me' (Lev. 25.23).[b] When Israel no longer dwells in the land, the status of sojourner is lost and with it all rights to the land's bounty bestowed by the landlord. The 'return to Egypt' (7.16; 8.13; 9.6; 11.5, 11) is the right punishment for those who do not 'return' to Yahweh. The salvation-history will be cancelled, Israel's past with Yahweh erased, and they will find themselves once again where they were when Yahweh called them (11.1f.). The

[a] G. E. Wright, *Biblical Archaeology*, 1962, pp. 183, 185, and plate on p. 186.
[b] Cf. also Josh. 22.19 and G. von Rad, *Theology of the Old Testament* I, 1962, pp. 299f.

pairing of Egypt and Assyria (7.11; 11.5, 11; 12.2) is frequent in Hosea. After 733 some Israelites had already been carried into exile by Assyria and he expected others to flee as refugees to Egypt. Then the Israelites would have to eat the food of a foreign land ruled by a strange god; what was unclean would be their lot (Amos 7.17; Ezek. 4.13 and the problem of 'unclean land' in Josh. 22.19).

[4] When the celebrants end up in foreign lands, the cult will end. They will offer no libations (Num. 15.1–12; Ex. 29.40; Lev. 23.13). Sacrifice will cease because there will be no shrines to Yahweh. Their food will make them unclean like the food in the mourners' house where contact with the dead has made all unclean (Num. 19.11ff.). Eating unclean food in an unclean land, they will be ineligible for the worship of Yahweh (Deut. 26.14). Verse 4b poses difficulties in this context. 'Yahweh's house' means the land or region of Yahweh in Hosea (8.1; 9.15) but here obviously refers to a temple. Israel had no temple called 'House of Yahweh', but the phrase was common for the Jerusalem temple. Moreover, if Israel were in exile, visiting a cultic centre in Israel would be out of the question. The line is probably a contribution of the Deuteronomic editor (HAT, BK), who thereby sets limits on the use of the Jerusalem temple by exiles lest they profane it.

[5] Of the three pilgrimage festivals celebrated in Israel since the days of the tribal league, the feast of Ingathering ('āsîp) or Tabernacles (sūkkōt) was the most significant. It was called the 'feast of Yahweh' (Judg. 21.19; Lev. 23.39). When Jeroboam I founded Bethel as a state sanctuary for the northern kingdom, he established a celebration of the festival (I Kings 12.32f.) in competition with the one held in Jerusalem (I Kings 8.2). Hosea's cutting question is the final blow against the cult of Israel. When these mirthful, celebrating Israelites are in Egypt and Assyria, what will they do when the time comes for assembly to hold the feast of Yahweh? His judgment will put an end to their worship of him, and in this punishment they will learn that the festival itself was harlotrous blasphemy against the covenant God. What will they do? There was no answer to that question, and the silence which the question creates is the beginning of the end of all their celebration.

[6] 'Behold' introduces a final picture of disaster, forcing the audience to look beyond their present assembly for rejoicing to another kind of gathering – a being gathered for burial. The verse takes up the theme of v. 3b, the return to Egypt and the reversal of the salvation-

history. When destruction (cf. *šōd* in 10.14) ravages their land, those who can will flee as refugees to Egypt. But their flight will be an escape to death. They will find no future except being collected for burial in the famous ancient graveyards of Memphis.[a] 'The thing of desire' is Egypt to which Israel's leaders had turned so often seeking an escape from Assyria. The nation of their hopes will be the instrument of their humiliation. The shrine that is so full of celebrating people will be left deserted, abandoned to silence and weeds.

20. THE FOOL FOR GOD: 9.7–9

9 7The days of punishment have come.
    The days of requital have come.
    Israel shall know (it).
  'Stupid is the prophet,
    crazed the man of the spirit.'
  Because of the greatness of your guilt,
    the hostility is great.
  8The prophet[b] is the watchman[c] of Ephraim with my God;
    (but) a fowler's snare (is set) on all his ways,
    hostility is in the house of his God.
  9They have acted basely[d]
    as in the days of Gibeah.
  He will remember their iniquity,
    he will punish their sin.

This saying is the only direct clue in the entire book of Hosea to the prophet's reception by his countrymen. The window which it opens on his life is however opaque. The speech is tantalizingly brief and at one point (v. 8a) exceedingly difficult to follow. There is no accompanying narrative (as in Amos 7.10ff.) to describe the circumstances of Hosea's persecution. Yet the lines bear witness clearly enough to the scorn, hostility, and danger which surrounded him as he announced the end of the covenant, the rejection of Israel's culture and cult, and the terrible punishment about to fall upon the nation. His own people to whom he was sent by their God slandered him with the charge of madness and plotted his downfall throughout the

---

[a] See 'Memphis' in *IDB* III, pp. 346f.
[b] According to MT's punctuation 'prophet' is a *casus pendens* that goes with v. 8b.
[c] *ṣōpēh* for MT's *ṣōpeh*.
[d] On this translation of the two verbs unconnected by a copula, cf. *GK* 120g.

land. The saying is a speech of disputation in which Hosea ('my God' in v. 8a) answers the slander and rejection of his audience ('your iniquity' in vv. 7f.). He begins by insisting that his message of judgment is true because the days of punishment have already begun (v. 7a); probably the time is the reign of Hoshea ben Elah after the partial exile of Israel in 733. He quotes what his opponents say about him and turns their slander into further evidence of their own iniquity (v. 7b). Though he is Ephraim's watchman who works in the service of his God, they beset his way through the land of Yahweh with danger and enmity (v. 8). In v. 9 the disputation speech shifts to an announcement of judgment with indictment and sentence which Hosea utters in his own right. His opponents' treatment of him is like the shameful deed of Gibeah; Yahweh will punish them for their sin.

[7] The repetition used in the first two sentences is aggressively emphatic. The insistence is probably a rejoinder to fellow Israelites who mock him concerning his prediction of destruction for the nation. He answers that the days of punishment and requital are indeed at hand. What was started in 733 by the Assyrians will be completed; let Ephraim not be deceived by the current temporary respite. For a process is in operation that is more than the human fact that they still survive. Yahweh has not finished what he began. Punishment is due their iniquity; requital must be worked upon their sin. If they do not realize it now, they will know it in the end. The scornful dismissal of the prophet (v. 7b) is almost certainly a quotation of what the prophet's opponents say; as in 6.1–3, the words of the audience are incorporated into the saying without introduction.[a] The stupid ('*ewîl*) man is a favourite foil of wisdom in proverbial sayings (13 times in Prov. 1.7–27.22). Hosea's audience see themselves as the wise man who has to deal with a fool; 'When a wise man has a case with a fool, he only rages and laughs . . .' (Prov. 29.9). 'Crazed' (*mešuggāʿ*) is even stronger disparagement; it is the word for a man who has lost his sanity (I Sam. 21.12–15), was applied scornfully to prophets by those who deemed them irrational and unreliable (II Kings 9.11; Jer. 29.26). 'Man of spirit' (*ʾîš hārûaḥ*) is a not-so-complimentary alternative title for 'prophet'. It was possession by the spirit which produced the ecstatic raving of the old *nebiʾim* (I Sam. 10.6); the gift of the spirit was a special characteristic of the northern prophets (I

[a] See H. W. Wolff, 'Das Zitat in Prophetensprach', in *Gesammelte Studien zum Alten Testament* (Th. Büch. 22), 1964, pp. 56ff.

Kings 18.12; 22.21; II Kings 2.9, 16). The title was probably a conventional synonym for 'man of God', the popular title for 'prophet' found frequently in northern sources. Its application to Hosea does not prove that the irrational ecstasy was a feature of his prophetic activity. It is rather the public's scornful way of putting the prophet in his place. They classify in order to dismiss. The remark has the flavour of assumed sophistication, the odour of the leading class in Israel who see Hosea as one more of the old *nebi'im* who is carried away by ecstatic possession. They are enough in awe of his supernatural status not to slay him, but so little impressed with his message that they scorn him. Hosea answers their attack by pointing to its real cause. They rage at him because they are guilty. They are hostile because he makes them hear and know what they had rather forget; the conscience cannot bear his message. They could repent, but it is easier to hate the man who uncovers their guilt and plot his downfall.

[8] There is little agreement about the right understanding of v. 8a.ª The translation adopted above holds to MT's consonantal text ('prophet' can be read with v. 8a or 8b without affecting the sense) and attempts to understand the text as it stands, since resort to conjecture only increases the uncertainty. Apparently Hosea continues his answer to the slander of his audience; their hostility is a manifestation of their guilt while the prophet whom they call stupid is in fact the divinely appointed watchman over the nation. The impersonal 'prophet' picks up the title from the quotation while with 'my God' Hosea shifts for a moment to first-person speech because of his passionate sense of belonging to Yahweh. Several of the prophets were called 'watchmen' (Jer. 6.17; Ezek. 3.17; Isa. 56.10); the role of the guard who warns of approaching danger from his position of vantage (I Sam. 14.16; II Sam. 13.34; 18.24–27; and the classic description in Ezek. 33.1–6) was a likely and apt image for the prophetic function. Hosea himself uses the image twice in his sayings (5.8; 8.1). That the prophet is watchman 'with God' is a way of saying that the office is carried out in the presence of, from the sphere of God (BK cites Ex. 34.28; I Sam. 2.21; Deut. 18.13 as analogies for the phrase). Moreover, the watchman is there for 'my God' and not to serve the nation; the hostility of the audience at Hosea's message from Yahweh leaves him with his God over against the nation, so he is the object of plots and hatred. Ephraim lays traps for its own watchman,

---

ª See the discussion and the review of the many proposals by R. Dobbie, 'The Text of Hosea 9.8', *VT* 5, 1955, pp. 199ff.

schemes against the guardian of its own safety. He is treated as though he were no better than a wild creature. Everywhere he goes in the land ('house of his God' means the region of Canaan; cf. 8.1; 9.15 and 'land of Yahweh' in 9.3) he is confronted with implacable hatred.

[9] In their conduct toward Hosea the people have continued to act as they did in the 'days of Gibeah' (10.9). The comparison points back to some historic incident when Israel's deed was base and ruinous. Gibeah in Benjamite territory near the border of Judah (cf. 5.8) was the residence of Saul as king (I Sam. 10.26; 11.4). Hosea viewed Israel's kingship as one of her 'original sins' (3.4; 8.4; 9.15). But its inauguration occurred at Gilgal and it does not serve well as a term of comparison for the treatment of the prophet. Probably Hosea refers to the notorious and shameful episode told in Judges 19–21, the wanton crime against the Levite and concubine that almost led to the extermination of the entire tribe of Benjamin. So basely does Ephraim now act toward the prophet and so ruinous will be the consequences, that Yahweh will himself assume the duty of punishment which the tribal rally carried out in the original incident. Their sin and iniquity will receive its punishment (v. 9b appears as verdict also in 8.13).

21. THE FALL TO BAAL: 9.10–14

9 ¹⁰Like grapes in the wilderness
    I found Israel.
Like early figs on the fig tree (in its beginning) ᵃ
    I saw your fathers.
But they came to Baal-Peor,
    consecrated themselves to Shame,
    and became an abhorrent thing like their lover. ᵇ
¹¹Ephraim! their honour shall fly away like a bird –
    no birth, no pregnancy, no conception.
¹²Even if they rear their children,
    I will bereave them to the last man.
Yea, woe also to them
    when I depart ᶜ from them.
¹³Ephraim, as I have seen,
    ᵈhas made his sons a hunter's prey.ᵈ

ᵃ The phrase is a gloss; it is superfluous in sense and metre; cf. the comment below.
ᵇ Reading *'ōhᵃbām*.
ᶜ Taking *šūr* as a form of *sūr*.
ᵈ⁻ᵈ MT is corrupt. G presupposes *lᵉṣayid šātū bānāyw*.

> Ephraim shall bring forth
> his sons to slaughter.[a]
> ¹⁴Give them, O Yahweh –
> what you will give them!
> Give them a childless womb
> and shrivelled breasts!

This oracle opens a new section of the book characterized by the repeated use of history to establish the perspective in which the present is to be understood. Up to this point the past has been mentioned, if at all only in passing (cf. 9.9; allusions to Egypt in 2.15; 8.13; 9.3), but now references to the historical background become regular and significant. Verse 10 is typical. The oracle begins in the style of the divine saying; Yahweh tells first of his pleasure in Israel during the wilderness epoch and how that epoch ended as soon as Israel reached the first outpost of Canaan's cult. This contrast between the Israel of the wilderness and the one at Beth-Peor is the reproach, and the oracle proceeds directly to announcement of the punishment for the contemporary Israel. Because Israel fell to the fertility god and still worships him (that is the obvious presumption), the women shall become barren (v. 11) and the children already alive will perish (v. 12). Verse 13 appears to be a prophetic saying in which Hosea acknowledges that the judgment through the sons is already under way. In v. 14 he breaks out into intercession, but can only petition for the barrenness which Yahweh has already announced. The divine-speech style and the references to Gilgal in v. 15 mark the beginning of a new unit.

[10] With an almost wistful nostalgia Yahweh recalls the beginning of Israel's life with him. It was a time of surprised joy and fresh delight for him. He remembers his emotions like a man recalling the best time of a life that is past and gone; its sweetness is reinforced by the contrast of the present. Both metaphors create this feeling of an unexpected pleasure that lives on in memory. Grapes do not grow in the wilderness; if a wanderer were to come upon them in its barren stretches he would be amazed with pleasure. The fig tree produces fruit which ripens in the spring from the late shoots of the previous season, '. . . a first-ripe fig before the summer; when a man sees it, he eats it as soon as it is in his hand' (Isa. 28.4; cf. Micah 7.1; Jer. 24.2). In the days before Canaan Yahweh found Israel just as delightful as that! The language is human and poetic. The people are

---

[a] Cf. G.

addressed as the children of fathers with whom Yahweh initiated the salvation-history, and who therefore are involved in the continuity of its unfolding. 'In the wilderness' is an element of the first metaphor and does not necessarily point to a special tradition about the beginning of the salvation-history, though there is a hint of such a tradition in Deut. 32.10 ('He *found* him in a desert land . . .'). Hosea consistently names Egypt as the locus of the beginning (2.15; 11.1; 12.9, 13; 13.4). In contrast to the pentateuchal tradition Jeremiah follows Hosea in regarding the wilderness period as a halcyon time in Israel's relation to Yahweh and also emphasizes the pleasure which Yahweh found in his people then (Jer. 2.2f.). The gloss (p. 131 n. *a*) is an explanatory comment to clarify the unusual word (*bikkūrā*) for early fig. The wilderness idyll came to an early end in Israel's first contact with the religion of Canaan. The story of how the fathers yoked themselves to Baal-Peor is told in Num. 25.1–5. The mountain (Num. 23.28) and the sanctuary to which Peor's name was given (Beth-peor; Deut. 3.29; 4.46, etc.) were located some ten miles north-east of the Jordan's mouth. The account in Numbers clearly suggests that Israel became involved in the sexual rites of the fertility cult (Num. 25.1f., 6, 8). Those whom Yahweh had found with such pleasure set themselves apart in ritual consecration to a deity who would create fertility for them in the land which they entered. 'Shame' is an abusive name for Baal (cf. 2.5; 10.6); the practice of replacing Baal's name with 'Shame' may well have begun with the derisive interpretation by Hosea (so BK). 'Abhorrent thing' (*šiqqūṣ*) is also a derogatory noun often used for idols. The fathers took on the character of Baal-Peor by their consecration to him. Their identity was changed, and in Hosea's view they have lived out that identity of shame ever since they came into the land. The salvation-history ended on the farther side of Jordan; Israel's story in Canaan is a history of sin.

[11] The oracle moves from accusation to punishment, and the time changes from past to present. Ephraim is the true heir of Israel, the sons of the fathers. They still devote themselves to shame in hope of fertility, so appropriately the fertility of their bodies shall be frustrated and ended. The 'honour' (*kābōd*) of Israel is their dignity and splendour as a proud people, specifically as the following lines show, their children in whom they glory, seeing in them their future and strength, and the blessing of the fertility cult. Now that honour will depart like a bird winging across the horizon. Fertility shall cease. 'Birth, pregnancy, and conception' follow the process of bearing

children backwards to its beginning to negate the whole. Through the end of the human fertility, Ephraim will face a convincing rebuttal of their devotion to the Baals.

[12] The circle of judgment's threat widens beyond the unborn to include the living children and the parents themselves. Let Ephraim take no comfort in the children they already have! By battle, deportation, and famine Yahweh will strip away the last of them. And for the adults who are left there will be only the sorrow and suffering; Yahweh saves his ominous 'woe' for them. He will abdicate his place as their God and their ultimate extremity shall be the silent, vacant emptiness above and around them (cf. 5.15). The true salvation-history ended at the shrine of Baal-Peor; Yahweh's departure will show that what has happened since has been a history of apostasy.

[13] The text of 13a is corrupt; the suggested translation is based on G, which stands at some distance from MT, and so must remain quite tentative. The fate of Ephraim's children is the theme of vv. 13b and 14, so the reconstruction is plausible to its context. Verse 14 is clearly a prayer addressed by the prophet to Yahweh. Verse 13 is best understood also as the speech of the prophet (ATD) rather than the continuation of the divine saying of judgment in vv. 10–12 (BK). Hosea responds to God's word announcing the end of fertility in Ephraim and the loss of all their children. He confirms Yahweh's judgment by his own observation. Already he has seen Ephraim expose his sons to the danger of pursuit and slaughter as though they were hunter's game. Probably he thinks of the war with the Assyrians under Pekah when Israel's troops were decimated in hopeless struggle against the overwhelming might of Tiglath-pileser. That catastrophe, he now knows by divine revelation, was not end but beginning. The word of Yahweh will be fulfilled; Ephraim will try once again to muster his sons for war that will end in their slaughter.

[14] In the face of what he has already seen and expects to happen, Hosea breaks forth into prayer. Prophet though he be, he is also a part of Ephraim, a son of the fathers, living by faith in Israel's election. Like Amos (Amos 7.3, 5) and Isaiah (Isa. 6.11) he cannot bear to hear this word of Israel's total extinction in resignation. He assumes the office of intercession for the people of God and begins his appeal to the covenant Lord: 'Give them, O Yahweh . . .' But his prayer hesitates, hanging unfinished. How can he be both prophet and intercessor, stand on God's side and Ephraim's side, speak to Israel of judgment and for Israel in hope? What shall he ask from the giver

of all Israel's blessings for this sinful, rebellious people who are already under the verdict of God? Then his tortured mind finds a way and the faltering prayer resumes. He prays that no more children be born. The prayer accepts the announced punishment in part (v. 11) as a kind of blessing for which he could pray. In the terrible days to come the curse of barrenness would be a merciful blessing. Better that mothers bear no children than to see them slaughtered (see Luke 23.29). Better for wives not to conceive than for husbands to watch them ravished and split open. The prophet can ask for no more than this curse.

22. LEADERS WHO MISLEAD: 9.15-17

9 15All their evil is in Gilgal.
    Yea, there I hate them.
  Because of their wicked deeds
    I will drive them out of my house.
  I will love them no more.
    All their leaders are misleaders!
16Ephraim is blighted,
    Their root is dried up,
    they will yield no fruit.
  Even though they give birth,
    I will slay their darling offspring.
17My God will reject them,
    for they have not obeyed him;
    they shall be wanderers among the nations.

Yahweh announces in blunt, unqualified language that his relation to Ephraim is at an end. Because of the evil that occurs in Gilgal, his love is withdrawn, and in its place there is hate and rejection. The blessing of life in the land is already withheld. Ephraim has no future except to become nameless fugitives drifting among the nations of the world. The divine saying extends through vv. 15 and 16; in v. 17 the prophet takes up the word, perhaps in answer to those who dispute the message in the name of a false faith in Yahweh. In the present arrangement of the material, vv. 15-17 are closely connected with vv. 10-14. The third person plural pronouns in v. 15 presuppose the antecedent Ephraim in vv. 11 and 13. Verse 16 returns to the theme of infertility and death of Ephraim's children (vv. 11f.) as though to reiterate the punishment whose announcement had evoked the prayer in v. 14. Probably the two oracles with their accompanying prophetic words belong to the same time and situation.

[15] The first line of v. 15 can be translated in either past or present tense. If past is correct, Yahweh refers to some incident at Gilgal in Israel's history, which like the fall to Baal-Peor (v. 10) has burdened Israel with a sin for which they must now pay. The only noteworthy incident at Gilgal preserved in the tradition of the Old Testament is the inauguration of Saul's kingship (I Sam. 11.14f.). Hosea considered Israel's monarchy to be one of the nation's primary offences against Yahweh (3.4; 7.3–7; 8.4; 10.3, 7, 15) and it is possible that he pairs the beginning of the monarchy with Israel's first participation in the cult of Baal as the two initial sins against Yahweh from which all the rest of Israel's rebellion flows.ᵃ However, the other two texts in Hosea which mention Gilgal deal with the cult conducted there (12.11; 4.15; cf. also Amos 4.4; 5.5) and the rest of the passage is more coherent with an attack on the cult. Gilgal, 'on the east border of Jencho' (Josh. 4.19), probably the mound called *Khirbet Mafjar*, was one of the original amphictyonic sanctuaries; its cult probably celebrated the conquest of the land; it continued to attract pilgrims. But Israel under the influence of Canaanite theology worshipped Yahweh as though he were the Baal of the land. 'All their evil' is the confusion of Yahweh with Baal, and the subsequent perversion of their understanding of his lordship over them. They thought of him as a divine 'lover' (2.5, 7, etc.) to be wooed and won with sacrifice and fertility rites. Yahweh rejects these ritual seductions and hates them as a husband 'hates' an unsatisfactory wife (Deut. 22.13; 24.3; cf. Jer. 12.8). He will drive the rejected wife out of 'his house' and bring the marriage to an end. Yahweh's 'house' is a metaphor for the land (8.1; 9.8). Israel's God declares that his love has reached its limits! The leaders (*śārîm*, royal officials) who assume the prerogatives of guiding the people are like the blind leading the blind, for they are guilty of being the leaders of this rebellion against Yahweh (cf. 5.1f.). The measure (v. 15bβ) contains an alliteration (*kol-śārēhem sōrᵉrîm*) which the translation attempts to reproduce; literally 'all their court officials are rebels' (cf. Isa. 1.23).

[16] The effects of Israel's faithlessness are already visible in the withering national life. Ephraim is like a plant whose leaves fade because its roots find no moisture. Such a plant can yield no fruit.

ᵃ See the discussion in E. Jacob, 'Der Prophet Hosea und die Geschichte', *EvTh* 24, 1964, pp. 283f.

The very goal of their worship, the thing above all else that they sought in their religion, is already taken away. Even if pregnant women bear children, Yahweh will slay the precious products of their fertility (9.1a).

[17] The possessive in 'my God' (cf. 'the house of his God' in 9.8) indicates that the divine saying ends with v. 16 and the prophet himself takes up the word (as in vv. 13f.). Yahweh is Hosea's God in a special and personal way, because as prophet he has been drawn in the service of Yahweh and set in opposition to his own people. Ephraim may make their own claims upon Yahweh and reject the message of Hosea, but the prophet answers their false faith and hostility (9.7f.) with a confessional claim based on his call and knowledge of Yahweh's decision. He knows what he speaks, for Yahweh is 'my God'. Ephraim's rejection has been decreed. In spite of their piety and ritual they have failed in the one requisite response under the covenant – obedience! (6.6; Ex. 19.5). Because their existence as a people depended on the covenant, they have no future as a nation. As homeless refugees they shall wander among the nations – a folk without land or nation of their own who have lost their identity. 'Hosea glimpses here something of the profound relation between the absence of God and homelessness, and is the first to point toward the problem of the "eternal Jew" which later takes on historical reality in the exile . . .' (ATD, p. 77).

23. THEY SHALL DWELL WITHOUT CULT OR KING: 10.1-8

10 ¹Israel was a flourishing vine
    which always bore ᵃ fruit.
As his fruit increased,
    he increased altars.
As his land made good,
    they made good pillars.
²Their heart is tricky.
    Now they shall bear their guilt.
He himself will break their altars
    and destroy their pillars.

³Yea, now they shall say,
    'We have no king,

ᵃ On *šwh* see Nyberg.

for we do not fear Yahweh,
    and thc king! what can he do for us? –
[4]mouth[a] words –
    swear falsely –
    make a covenant –
so that justice sprouts like poison-weed
    in the furrows of the field.'

[5]The residents of Samaria tremble
    for the bull[b] of Beth-awen.
Yea, his people mourn over him,
    and his idol-priests (mourn) over him.
They howl[c] because of his splendour
    for it has departed from him.
[6]Even it itself shall be borne to Assyria,
    a tribute for the great king.[d]
Ephraim shall experience shame;
    Israel shall be confounded because of its idol.[e]
[7]From[f] Samaria its king shall be eliminated
    like a broken branch upon the torrent,
[8]and the high places of wickedness shall be destroyed,
    the sin of Israel.
Thorn and thistle shall overgrow
    their altars.
They shall say to the mountains, 'Cover us!'
    and to the hills, 'Fall upon us!'

10.1–8 portrays the judgment of Yahweh as it falls upon every significant institution of Israel's religious and national life. Altar and pillar, king and capital, idol and high place – one by one they are blotted out until the people are left alone to face the wrath of Yahweh, crying out for the sanctuary of death in consternation. Whether the sequence is an original unit of speech or a tightly woven compilation of shorter sayings and fragments is difficult to determine. The metaphor of Israel as a flourishing vine (v. 1) used to characterize its history in the land clearly marks a new beginning. The themes of cult (vv. 1f., 5–8) and king (vv. 3f.) alternate without serving as convincing guides by which to distinguish independent sayings. Verses 1f.

    [a] *dabbēr* for *dibberū* to correspond to the parallel absolute infinitives following; cf. G.
    [b] Cf. BH.
    [c] *gīl* in the sense of 'howl, shriek' is used as a word-play on *gālā*; cf. *HAL*, p. 182.
    [d] *malkī rab*; cf. 5.13.
    [e] Reading *mēʿoṣbō* for MT's 'because of its plan (counsel: *ʿēṣā*)'; G. R. Driver translates MT 'disobedience, rebellion' (*Nötscher Festschrift*, 1950, p. 54).
    [f] *miššōmerōn* with Rudolph.

make up an oracle of judgment against Israel's investment of her prosperity in cultic equipment; it is complete in itself. But the opening 'now' of v. 3 picks up the 'now' in v. 2b and the antecedents for its pronouns are found in vv. 1f. Verses 5f. foretell the fate of the bull-image at Bethel. Verse 7 probably continues the same subject, if 'king' is a title for Baal. An announcement of the desolation of the high places (v. 8) completes the agenda of judgment, and the whole is brought to a climax with the people's cry of terror. The style of the divine saying is missing throughout; the accusations and indictments seem to be prophetic sayings.

[1] With another of his numerous metaphors Hosea portrays an Israel that has prospered, and in its success come to failure. He uses the name 'Israel' instead of Ephraim because with the metaphor he surveys all the time since the people came into Canaan. Israel was like a vine planted and cultivated by Yahweh (cf. Jer. 2.21; Isa. 5.1–7), and therefore it bore much fruit. That the produce of the land is the gift of Yahweh is almost a dogma for Hosea (2.8f.). And in its own way Israel viewed its prosperity in Canaan from a religious perspective; the growth of wealth was paralleled by an expansion of cult. The more the land yielded, the more altars were built. Prosperity was memorialized in embellished and decorated pillars (on *maṣṣēbā*, see the commentary on 3.4). This co-ordination of welfare and cult shows that Israel saw a functional relation between the two; the development of cultic sanctuaries was simply turning part of the profit back into the business. Altars and pillars were the holy machinery which produced the prosperity – a typically Canaanite understanding of cult. And therefore the altars had become the instruments of sin (8.11). [2] The heart of Israel was neither whole nor faithful toward Yahweh; they worshipped him, but what they really had in mind was the produce of grain, wine, and oil which they thought their worship would secure. Instead of encounter with their God, the cult had become an evasion of him.

'Now' introduces the verdict of Yahweh, as it often does in Hosea's oracles (5.7; 8.10, 13). Yahweh himself shall bring upon them the consequences of their guilt and in his terrible action end the evasion and create encounter. The altars and pillars will in the end serve as a place of knowing Yahweh's nearness – when they are shattered and destroyed! Then their false heart will have no way to pretend to seek Yahweh while only pursuing its own desires.

[3] Verses 3f. take up the subject of Israel's king, a theme to which

Hosea returns frequently because he regards the kingship in Israel as a primary manifestation of their faithlessness and rebellion against Yahweh (3.4; 7.3–7; 8.4, 10; 10.7, 15; 13.10f.). By means of a quotation the prophet dramatizes the despair which grips Ephraim when their king is gone and they realize that they are without king or God. The significance of the quotation is ambiguous. Does the prophet repeat in an ironic taunt what the people are already saying? Or is the quotation a portrayal of their future situation when judgment has left them without a king? It is conceivable that after the murder of Pekah some of the people attributed their desperate circumstances during the Assyrian invasion to his assassination. But the second possibility is the more likely interpretation. 'Now' in Hosea frequently introduces the announcement of imminent punishment (10.2; 5.7; 8.10, 13). The fall of the king is predicted in the context (10.7, 15). And it is difficult to imagine that the audience to which Hosea speaks would readily admit that the king was no help and they actually had no reverence of Yahweh. The quotation reports what Ephraim will soon have to say when Yahweh's judgment drives them to self-knowledge and penitence. They will confess they are a people without their own king. They did not let Yahweh rule them. And the man they have as ruler is a delusion. What can he as king do for them? No more than he has always done.

[4] 'What can the king do for us?' The answer to this disillusioned question comes tumbling out in a torrent of staccato expressions. The embittered phrases add up the sum of Israel's actual experience with their kings. Each of the three measures in the first line is a way of saying that the king betrays the obligations of his inauguration. 'Speak (mere) words' means empty speech that carries no authenticity, is followed by no fulfilling act (cf. Isa. 8.10). 'Swear falsely' refers probably to the oath taken before God to serve the best interests of the people. 'Make covenant' points to the pact of relationship established between king and people at his enthronement (II Sam. 3.21; 5.3).[a] In Israel the king had assumed the responsibilities which the judge bore in the era of the tribal league; it belonged to the royal office to judge the people by saving them from their foes and by maintaining the right order of life within the community. Justice (mišpāṭ) was his peculiar responsibility.[b] But the harvest of royal treachery had been

[a]So G. Fohrer, 'Der Vertrag zwischen König und Volk in Israel', ZAW 71, 1959, p. 17.
[b]See A. R. Johnson, Sacral Kingship in Ancient Israel, 1955, pp. 3ff.

a false justice that killed rather than saved. The fields of the nation bore poison weed instead of grain. The metaphor is quite similar to the one used by Amos (4.15; 8.14) and may be borrowed from him or could reflect a saying that was current among those who suffered under the king's justice. In the coming judgment all Israel would learn to speak such bitter words and their lament would announce their own guilt in making kings in autonomous independence of Yahweh.

[5] Verses 5f. return to the theme of Israel's cult and deal specifically with the odious object which stood at its centre, the bull in the sanctuary at Beth-awen, Hosea's scornful nickname for Bethel (cf. 4.15). On the nature of the image and its role in Israel's cult, see the commentary on 8.5. Though it had been designated as a pedestal for Yahweh's invisible presence, the bull had such intimate connections with the cult and mythology of Canaan that it obscured the reality of Yahweh and opened the door on pagan syncretism. Israel adored the thing itself with sacrifice and ritual kiss (13.2). In a taunt that rises to the level of Deutero-Isaiah's eloquent scorn at Babylon's frantic anxiety over the safety of her deities (Isa. 41.5ff.; 44.9ff.), Hosea describes the apprehension that runs like contagion through the devotees of the bull as the Assyrian menace fills their horizon. The leading circles of the nation who live in the capital city of Samaria are gripped with dread as their confidence that the power of their deity can preserve them melts, and they begin to wonder how they can protect him. People and priests assemble at the sanctuary to hold services of lamentation concerning their endangered god. Normally such ritual lamentation would bewail the absence of the god during the long dry season. But now the lament is tinged with a fear for the idol itself. 'My people', the elect of Yahweh, show themselves to be 'his people', the folk who belong to the bull. Hosea calls the clergy of Bethel 'pagan priests' (kōmer), a name that designates the priests of idols in its other appearances in the Old Testament (II Kings 23.5; Zeph. 1.4). The splendour (kābōd) of the bull is the costly ornamentation and gilding decorating the idol; apparently the sanctuary has already been stripped in order to pay the tribute levied by the Assyrians in 733. The last measure is reminiscent of the cry of Eli's daughter-in-law concerning the loss of the ark to the Philistines: 'The glory (kābōd) has departed from Israel' (I Sam. 4.22).

[6] Such a fate is in store for the bull. In the days ahead the image will follow its trappings and end up in a caravan on the way to the

court of the Assyrian king. The folly and uselessness of Bethel's bull will then be apparent. Ephraim will be left exposed to the disgrace of having worshipped a powerless fraud.

[7] The reference to Samaria's king seems to indicate that v. 7 is a fragment which reverts to the subject of Israel's royalty (vv. 3f.). But v. 7 is set within sayings about the cult; indeed v. 8 appears to continue its literary pattern directly (. . . . shall be eliminated . . . and shall be destroyed). The best solution is to understand 'king' as a title for the bull image of vv. 5f. The verse then continues the thought of v. 6, describing with a comparison the disappearance of the image. It will be swept away by the Assyrian forces as a branch broken from a tree is carried away in a flood.

[8] The loss of the bull image will lead to the desertion of the high places (*bāmōt*). The high place was the site for worship out in the countryside; every town of significance was likely to have one. An altar was placed on an elevated place; usually there was a sacred grove or tree, apparently the symbol of the mother goddess Asherah, and the sacred pillar or *maṣṣēbā* which may have represented Baal. Many of the high places were taken over from the Canaanites and their cult was continued with little change.[a] Hosea describes the ritual of the high place as he knew it with outraged disgust in 4.11–14. Here he names them the 'high places of wickedness'. Because their religion was so absolutely out of accord with authentic Yahwism of the covenant he regarded them as the 'sin of Israel' par excellence. Destruction would come upon them and the wild growth of brambles would soon cover them from sight. The people will then be left without altar, pillar, or high place, without king or deity. All the supports and instruments of national and religious life gone, they will cry out in terror for the hiding place of death. Hosea depicts the dread of the time by quoting what the people will say (as in v. 3); they will implore mountains and hills to erupt in earthquake and cover them lest they be left in their nakedness to face the wrath of God (cf. Luke 23.30; Isa. 2.10, 21).

24. THE DOUBLE INIQUITY: 10.9–10

10 [9]Since the days of Gibeah you have sinned, O Israel!
    There they have remained.

[a] See W. F. Albright, *Archaeology and the Religion of Israel*, 1956, pp. 105–107; G. E. Wright, *Biblical Archaeology*, 1962, pp. 114f.

> Shall war not overtake them in Gibeah?
> Against sons of wrong[a] [10]I have come[a] that I may chastise them.
> Peoples shall be assembled against them
> when they are chastised[b] for their double iniquity.[a]

Invoking once again 'the days of Gibeah' (9.9) as a historic point of departure for Israel's career in the land, Yahweh announces that the coming war against them will reach even to this town on the southern borders of the kingdom. The oracle is an announcement of judgment with indictment (v. 9) and verdict (v. 10). The divine word opens in the style of direct address, but shifts to the third person plural for Israel in the second measure. The state of the text limits confidence about interpretation at points.

[9] As in 9.10 Hosea uses the old tradition of incidents in Israel's first years in Canaan to establish the character of the contemporary nation. In such historic deeds Israel disclosed its corporate soul and entered into a way that determined its subsequent life in the land. History is significant because it provides a typology by which to interpret and evaluate the present. On the original sin of Gibeah see the commentary on 9.9. Hosea probably refers to the shameful deed of the Benjamites (note Judg. 19.30) against the visiting Levite which provoked a tribal assembly against them and led to their near extermination (Judg. 19–21). Gibeah later became the residence of Saul during his kingship (I Sam. 10.26f.; 11), and because of Hosea's negative view of Israel's kings it is possible that he has the beginning of the kingship also in mind. But the beginning of kingship is associated with Gilgal in Israel's tradition (see the commentary on 9.15). Gibeah, not the wilderness and the Exodus, is the central clue to the history of which Israel is the primary subject. What happened there continues to be present. Gibeah has become a location in a geography of the spirit; 'there' designates a way of life. The Israelites of Hosea's day are the heirs of what their fathers did and as 'sons of wrong' ('awlāh) they continue to live out their heritage. Will it not be just and appropriate that the war of Yahweh's judgment should overtake them as they live on in this 'city of violent and shameful wrong'?

[10] Their punishment is already under way! The parallelism between 'I have come' and 'peoples are assembled' co-ordinates divine act and external public history. In the assault of foreign nations

---

[a] Cf. BH.
[b] A passive of *ysr* is suggested by GSV.

('peoples' for foreign folk in 7.8; 9.1) upon Israel Yahweh is the present acting subject. As the Lord of world history he assembles the nations to be the instrument of his chastisement of Israel (cf. Isa. 10.5). As the tribes rallied in assembly against Benjamin (Judg. 20.1f.), so the nations assemble against Israel. The old amphictyonic process for maintaining covenant order has been translated into the process of world history in order to chastise Israel for breach of covenant. If Hosea does have Saul's kingship also in mind in the reference to Gibeah, the 'double iniquity' could be the sum of the incidents in Judges 19–21 and Saul (HAT, ATD). But Hosea may see 'then' and 'now', the original deed and its subsequent continuation, as two phases which double the iniquity (BK).

25. THE FARM OF GOD: 10.11–13a

¹¹Ephraim was a trained heifer
   that loved to thresh,
but I ªlaid a yoke
   uponª her lovely neck.
'I will harness Ephraim;
   Judah^b shall plough;
   Jacob shall harrow for himself.'
¹²'Sow righteousness for yourselves;
   reap according to devotion.
Break up new ground for yourselves;
   it is time to seek Yahweh
that he may come and rain salvation on you.'
¹³You have ploughed wickedness;
   wrong you have reaped;
so you have eaten the fruit of falsehood.

10.11–13a is an oral unit held together by the use of agricultural imagery to interpret Yahweh's tragic disappointment with Israel. In spite of the third-person references to Yahweh in 12b, the whole speech is a divine saying. Yahweh describes the Israel of the wilderness as a trained heifer loving its work and tells of his plan to yoke the beast for work in Canaan (v. 11). The direct address in v. 12 continues the story by reviewing the task which Yahweh set for his people.

ª–ª For MT's ʿābartī ʿāl, certainly an incomplete expression, read ʿibbartī ʿōl ʿāl-; see Rudolph.
^bThe addition of the redactor; Judah does not fit in the sequence.

Verse 13a breaks off the narrative about the past to speak directly to the contemporary nation; what they have done is the very opposite of the vocation given them. Verse 13b turns to another subject and opens a new oral unit. The redactor has placed 10.11–13a after 10.9f. because of the catchword 'wrong' ('*awlā*) in v. 9 and v. 13.

[11] The saying begins with one of the metaphors at whose formulation Hosea was so apt. Portraying Ephraim as a young cow (note the 'balky heifer' in 4.16) Yahweh speaks of his relation to Israel in the form of a parable about a strong useful animal and the man who harnesses it to work his land. The heifer already belongs to the man and has been trained to thresh, work that she does willingly. Presumably the kind of threshing in mind was not the work of pulling a threshing sledge – that would have involved a yoke, but rather the easy, pleasant method of having the animal walk around over the cut grain spread on the threshing floor until the grains were loosened from the ear. The animal was left unmuzzled and free to eat as it worked (Deut. 25.4). The owner decides that the heifer is ready for harder work and puts a yoke on the neck that had not been rubbed and chafed by its weight and pull before. In v. 11b the owner speaks directly of what he has in mind. The heifer that had hitherto had only the light work of threshing to do must now do the harder work that produces the grain – ploughing and harrowing. The meaning of the parable is clear. The time when Israel did its work for Yahweh willingly was the wilderness era (cf. 2.25; 9.10). The harder work of ploughing and harrowing is the life in Canaan where Israel was expected to fulfil the promise of the wilderness and serve Yahweh with faithful labour. The agricultural imagery fits the beginning of the life of peasants in Canaan, but that is not its point. The images are only metaphors and already in 11b the image of the trained heifer is dropped for the names of the nation. What Israel was to work at is made plain by the covenant terms in v. 12; the new life in Canaan was to have been a period when Israel fulfilled the plan of Yahweh to have a people who were truly his own. The appearance of 'Judah' in the sequence between Ephraim and Jacob is surprising. Hosea did on occasion address oracles to both Israel and Judah (e.g. 5.9ff.) and the parable deals with a period in which all Israel would have been involved, but Judah does not fit here; the agricultural metaphors require that all three of the names refer to the same people. 'Judah' is the work of a Judean redactor who probably substituted it for the name 'Israel'.

[12] With v. 12 the style shifts to direct address and exhortation. But the imperatives are not the prophet's summons to his audience; they are rather meant to be heard as part of the story begun in v. 11. Yahweh continues to speak and quotes what he said at the time Israel was yoked for work in Canaan. The exhortation is Yahweh's charge in which he delineates the purpose for which he brought his people into the land. The reference to Yahweh in the third person in v. 12b is due to the fixity of the expression 'to seek Yahweh' and the tendency of the hortatory style itself whose idiom was shaped in its didactic use (12.6; 14.1ff.; 4.15?). The metaphor of the heifer is dropped but the agricultural terms introduced in v. 11b are continued as the metaphors for Israel's assigned task. The terms (sow, reap, break up new ground) do not represent separate stages or phases of Ephraim's vocation. Each stands on its own for the service of Yahweh. The language of agricultural work is woven together with the normative terms for covenantal life to show the meaning and purpose of Israel's career as a peasant folk in Canaan was the creation of an existence in which Yahweh's election would be actualized and fulfilled. Life for Israel was to be a matter of righteousness and devotion, of seeking Yahweh. For other lists of covenantal values, see 2.19f.; 4.1; 12.7. Righteousness (*ṣedāqā*) is the quality of an act whose rightness lies in the fact that it vindicates a relationship, i.e., the covenant (see the commentary on 2.19). Devotion (*ḥesed*) is a near synonym of righteousness; it means the concern and responsiveness to do in a given relation what another can rightfully expect according to the norms of that relationship (see 2.19; 6.4; 6; 12.6; and the commentary on 4.1). Practising righteousness and devotion is seeking Yahweh; that means, not inquiring by cultic divination or augury (4.12) or visiting a shrine to bring animal sacrifice in hope of the blessing of fertility (5.6; 7.14), but setting one's attention on Yahweh's *tōrā* and *dābār*, the true instruction of priest and word of prophet, as the answer to life's questions and needs. Upon the ground cultivated in such fashion Yahweh will send the rain of his salvation. The word for salvation is *ṣedeq*, Yahweh's own active righteousness of maintaining and blessing his people in vindication of his election of them (see comment on 2.19). Israel is to work the soil; Yahweh sends the rain. The agricultural imagery allows for a marvellous portrayal of the mutual involvement of God and people in realizing the divine purpose. Canaan is the farm of Yahweh on which he set Israel to produce for him a harvest of righteousness and devotion that God's

own righteousness might find its fulfilment in blessing the earth. The picture of Yahweh as one who 'rains' his salvation is daring for Hosea in the light of the conception of the activities of Canaan's gods. Indeed he probably had a model for such language in the cult of Canaan. Baal once sent a message to Anath: 'Banish war from the earth, put love in the land; pour peace into the bowels of the earth, rain down love into the bowels of the fields.'[a] Yahweh's charge to Israel is at the same time a polemic against the Canaanite interpretation of life. The devotees of Baal saw the consummation of work and worship in the produce of the land. Israel is to live as holding the land from Yahweh, whose purpose is made known in the covenant.

[13] Verses 11f. are an interpretation of Yahweh's relationship with Israel throughout her history that shows what he expected. Verse 13 states what happened. The contrast between expectation and result, between divine purpose and human performance, is quite like that created by Isaiah in his song of the vineyard (Isa. 5.4, 7). The agricultural imagery continues in the verbs, but now the opposites of the covenant value terms are the objects of the verbs. Wickedness (reša') is the opposite and contradiction of righteousness, the autonomous, heedless violation of the valid norms of life. There is a dimension of violence in the word 'wrong' ('awlā; cf. 'sons of wrong' in 10.10) which puts it in contrast to devotion. Falsehood has been the fruit of their existence – treachery against their fellows (4.2) and in the politics of the kingdom (7.3), and against Yahweh himself (11.12). Ephraim's existence in the land has frustrated Yahweh's election and perverted their vocation. 'You have eaten' indicates that Israel has already 'enjoyed' the fruit of their failure, and probably refers to their experience of the absence of salvation in the Assyrian crisis. So the saying is really a tale of two disappointments – Yahweh's and Israel's; but the guilt belongs to the farmers.

26. THEY THAT TAKE THE SWORD: 10.13b–15

13b Because you trust in your chariots,[b]
    in the number of your warriors,

[a] Cf. ANET, pp. 136f.; the translation is that of M. Dahood, Psalms I, 1–50, 1966, p. 281.
[b] be rikbe kā which affords a better parallelism with 'warriors'; so G instead of MT's 'in your way' (be darke kā).

[14]a din shall arise among your people,
     and all your fortresses shall be destroyed –
like Shalman's destruction of Beth-arbel
     when in the day of battle
     mother was dashed over sons.
[15]Just so it will be done[a] to you, O house of Israel[b]
     because of the evil of your evil.
In the dawn the king of Israel
     shall surely be cut off.

The Hebrew text of v. 13b begins with the particle *kī* which could be translated 'for' so as to connect v. 13b with the first line of the verse as an illustration of Ephraim's weakness and falsehood. But vv. 13b–15 stand as a separate saying with its own theme and structure. It is an oracle of judgment against Israel's false faith in military power with indictment (v. 13b) and punishment (vv. 14–15). The style is ambiguous; it could be a divine saying or a prophetic announcement. In contrast to the second person plural pronouns in the foregoing unit, the 'you' here is singular in vv. 13b and 14, shifting to plural in v. 15. Israel's confidence in her military power may belong to the period in the reign of Hoshea ben Elah when he was beginning to think of revolt against his Assyrian masters, perhaps just before the end of Tiglath-pileser's reign.

[13b] Making military prowess a basis of self-confidence is a crime against Yahweh (cf. Amos 6.13; Isa. 31.1). The offence lies, not in the possession of armies, but in the trusting (*bāṭaḥ*), hoping to find one's security in them. Like Judah in a later crisis, Israel in the face of the Assyrian threat relies on chariots and 'does not look to the Holy One of Israel or consult Yahweh' (Isa. 31.1). The crisis brings to light their real secularity; their fundamental confidence that they can look after themselves. The old faith in Yahweh as the one who acts in their behalf in the battles of Holy War has been replaced by a dependence on the king's military establishment. And that confidence supplies a security which allows them to ignore the prophet's message of Yahweh's coming judgment; their trust in chariots and warriors is ultimately a faith against Yahweh. Chariots were the most fearful weapon in the wars of the time, and chariotry had played a major

---

[a] Read *yēʿāśeh* with van Hoonacker; MT's *ʿāśā* could be a prophetic perfect ('he will do. . .').

[b] MT has 'Bethel' for which Hosea usually says 'Beth-awen'; the saying clearly deals with the nation, not the shrine. Cf. G.

role in Israel's military establishment.[a] Shalmaneser III reported that Ahab brought two thousand chariots against him at the battle of Qarqar, more than any of the other allies in the coalition formed to resist him.[b] Sargon II listed fifty chariots as part of his booty when he captured Samaria in 721.[c] Warriors (*gibbōrīm*) are professional soldiers of the royal army. It would appear that Israel's army had recovered from the disaster of 733 sufficiently to give Hoshea a growing confidence that he could break away from Assyria's grasp – which he attempted in the first years of Shalmaneser's reign (II Kings 17.4).

[14] Yahweh announces that Israel's faith in chariots and warriors will bring disaster upon them. A din shall arise in their midst! – the tumult of war with its clanging weapons, shout of combat and shriek of pain from the surging mass of armies. 'Your people' may refer to the army itself (cf. Num. 20.20; 21.33; Josh. 8.3, etc.). The destruction of their fortified cities means complete defeat, the total loss of their system of defence. To intensify their awareness of the scope and terror of the coming devastation, Hosea compares it to an event which must have been well known to his audience. But no other record of Shalman's conquest of Beth-arbel is known, and several proposals about the allusion have been made. Some emend the text in dependence on G to read 'Shalman's destruction of the house of Jeroboam' and connect the event with the assassination of Jeroboam's son, Zechariah (II Kings 15.10); but this royal murder hardly furnishes an example of the destruction of a city. Others take Shalman to be a corruption of Shalmaneser and place the incident in the time of his campaign against Samaria in 722; but this solution dates the event too late for an oracle of Hosea. Tiglath-pileser III names a Salamanu of Moab among those who have paid him tribute,[d] and it is possible that the incident belongs to one of the fierce border wars fought in Transjordan (cf. Amos 2.1–3). Beth-arbel has been tentatively identified with the mound of Irbid in Gilead. Beth-arbel was remembered because of a particularly vicious instance of the mass murder of children which was practised by conquerors seeking to wipe out a population (13.16; II Kings 8.12; Isa. 13.16; Nah. 3.10; Ps. 137.9).

[15] The devastation of Israel will come with similar horror.

[a] R. de Vaux, *Ancient Israel*, 1961, pp. 222ff.
[b] *ANET*, p. 279.
[c] *ANET*, p. 284.
[d] *ANET*, p. 282.

Yahweh will be the one who acts in gruesome devastation against these whose faith makes them secure against his judgment and independent of his power. Autonomy as a state in violation of their existence as the covenant people is 'the evil of their evil'. The king to whom the army belongs and who therefore incarnates their independence of Yahweh will be the first to fall. In the dawn's first light, when the battle has hardly begun, he shall be cut off.

27. THE DIVINE FATHER: 11.1–11

11 ¹When Israel was a lad, I loved him;
        from Egypt I called my son.
     ²The more I ª called them,
        the more they went away from me. ª
     They sacrificed to Baals,
        to idols they burned offerings.
     ³I myself taught Ephraim to walk;
        I ª took them up in my ª arms,
        but they did not acknowledge that I healed them.
     ⁴With human cords I drew them,
        with bonds of love.
     I was to them like those who lift a baby ᵇ to their cheeks;
        I bent down to him that I might feed him. ᶜ
     ⁵He returns to the land of Egypt;
        Assyria – he is his king!
        because they refuse to return (to me).
     ⁶The sword whirls in his cities,
        puts an end to his oracle-priests, ᵈ
        and devours because of their counsels.
     ⁷My people grow weary in ᵉ their apostasy from me.
        To Baal ᶠ they call ᵍ
        but he ᵍ does not raise them up at all. ʰ
     ⁸How can I give you up, O Ephraim?
        surrender you, O Israel?
     How can I make you like Admah?
        treat you like Zeboiim?

ª Cf. BH.
ᵇ *ʿūl* for MT's *ʿōl* ('yoke'), with van Hoonacker, Wolff.
ᶜ Moving *lōʾ* from the beginning of v. 5 to the end of v. 4, and reading *lō*.
ᵈ So *bad* V, *HAL*, p. 105. The word is a problem; Wolff translates 'boasters' (cf. *bad* II, *KB*, p. 108); others emend.
ᵉ Reading *nilʾā*; MT's *tᵉlūʾîm* ('hung up') does not fit in the context.
ᶠ *baʿal* for *ʿal*.
ᵍ Taking the verbal object (*-hū*) as the subject of the next sentence (*hūʾ*).
ʰ Cf. *yaḥad* in v. 8.

My heart has turned itself against me;
    my compassion grows completely warm.
9I will not execute my burning anger;
    I will not again destroy Ephraim.
For God am I, not man,
    the Holy One in your midst.
    I will not come to consume.[a]
10After Yahweh they shall go;
    like a lion he shall roar.
Because he roars
    sons shall come trembling from the west.
11They shall come trembling like a bird from Egypt,
    like a dove from the land of Assyria;
and I shall return them to their houses.
    Saying of Yahweh.

Yahweh's self disclosure through the speech of Hosea reaches an unusual level of intensity and power in this chapter. Anthropomorphism is Hosea's stock-in-trade, but the portrayal of Yahweh as a father caring for a son achieves an explicit tenderness and detail unmatched in the Old Testament. Yet that portrayal is followed by a soliloquy of God which comes to a climax in the surprising disavowal, 'I am God, not man . . . .' Like a human father Yahweh loves his son Israel, but that love can and will bring salvation out of sin only because it is God who loves. The emotion and commitment of love is introduced as the basis and power of Yahweh's way with Israel; and a theme of revelation appears which finds its climax finally in the New Testament. In the oracle Yahweh surveys the entire life story of Israel as the son of God; and, as the story unfolds, the history of Israel becomes an astonishing witness to the very life of Yahweh himself. Verses 1–4 tell of Israel's past, weaving together the saving acts of Yahweh and the sin of his people. Israel's election was an act of love, of Yahweh's will to have Israel as his son. Though the son proved prodigal and faithless, that love was not exhausted in repeated deeds of fatherly tenderness. Verses 5–7 sketch the present plight of the people who have left their God. They are on the verge of being swallowed up by the great powers of history, shattered by the ravages of invasion, and yet clinging to another god who cannot save them. In vv. 8f Yahweh reveals the suffering agony which Israel's faithlessness has brought upon him; but his love will not let them go. In the

---

[a] Reading *leḇāʿēr*; perhaps MT's *beʿīr* could be translated 'in the agitation (of wrath)' (*ʿīr* II in *KB* and Jer. 15.8).

sovereign freedom of his being God he refuses to permit the sin of Israel to lead to their annihilation. Verses 10f. look to the future which the power of Yahweh's love will create.

The entire oracle has the style of a divine saying except for v. 10. After the report of Israel's past and present (vv. 1–7) Yahweh begins to speak directly to Israel with second person singular pronouns as he faces in agony the possibility of losing his son. The report of the future (vv. 10ff.) reverts to third-person speech about Israel. Except for v. 10 (see the comment below), the chapter can be taken as an original unit in spite of its unusual length. The metaphor of parent and child established in v. 1 continues in v. 3 and probably in v. 4. The painful dilemma of Yahweh expressed in the anguished questions of v. 8 presupposes the history of love in vv. 1–4 as its background. The issue of whether Yahweh will give Israel up is based on the picture of Israel's hopeless predicament in vv. 5–7. After Yahweh's decree that he will not abandon Ephraim (v. 9) some resolution of the impasse by an announcement of salvation (v. 11) is required.

The oracle could well belong to the middle years of Hoshea's reign when Israel's king had provoked the retribution of Shalmaneser V (727–722) by withholding tribute and appealing to Egypt (II Kings 17.4) and the final end of the nation was all too obvious. Verse 11 assumes the presence of refugees in Egypt and exiles in Assyria, while v. 5 asserts that the Assyrian is in unquestionable control of Israel. The announcement that Yahweh's wrath and judgment will find its fulfilment in a restoration of Israel as the covenant people is a feature of the composition in 2.2–15, the oracles in 2.16–23, and the report in ch. 3. But in chs. 2 and 3 judgment brings Israel to repentance as the basis of restoration. Here it is out of the divine nature of Yahweh and his love alone that salvation comes, a shift which brings this oracle nearer to 14.4 than the other messages of salvation. This change may come out of the fact that judgment is already in progress (vv. 5f.) without any repentance in Israel (v. 7) having appeared (so Wolff).

[1] Once again Hosea reaches back into the historical tradition to establish a point of vantage for interpreting the meaning of the present (cf. 9.10; 10.1, 9, 11). The earlier references went back to the wilderness and to first sins in the land; now the interpretative narrative begins with Egypt and the beginning of Yahweh's relation to Israel (2.15; 12.13). In Hosea's theological vocabulary Yahweh's identity is disclosed in the formula: 'I am Yahweh your God from

the land of Egypt' (12.9; 13.4). Both the knowledge of Yahweh and Israel's unique relation to him were created in the event of Israel's rescue from Egypt. Yahweh tells the narrative himself, portraying Israel as a young boy and himself as a man who comes to love the lad and makes him his son. Exodus, the basic element in Israel's credo, is translated into a metaphor which clothes the event with all the feeling and personal involvement that belong to a father's relation to a beloved child. The period of Egypt and the wilderness was the time of Israel's youth (2.15; Jer. 2.2; cf. the contrasting image of Israel's senility in 7.9). 'Lad' (na'ar) can be used for a young person of any age from babe to adolescent; here the basic notion is helpless dependence on an adult. The verb wā'ōhᵃbēhū ('I came to love him') marks the beginning of a biblical motif which reaches its climax in the New Testament. So far as one can tell from the Old Testament Hosea is the first to base Yahweh's relation to Israel on his love (cf. 'bonds of love' in 4). The Deuteronomist in his programmatic use of love as a theological theme (Deut. 7.8, 13; 10.15; 23.5) is his heir. The genesis of the motif is possibly to be found in the divine command to enact Yahweh's situation with faithless Israel by loving an adulterous woman (3.1) and in the general symbolism of man and wife for Yahweh's covenant with Israel (chs. 1–3). However, Hosea could not answer the question about the beginning of this love in terms of Israel's life in Canaan (cf. 9.15) by analogy to the sexual cult and theology of the religion of the Baals. Since Israel's relation to Yahweh was founded on the Exodus, he must go to the salvation-history for an answer. So he removes the motif from its sexual-cultic setting and gives it a historical locus in an imagery that fits the election of Israel far better – father and son. 'Called' is an election verb; it means 'summon into a relation'. The representation of corporate Israel as Yahweh's son understands the election in terms of adoption (cf. the bestowal of sonship on the Davidic king in Ps. 2.7). The portrayal of Yahweh as father of the tribe or people goes back into Israel's earlier history as is evident in theophoric names such as Abijah, which combine the elements of 'father' and 'Yahweh', and in such texts as Ex. 4.22f. and Deut. 32.6.[a] The image was used by Isaiah (Isa. 1.2f.; 30.9) and Jeremiah (3.19, 22; 4.22; 31.9, 20). In the symbolic language of ch. 2 the nation is called the 'sons of harlotry' (2.4); here sonship is a metaphor for the covenant itself.

---

[a] On the divine Father motif in the OT, see *TWNT* V, pp. 959ff.

[2] The narrative moves directly from election to rebellion, from the history which Yahweh made in the Exodus-wilderness epoch to the one Israel made in the land. The two are put in juxtaposition to heighten the contrast; the beginning has no proper sequel, only a contradiction. No sooner is the 'son' in the land than the relation of dependence and obedience is broken (9.10). Yahweh kept on calling; Hosea sees the acts of care and help which follow the Exodus as re-enactments of the original call; each is a validation and renewal of election that makes the Exodus a constantly contemporary reality for Israel. But now the answer does not come; the son is prodigal. He dwells no longer in the father's house and is to be found in the sanctuaries of the land making sacrifices to the Baals. On 'the Baals' see 2.13, 17. In becoming cultic devotees of another god, the Israelites break the fundamental ties of the sonship, i.e. covenant relation (Ex. 20.3f., 23; 22.20; 34.17).

[3] How could the people reject Yahweh when he like a father had held them by the hand while they made their first faltering steps, gathered them up in his arms when they fell, and healed their hurt? The poignancy of the image is intensified by the picture of a father who aids, cherishes, and heals his child as he grows to maturity (cf. Isa. 1.2). The image may cover the wilderness ('taught to walk') and the time after the conquest when Yahweh fulfilled his fatherly role in spite of Israel's disloyalty. His acts of love carried them through crisis beyond their strength to meet. But alas, they were obstinate and would not see their continuing history as the manifestation of Yahweh's saving help. 'Heal' is used by Hosea as a verb of redemption from historical threats and dangers to the nation (5.13; 6.1; 7.1; cf. the different meaning in 14.4).

[4] The imagery of v. 4 is not clear. Its unusual expression and the state of its text hamper interpretation. Does the metaphor of father and child continue (ATD, BK) or is there a shift to the image of a beast of burden and its master (ICC, HAT)? The latter is possible and is suggested by MT's 'yoke'; Hosea compares Israel to a balky cow in 4.16 and uses the imagery of ploughing for covenant vocation in 10.11. The issue turns around the consonants '*l*, which MT vocalizes as 'yoke' ('*ōl*), but which could be translated 'baby, suckling' if pronounced '*ul*. The latter continues the metaphor already established in v. 3 and fits better with the rest of v. 4b. The translation '. . . like those who lift the yoke from upon their jaws' requires an emendation of MT's '*al* ('upon') to *me*'*al* ('from upon') and leaves the problem of

the position of the yoke on the jaws when it would normally be on the neck of the animal. The imagery continues the narrative of Yahweh's kindly dealing with Israel. In the early epoch of the wilderness he drew them with the power of humane gentleness and compelling affection. The picture of the parent lifting up a child to its cheeks for an embrace is an incomparable image for the most tender feeeling – parental devotion concentrated in one gesture! He bent down to feed the child who could not provide its own food or eat alone – divine condescension dramatized as fatherly care! Does the image allude to the divinely given food of the wilderness?

[5] In contrast to the time of the beginnings when Israel's existence was the work of Yahweh's fatherly love and care, the present situation is perilous and tragic. The consequence of Israel's apostasy (v. 2), their heedless disregard of the help of Yahweh (v. 3b), is already destroying the nation. The 'return to Egypt' is a theme of coming punishment in 8.13; 7.16; 9.6. Here the expected judgment seems under way. The circumstances described in vv. 5f. fit the situation of Israel during the reign of Hoshea ben Elah. The fact that v. 7 speaks of Israel's contemporary situation, and that v. 11 presupposes that there are already Israelites in Egypt and Assyria, strengthen the possibility that vv. 5–7 depict the current plight of Israel which provokes the divine self-questioning in v. 8. The 'return to Egypt' refers either to the pro-Egyptian policy of Hoshea who hoped by alliance with Pharaoh to get free of Assyrian rule (II Kings 17.4) or to the refugees who had already fled to the south during the disaster of 733 when Tiglath-pileser III took over most of Israel's territory. What pitiful irony that the people whom Yahweh brought up from the land of Egypt should end up returning there. Assyria is now their real ruler; Hoshea is only a vassal and figurehead, a creature of the Assyrian empire. A tyrant's iron hand has replaced a father's tender help as the first fact of Israel's history. All this is the result of Israel's inexplicable obtuse stubborness. Returning to Egypt instead of returning to Yahweh! Their one hope is the one possibility which they ignore.

[6] The sword of the Assyrian armies had already done its bitter work during the campaign of 733 (II Kings 15.29). If Hoshea had by the time of this oracle already withheld tribute and sent to Eygpt for assistance (II Kings 17.4), then the retribution of Shalmaneser was imminent. If 'oracle-priests' is the correct meaning of bad (cf. also Isa. 44.25; Jer. 50.36), the survey of Israel's descent into the abyss includes an ironic observation that the catastrophe had also swept

away the diviners whose counsels had doubtless supported the appeal to Egypt and revolt against Assyria. What their divine oracles had recommended turned out to be a plan of execution for them.

[7] The verse is a fabric of obscure expressions and uncertain reading; comment must be tentative on particulars. Because of Israel's suffering, they show signs of exhaustion in their apostasy; yet the spirit of rebellion continues to dominate them (5.4). They are the elect of Yahweh ('my people'), yet the folk who are bound by covenant to have no other god persist in calling on Baal (cf. v. 2) in their need. But there is no rescue forthcoming from Baal. On 'raise up' as a verb of saving from disaster, cf. Amos 5.2. What Yahweh has done for Israel in the history of their relationship with him, the chosen people now expect from Baal! The verse carries the mood of a lament, Yahweh's sorrowing over his people, a preparation for the intense self-questioning which breaks forth from Yahweh in v. 8.

[8] A shift in the style of the divine saying marks a transition from the narrative about Israel's past and present to an impassioned self-questioning by Yahweh. Now the elect people are addressed directly as though the beloved prodigal son stood in the presence of his father to hear what he shall say about his failure. The complaint against him (vv. 1–7) has been spoken; the word of complete punishment is expected. But instead the father pours out mingled sorrow and love in rhetorical questions which deny just punishment. Yahweh draws back from a complete rupture with his son. The radical character of this refusal to execute punishment stands out the clearer in light of the law that a son who persists in stubborn rebellion against his parents is to be put to death by stoning (Deut. 21.18–21). Just as Yahweh as husband deals with Israel as adulterous wife in extra-legal fashion (see the commentary on 3.1), so, in bringing his rebellious son to account, covenant rights are transcended by the love which originated the covenant. The questions are simultaneously an anguished lament that Yahweh and Israel have come to the point of final separation, and an assertion that Yahweh will not desert them. As a literary expression of the suffering into which the covenant God has been drawn by Israel's faithlessness, the questions are similar to those in 6.4. The issue is whether Yahweh will deliver Israel finally and completely to the destruction already in progress (vv. 5–6) and leave them caught in their fatal fascination with Baal who cannot save them (v. 7). Admah and Zeboiim stand for total annihilation; the two are listed with Sodom and Gomorrah in Gen. 10.19; 14.2; 8; and Deut. 29.23

also knows of their complete devastation. To be like Admah and Zeboiim is to exist only as a memory of swift and final calamity. In face of such a fate for Israel Yahweh has become like a man in whose self-consciousness wrath and love do battle with each other. His heart, the seat of consciousness and will, assumes a hostile position against the punishment which he has already announced (9.6, 11–13; 10.8, 14f.). Compassion, the tender emotion which parents feel toward the helpless child, grows increasingly strong and displaces wrath (cf. Jer. 31.20). Yahweh speaks of himself in the human genre to disclose in emotional terms that his election of Israel is stronger than their sin.

[9] Responding to the desire of his heart and poignancy of his compassion Yahweh declares three times that his wrath shall not have the final word about Israel's destiny. God's wrath is his active refusal to let Israel go her own way, oblivious of his claim upon her, and therefore is an expression of the election of Israel. Its limit is set within God himself by its purpose of punishing and disciplining 'my people' to wrench them back into the covenant position. So wrath cannot be the final decree. Yahweh will not turn from his election of 'my son' and destroy the Ephraim created by his saving acts. This refusal to execute his wrath is based on an amazing self-identification (v. 9b). Such a formula for Yahweh's identity comes as a surprise in this context. The salvation-history was portrayed by the most intimate and tender of human relations (vv. 1, 3f.); in v. 8 Yahweh speaks as a man incapable of action because of his divided feelings, caught by the growing power of desire and emotion which oppose what he must do. But now the resolution of Yahweh is grounded on his utter difference from man. The apparent inconsistency is a warning that Hosea's many anthropomorphisms are meant as interpretative analogies, not as essential definitions. The metaphors are incarnations in language. The actions and feelings of Yahweh can be translated into representations of human, and even animal, life. In the dramatic metaphor the personal reality of Yahweh's incursion into human life and history is present and comprehensible. But he transcends the metaphor, is different from that to which he is compared, and free of all its limitations. He is wrathful and loving *like* man, but *as* God. The future of Israel rests wholly on the identity of Yahweh – that he is God (*'ēl*) instead of a man, and that he is the Holy One (*qādōš*) in their midst. A stark contrast between God and man appears in three other texts of the OT (Isa. 31.3; Ezek. 28.2; Num. 23.19); in each case the contrast is used to show that the limita-

tions which qualify man do not affect the sovereign freedom and power of Yahweh. In this text the significance of Yahweh's power and freedom is interpreted in the title 'the Holy One in your midst'. The designation of Yahweh as 'the one in the midst of Israel' is a way of speaking of the election. See Num. 14.14; Josh. 3.10; Isa. 12.6 where the expression speaks of Yahweh's presence with Israel as the ground of their security and joy. 'Holy' is a synonym for God; it indicates the numinous and dynamic, the *mysterium tremendum*, the incomparable awesome force of the divine. 'The Holy One in your midst', then, is really an alternate title for 'Yahweh your God from the land of Egypt' (12.9; 13.4). The title is very like Isaiah's 'Holy One of Israel', who will act with such splendour that he alone will be exalted, and yet by his exaltation create a purged and penitent Israel (cf. especially Isa. 8.11–18; 10.20, 17; 30.15). Yahweh's refusal to destroy Israel is no concession to their sin, no curtailment of discipline; but it is a declaration that his relationship in history with Israel shall not end because of their sin and his wrath. The call of the son shall have its fulfilment in a future which unfolds out of the identity and power of God himself.

[10] How that future will come about is described in vv. 10f. The style, vocabulary, and assertions of v. 10 suggest that it is a non-Hoseanic piece which has been inserted to expand the description of Israel's rescue in the terms of a later Judahistic theology of salvation. The style of the divine saying which continues in vv. 1–9 and 11 is dropped. Though Hosea compares Yahweh to a lion in 5.4 and 13.7, the noun used here (*'aryēh*) is different; and the metaphor in the other texts is used to depict the ravaging wrath of Yahweh. 'Like a lion he shall roar' is similar to Amos 1.2; 3.8; Jer. 25.30; Joel 3.16. In v. 1 the people are 'my son', but here the Israelites are 'sons', and are said to be in the west, the location of which is quite uncertain (cf. Isa. 11.11). In the tradition which spoke of 'the lion's roar of Yahweh'[a] the divine noise was a signal of hope. It was the sound of Yahweh coming forth to do battle with the threatening foes of his people. When those who have fled from the destroyed land to the west hear the roar, they will know their redemption is at hand. Once again they will go behind Yahweh instead of following other gods. They will come trembling with awe and joyous anticipation from their dispersal, prodigal sons returning to the divine father in fear and hope.

[11] Verse 11 completes the divine saying of vv. 1–9 by describing

[a] See J. L. Mays, *Amos* (OTL), 1969, pp. 21f., on Amos 1.2.

the future whose possibility is created by Yahweh's faithfulness to the election of Israel. Its themes are typical of Hosea. The metaphor of the dove (7.11), the pairing of Egypt and Assyria and their role in Israel's current politics and future punishment (7.11; 8.8f., 13; 9.3, 6), the return to Yahweh in awe (3.5), the land as the place of restoration (2.15, 20) are all motifs of Hosea's prophecy. The restoration does not cancel judgment. This description of salvation assumes that refugees have fled to Egypt while deportees are living in exile in Assyria. The nations to which Israel turned in frantic search for a solution to her national crisis have become the places of punishment and humiliation. Chastened and awed, they shall come back to the land like a bird returning to its nest. But the return is not their achievement; it is the action of Yahweh. Once again he is the subject of Israel's history and once again by his act they are brought to their homes. Residence in the land is the realization of Yahweh's salvation in Hosea's eschatology because that residence is the form of Israel's existence as the covenant people (2.15, 18, 22; 14.7).

28. A POLICY OF FUTILITY: 11.12–12.1 (Heb. 12.1–2)

11 12Ephraim has surrounded me with deceit,
    the house of Israel with falsehood.
  ⁿBut Judah still roams with God,
    is faithful to the Holy One.ᵃ
12 1Ephraim befriendsᵇ the wind,
    pursues the east wind all day long;
    lies and destruction he multiplies.
  They make covenant with Assyria,
    bearᶜ oil to Egypt.

11.12–12.1 is a divine saying that stands apart from its context as a separate oral unit. The reproach against Ephraim's deceit in 11.12a clearly marks the beginning of a new saying; in 12.2 a prophetic saying opens with the announcement of Yahweh's complaint against Judah (?). Uncertainty about the interpretation of 11.12b and the originality of the name Judah in 11.12b and 12.2a encumber the literary analysis. Depending on decisions about these problems other groupings of the material are possible (see Ward, Rudolph, Wolff).

ᵃ⁻ᵃ This is only one of the possible ways to translate MT; see the comment.
ᵇ Cf. *rāʿāh* II in *KB*, p. 899.
ᶜ Cf. BH.

According to the interpretation adopted below the saying is in the divine style throughout, is a reproach (without accompanying announcement of punishment) against Ephraim's religious (11.12) and political (12.1) betrayal of Yahweh.

[11.12] It is Yahweh who speaks and complains that wherever he turns in Ephraim he is faced with deceit (cf. 7.2), and not the prophet (so Wolff, referring to 9.8). In dealing with Ephraim Yahweh finds himself in the midst of a folk who practise treachery and evade truth. Deceit (*kaḥaš*) is a primary feature of Israel's unfaithfulness (7.3; 10.13; cf. the verb in 4.2; 9.2). In this text it could refer to the nation's political policy of seeking a solution for their danger by manoeuvring between Assyria and Egypt (12.1). Probably the general terms 'deceit' and 'falsehood' are illustrated by the conduct described in v. 12b. Verse 12b is an enigma. The above translation is one way to interpret MT; it takes the unexpected '*ēl* as the noun for God (cf. 11.9), *qedōšîm* as an intensive plural meaning the Holy One (so Prov. 9.10?), and the initial conjunctive as an adversative. The line sets Judah's faithfulness in contrast to Ephraim's deceit as a way of heightening the reproach against Ephraim. But a complimentary word about Judah is completely unexpected from Hosea (see 5.8ff.) and the use of '*ēl* and *qedōšîm* conflict with Hosea's usage in 11.9 where the first is a generic and *qādōš* is used for the Holy One. The line could be the contribution of a Judahistic editor who enters the caveat that Judah in his time remains faithful. But the philological problems still remain. The versions are too distant from MT to help. Probably an editor has inserted 'but Judah' in the text which was originally a continuation of the reproach against Ephraim. It is possible, with a different understanding of '*ēl* and *qedōšîm*, to translate: 'He still wanders after El [the Canaanite high god] and is faithful to the Holy Ones [members of the heavenly court of El].'[a] The deceit and falsehood confronting Yahweh is then the religious apostasy in Israel.

[12.1] 12.1 is constructed of a metaphor (v. 1a) and its interpretation (v. 1b). The metaphor evokes the picture of an action that is futile and impossible; the interpretation applies the metaphor to Israel's current international politics. Wind represents the elusive and illusionary (cf. 8.7). The east wind is the fearful sirocco, the dry, searing blast that rises from the eastern deserts and scorches the coastal regions in its seasonal passage (cf. the description in 13.15). No man can befriend the wind, for it moves and shifts and goes where

[a] Cf. M. Pope, *El in the Ugaritic Texts* (VTS II), 1955, p. 13.

it will. Why pursue the sirocco, for its power and heat are inexorable and it simply destroys all that is in its path? But Ephraim does equally senseless things. Hoshea makes a vassal-treaty with Assyria (II Kings 17.3) and then turns to Egypt for help in breaking it (II Kings 17.4). Such a policy adds lie to lie and invites destruction. Making treaties and breaking treaties in autonomous efforts to find security through history is faithlessness against Yahweh; true faith means turning to him with the confession that salvation rests neither in another nation nor in their own power (14.3).

29. ISRAEL AT THE JABBOK: 12.2–6 (Heb. 12.3–7)

12 ᵃYahweh has a suit against Israelᵃ
     to punish Jacob according to his ways;
     according to his deeds he shall requite him.
³In the womb he deceived his brother,
     and in his manhood he struggled with God.
⁴He struggledᵇ against an angel and he prevailed;
     he wept and entreated favour.
 At Bethel he found him,
     there he spoke with him.ᶜ
⁵Yahweh, God of Hosts;
     Yahweh is his memorial.
⁶But you, with the help of your God you shall return;
     observe devotion and justice,
     and wait continually on your God.

A formal announcement of a legal suit (v. 2a) opens this prophetic saying and creates the verbal situation of a court scene. Yahweh is plaintiff and Israel is summoned as defendant. The case against Israel is made in terms of a report concerning Jacob's career.ᵈ Such a use of traditions about Israel's beginnings as a way of bringing the present under judgment is a frequent feature of the later chapters in Hosea,

  ᵃ MT has 'Judah'; see the comment.
  ᵇ Reading *wayyiśar* for MT's *wayyāśar*; cf. *KB*, p. 930.
  ᶜ On *'immānū*='with him', see M. Dahood, *Psalms II, 51–100*, 1968, p. 275.
  ᵈ The problems connected with Hosea's use of Jacob in this passage and in ch. 12 as a whole have provoked a series of studies. Among the more recent are: M. Gertner, 'The Masora and the Levites. Appendix on Hosea XII', *VT* 10, 1960, pp. 272ff.; P. R. Ackroyd, 'Hosea and Jacob', *VT* 13, 1963, pp. 245ff.; H. L. Ginsberg, 'Hosea's Ephraim, More Fool Than Knave. A New Interpretation of Hosea 12.1–14', *JBL* 80, 1961, pp. 339ff.; E. M. Good, 'Hosea and the Jacob Tradition', *VT* 16, 1966, pp. 137ff.

but it is only here that he goes back behind the Exodus. The interpretation of Israel's election in terms of the promise to the patriarchs to the neglect of the Sinai Covenant was probably still strong in the north, and Jacob would have been particularly emphasized at Bethel. So Hosea takes the figure of Jacob as a dramatic way of bringing to life the current deceitfulness and self-will of Israel (v. 3). He points out that even Jacob finally was brought to his knees by God (v. 4) and in an exhortation (v. 6) sets over against his contemporaries the life which God gave Jacob to live. Verse 5 is a liturgical formula for the pronouncement of the name of Israel's God, which was added to the text, perhaps as clarification of the sequence of unidentified pronouns in v. 4, or as a solemn introduction to the exhortation in v. 6.

[2] The opening formulary announcement proclaims that Yahweh has instituted legal proceedings in which his people will have to stand as defendant. On this formula for convoking a court to hear the case (*rib*) of a plaintiff, see the commentary on 4.1. In MT the accused is 'Judah' who can hardly have been the defendant in the original saying. Jacob as the ancestor of the whole people could stand for both Israel and Judah, but if Judah is particularized as the contemporary defendant, then Israel, Hosea's proper audience, is omitted. The Judean editor whose work may be seen in 11.12b and 12.5 changed the text as a way of applying the message to the other descendants of Jacob in the south (cf. also 10.11). The suit is against the contemporary nation (Israel), but the name of Jacob is introduced in preparation for vv. 3ff. where the career of Israel's ancestor is reviewed as a way of establishing the nation's guilt. What Jacob was and did corresponds to the liability of his descendants. Hosea is not working with any simple theory of inherited guilt. He is rather using a tradition about Israel's origin to disclose the character of the Israel of his day. They are chips off the old block, and in their pervasive deceitfulness (see 11.12) are living up to their heritage. In Jacob they must see themselves. The purpose of the complaint is to see that Israel receives an appropriate punishment (2b; cf. 4.9); but as the complaint draws to a close (v. 6) it is apparent that the plaintiff hopes for a reconciliation.

[3] In vv. 3f. Hosea is clearly referring to ancient Jacob-traditions which have also been recorded in the old patriarchal saga in Genesis. But his references are too brief and elusive to conclude that he knows or uses the tradition in just the form which was fixed in the Genesis stories. The connection, however, is quite close. Jacob's tricky career

began before his birth; while still in the womb he deceived (*'āqab* in the sense of 'go behind one's back to trick') his brother. This sounds like an allusion to Gen. 25.26: Jacob followed Esau from the womb grasping his heel (*'āqēb*) and so was called *ya'ªqōb*. But Hosea uses the verb *'āqab* in the sense it has in Gen. 27.36 (cf. Jer. 9.4), the only other occurrence; Jacob is well named because he is the one who deceives to supplant (*ya'ªqōb*). Like the story in Gen. 25.21–26, Hosea traces the name-character of Jacob back to his birth, but he speaks of an act in the womb, the supplanting itself, without the etymologizing reference to Esau's heel. To the brother one was bound by the closest ties of customary obligation, but Jacob violated the loyalty due his brother in the first sphere of his existence. Verse 3b picks up the word-play of Gen. 32.28. At the ford of the Jabbok Jacob's name was changed to Israel (*yiśrā'ēl*) because he struggled (*śārā*) with God ('*ēl*). The parallelism of womb and manhood shows that v. 3b is a pejorative statement; the narrative of Jacob's experience at the Jabbok in Gen. 32.22–32 is not, at least in its present form. What Jacob was before birth, he was in his maturity. First, he supplanted his brother, and then he undertook to overpower God himself – so passionate and absolute was his self-will.

[4] The interpretation of v. 4 is hindered because of the difficulty of deciding who is represented by the pronominal subjects and objects. Who prevails – angel or Jacob? Who finds whom at Bethel, and who speaks to whom? The Genesis narratives cannot be used as a sure guide because Hosea is not using that precise form of the tradition; one is left to untangle the movement of thought in this text. 'He prevailed' (*yūkāl*) appears to certify that the allusion to the Jabbok incident continues (Gen. 32.28), and supports the vocalization adopted in note *b* on the text. In Gen. 32.24 Jacob wrestles with a man instead of an angel (*mal'āk*). For angel as the form in which God appears to the patriarchs in the E tradition, see Gen. 21.17; 31.11; men as divine messengers (Gen. 18.1f.) shift to angels (Gen. 19.1). Angel is probably a feature of the tradition known to Hosea. In contrast to Gen. 32.28, 'angel' must be the intended subject of 'he prevailed'. In the story of Jacob's encounter at the Jabbok it is not obvious who won (cf. Gen. 32.25); the motif that Jacob 'prevailed' is clearly stated only in the etymology of the name Israel whose original meaning is probably not that of the etymology in Gen. 32.28 (see 'Israel' in *KB*, *BDB*). And it is certainly Jacob who weeps and entreats favour, not the angel; so Jacob must, by Hosea's account, have

ended up as suppliant (as he does in the prayer of Gen. 32.9–12). The weeping is possibly Hosea's embellishment; the Genesis story knows nothing of it. But Jacob does seek the favour of a blessing (Gen. 32.26). Is it possible that the weeping and seeking favour (Hithpael of *hnn*) allude to Jacob's meeting with Esau (Gen. 33.1ff.) where Jacob weeps (v. 4) and seeks favour (*hēn*), and so reintroduces *the brother* of v. 3a whom Jacob had deceived? In any case the Jacob whom Israel proudly claims as its representative ancestor was overcome by God and brought to tears and dependence. His deceitful self-will failed him in his climactic encounter with God. Here the Jacob story becomes appeal and warning, for Israel must find in Jacob a typology for their own treachery and trouble. As he could not, neither can they prevail against God. Tears and entreaty are their only future. God is the subject of the verbs in 4b. 'Find' is used as a verb of election; the choice of Jacob is spoken of as a discovery (cf. *māṣā* in 9.10). The tradition in Genesis reports two crucial visits of Jacob to Bethel (28.10ff. and 35.1ff.), but a theophany and election motif appear only in the first. Does Hosea think of 3b–4a as taking place at Bethel instead of at the Jabbok? Bethel comes to the fore as the one location mentioned in Hosea's Jacob narrative for two reasons. It was the sanctuary whose *hieros logos* proclaimed that Jacob was its founder.[a] This theology of its origin made it the place where Israel as sons of Jacob celebrated their claim on the land by right of their status as God's chosen in identity with their ancestor. Furthermore, it was the most important state sanctuary in Hosea's time (cf. Amos 7.13). Possibly Hosea addresses Israelites who are at Bethel to resurrect the Jacob tradition in hope that God will re-enforce his relation to father Jacob as an answer to their crisis. This would explain the topicality of Hosea's use of Jacob. The appeal to Jacob is an appeal to a deceiver who had himself to be overcome by God's power. Let them hear the word of God to the chastened Jacob as God's answer to their appeal (v. 6 is a quotation which cites the admonition of God to Jacob). It is interesting that the verbs in v. 4b shift from the narrative perfects and consecutives of vv. 3 and 4a to imperfects as if to bring the events of this line nearer to the audience. God still meets *them* at Bethel and speaks with *them* there!

[5] Between the report that God spoke with Jacob (v. 4b) and the quotation of his word (v. 7), the name of God is proclaimed with liturgical ceremony. This doxological announcement of the sacred

---

[a] G. von Rad, *Genesis* ET(OTL), 1961, pp. 278ff.

tetragrammaton sets the stage for the correct hearing of the following exhortation. The reader is summoned to reverence by the declaration of God's identity; he is Yahweh whose almighty power is manifest in his title as 'God of hosts'. God has given the name Yahweh to Israel as his 'memorial' (*zēker*) so that by its use his identity can be brought to mind and invoked through the generations (cf. *zēker* in Ex. 15.3; Pss. 102.12; 135.13). The ceremonious proclamation of Yahweh's name is quite similar to the forms used in the doxological insertions in the book of Amos (4.13; 5.8; 9.5a–6c; see the comment on 4.13).

[6] In the context of the story about Jacob v. 6 reports what Yahweh said to him at Bethel; but the exhortation is really the prophet's appeal for Israel to settle with Yahweh before he punishes them. For another case of an exhortation used to summarize the significance of the vocation given Israel by God, see 10.12. The admonition is Hosea's own interpretation of Jacob's election in terms of the covenantal values of devotion and justice; no such saying appears in the tradition in Genesis. By the help and power of his God Jacob must 'return'. In Jacob's life situation the summons to return really had no setting, but Hosea has contemporary Israel also in mind, who shall return from their rebellion and apostasy by the help of God's judgment (2.14f.; 3.5). Devotion (*hesed*) which acts loyally to maintain the relation to God, and justice (*mišpāṭ*) which keeps the order of God, are to be the hallmarks of Jacob's existence. On *hesed*, see 4.1; and on *mišpāṭ*, see 5.1; 10.4. Jacob-Israel is not to take his destiny into his own hands and seek to force the realization of his future by deceit and power. He is to wait in the humility of self-denying trust on the intervention of his God, making his own life continually the sphere of God's action alone. The command is dramatized as the word of God to Jacob, but it is meant for the ears of the Israel that calls itself 'Jacob'. They are to find no other meaning in their ancestor than this command, for in continuing his old life of deceit they are under the judgment of the command.

30. ISRAELITE OR CANAANITE? 12.7–11 (Heb. 12.8–12)

12 ⁷Canaan – false scales in his hand!
    He loves to exploit.
  ⁸Ephraim said, 'Yea, I am rich;
    I have found a fortune for myself.

[a]For all my gain there cannot be found in me
    any guilt that can be called sin.'[a]
9But I am Yahweh your God
    from the land of Egypt.
Once more I will make you dwell in tents
    as in the days of the festival.

10I spoke to the prophets,
    and I sent many a vision;
    so through the prophets I shall destroy.[b]
11If Gilead be evil,
    surely they have become worthless.
In Gilgal they sacrificed steers.
    So their altars shall be like stone-heaps,
    on the furrows of the field.

The vocative 'Canaan' marks the beginning of a new unit. In contrast to vv. 2–6 this oracle is a divine saying (v. 9). It begins with a picture of Ephraim as a Canaanite trader holding rigged scales (v. 7) and then lets him speak boastfully of his economic success (v. 8). Over against this picture Yahweh sets himself, the God of the Exodus, and announces the punishment he plans for such entrepreneurs – back to the tents! (v. 9). The editors have brought this picture of Ephraim as a Canaanite after the portrayal of Jacob the supplanter (vv. 2–6) because the two seemed to go so well together. Verses 7–9 make up a complete announcement of judgment. The style of divine speech continues in v. 10, but it is not so apparent that Yahweh's report of his activity through the prophets is part of the oracle in vv. 7–9. The prophet is the subject once again in v. 13, though it speaks of 'the prophet' against 'the prophets' of v. 10. Verse 11 with its focus on the cultic centres of Gilead and Gilgal is even more of an orphan in the context. Either the compilers have put together odd fragments or the material has got out of order. Rearrangements are often attempted among which the most promising is to move vv. 10f. after v. 13 (so most recently Rudolph; see the discussion by Ward, pp. 211f.).

[7] 'Canaan' is a scornful nickname hurled at Ephraim; it is a *double entendre*; it was originally the name for the Phoenician coastal

---

[a]-[a] So, freely translated, MT; the reconstruction which finds a reproach by Yahweh instead of the continuation of Ephraim's quotation (cf. RSV) depends on G.

  [b] *dmh* consistently means 'silence, cut off' in Hosea (4.5, 6; 10.7, 15); others translate 'make comparison, similitude, parables'. Cf. *dmh* I and II in *KB*.

region, and because of the Canaanites' famed reputation as travelling merchants 'Canaanite' came to mean 'trader, merchant' (Prov. 31.24; Job 40.30; Zeph. 1.11; Ezek. 17.4). Israel has taken on the character of the dwellers in the land and lost his identity as Israel. When God looks at him he sees only a Canaanite trader standing in the market place with crooked scales, avid to exploit by cheating for the sake of profit (cf. Amos 8.5). False balances were so common in the market place that their use was deplored by Wisdom and prohibited by law (Prov. 11.1; 16.11; 20.23; Job 31.6; Deut. 25.13; Lev. 19.36). The old Jacob of greed and trickery lives on in the people and makes a better Canaanite than Israelite. The ethic of the covenant has given way to the ethos of the unscrupulous trader.

[8] Ephraim's own statement is put in evidence against him. For other examples of a citation of the accused's words as a part of the indictment, see 6.1–3; 8.2; 10.3. Ephraim rejects every criticism of his conduct by pointing to the fact that his life has been quite profitable. Being rich is success enough and justifies the means of gain. The quotation sounds like the hollow boasting of the man who invited himself to ease because of his wealth (Luke 12.16–21; HAT). The crass assertion that riches gained by dishonesty and oppression involve no sin worth mentioning is a blatant rejection of the covenant's social norms. Here there speaks a people who see religion exclusively as a cultic ritual and the goal of worship as material prosperity. When a man is rich, his religion is vindicated. How can there be any talk of guilt and sin!

[9] With a solemn proclamation of his own name (13.4), Yahweh sets his own identity over against Canaanized Ephraim. He is Yahweh, not a Baal whose way with his people aims only at their prosperity. He is 'your God', God of the election and covenant, to whom they are inseparably bound by the historic deed of the Exodus (11.1). Their creation is his work in the normative history (11.1–4; 13.4f.) and they cannot hide from him within the security of their wealth (13.6). In the announcement of his name he is present, confronting them with his inexorable purpose. Their Canaanized life must end. He will break off their residence in the houses and towns of the cultivated land and make them live again in tents as they do annually at the festival of tabernacles. On the festival and the custom of dwelling in tents, see the commentary on 9.5f. The time of the wilderness which they recreate in the ritual of tabernacles shall become the situation of their lives; ritual of re-enactment shall become

a recapitulation of history. On the wilderness as the place of Israel's reconstitution see 2.14.

[10] The relation of v. 10 to its context is something of an enigma. Yahweh continues to speak of his acts in the style of the divine saying as in v. 9. But are the acts past events from the history of Yahweh with Israel (as in v. 9a), or are they coming deeds of judgment (as in v. 9b)? The verse has three different verb forms in Hebrew and can be translated either as past or future. If the future is used (ATD, HAT), then v. 10 can be read as the continuation of v. 9b. But Yahweh's action through the prophets is best understood as a reference to the past and the prophetic succession which began with Moses (12.13) and stretched across Israel's history in Canaan. The reference to the prophets in 6.5 points in that direction and Amos speaks of the prophets as one of the decisive acts of Yahweh in Israel's past (Amos 2.11). It does not then continue the announcement of punishment in v. 9b unless to say that destruction shall come by the prophetic word as oracles of help have in the past. Verse 10 has no apparent connection with v. 11, which can stand on its own as an independent saying, unless v. 10 provides a setting of salvation-history to accent the guilt of the sins cited in v. 11 (BK). With the exception of the questionable text in 4.5b, Hosea regards the prophets as an item in the salvation-history. Their office was defined by no less a person than Moses (13). They are the audience of Yahweh's direct speech and are granted visions (*ḥāzon*) of what he is about to do. By hearing and sight the prophet is privy to Yahweh's counsel, the unquestionable authority on his policy for his people. Their word is co-incident with the divine act, for the word is not simply meaning; it is also dynamic power, setting in motion the judgment which it announces, bringing punishment on the rebellious subjects of Yahweh (cf. 6.5).

[11] This verse is a doublet on Gilead and Gilgal, reporting the sin of each place and its punishment. The subject is cultic evil. The verse could be an individual saying; it stands isolated in its context and there is only a remote possibility that it continues v. 10. Like most of Hosea's references to places (e.g. 5.1f.; 6.7ff.; 10.9), these allusions to Gilead and Gilgal are vague because they presuppose a contemporary's knowledge of what was going on there. Hosea uses Gilead as the name of a town or cultic site; it is in parallel with Gilgal, and is used for a particular place in 6.8 where it is said to be the residence of evil-doers. 'Evil' (*'āwen* appears in both texts) is a category for cultic perversion (10.8); note Beth-awen as a nickname for Bethel in 4.15;

5.8; 9.5. On Gilgal, see the commentary on 9.15. The sacrifice of steers was not wrong in itself; the cult was pagan and the offerings dedicated to Canaanite deities. Gilead has already become an empty, worthless thing, perhaps a reference to its destruction by the Assyrians. Gilgal faces a similar fate. The day is near when its altars will be of no more significance than the stone-heaps that farmers make when clearing rocky fields for ploughing.

31. PATRIARCH OR PROPHET? 12.12–14 (Heb. 12.13–15)

12 ¹²Jacob fled to the Field of Aram;
    Israel served for a wife,
    for a wife he kept (sheep).
  ¹³But by a prophet Yahweh brought up
    Israel from Egypt;
    by a prophet he was kept.
  ¹⁴Ephraim has provoked (him) bitterly.
    He will leave his blood-guilt on him;
    his Lord will bring back his reproach on him.

In this prophetic saying Hosea resumes the discussion of the Jacob tradition; as in 12.2–6 he uses father Jacob as a model of what the sons of Jacob are and ought not to be. Verses 12 and 13 are formed as a study in contrasts with Jacob as the subject of the first and Yahweh of the second. The two poles of the contrast are held together by the use of repetition: Jacob acted for (*bᵉ*) a wife, Yahweh by (*bᵉ*) a prophet; Jacob kept (sheep); Israel was kept (as sheep) by Yahweh's prophet. The first picture (v. 12) shows how Jacob behaved when he was on his own; the second (v. 13) how Yahweh acted to save the people from being on their own, that is, by a prophet. Verses 12 and 13 thus clearly form a unit but their relation to v. 14 is not so apparent and belongs to the larger problem of the literary analysis of ch. 12; see the comment on 12.7–11, particularly vv. 10f. Verse 14 is a summary announcement of judgment; Israel's guilt is cited by using the general notion that they have provoked Yahweh to anger (v. 14a) and then their punishment is announced in equally general expressions about punishment (14b). If v. 14a cites the guilt illustrated by Jacob's conduct, then the reference to Jacob's service for the sake of a wife could be an allusion to Israel's proclivity for the sexual cult of

Canaan; the verb in v. 14a (provoke to anger) in its general usage describes Yahweh's response to Israel's worship of idols.

[12] Hosea's concern with Jacob (cf. 12.2ff.) as an issue between himself as prophet and his audience as the devotees of Yahweh probably grows out of a revival of interest among the Israelites in the religious role of the ancestor from whom their name came. Jacob's saga was intimately related to the cultic legend of Bethel (Gen. 28.11–22). In the Assyrian crisis some circles in the nation probably turned to the Jacob tradition with its promise of the land in perpetuity as a theology of last resort (cf. Gen. 28.13ff.). But for Hosea the fundamental point of departure for understanding Yahweh's way with Israel is the Exodus (13); the relation between God and people began only then (11.1; cf. 13.4). The flight of Jacob and his service to gain a wife clearly refer to the tradition concerning Jacob's return to the homeland of his mother (Gen. 27.43; 29.18; 30.31). Hosea's 'Field of Aram' is the equivalent of Paddan-Aram (Gen. 25.20, etc.). Hosea recreates Jacob as a completely human and vulnerable figure. He was a man whose conduct resulted in the necessity of flight; perhaps there is an allusion to his treachery against his brother (cf. 12.3). And he was willing to be a bond-servant to gain a wife! – is there here a covert reference to Israel's proclivity for the sexual cult as servants of Baal? How can Israel appeal to Jacob who fled from his brother and served his kinsman for a wife?

[13] Israel should not see themselves in Jacob, but instead in the identity given them in the Exodus. There they were the object of Yahweh's deliverance. There it was Yahweh who acted and did the keeping. While Jacob's life was determined by a wife, Israel's life was determined by a prophet. The reference must be to Moses. This identification of Moses as the first of the prophetic succession appears in Hosea and then recurs in Deut. 18.15ff., another clue that Hosea was connected with the circles whose thinking and faith constitute the background of the Deuteronomic outlook. The prophet, not the Jacob tradition, should receive the attention of contemporary Israel. It is to Yahweh of the Exodus and not the cult centres of patriarchal founding that Ephraim should look.

[14] But Ephraim, the contemporary sons of Jacob, have done just the opposite. They have continually and openly provoked Yahweh with bitter offence. The verb 'offend, provoke' (Hiphil of $k's$) is a favourite of Jeremiah, Deuteronomy, and the Deuteronomic history, [a]

[a] See *BDB*, p. 495, for its distribution.

and is used predominantly for the provocation of Yahweh by the cult of other gods. The cult of Canaan has been Israel's response to Yahweh and his prophets. Verse 14b announces the punishment for this offence. 'Blood (guilt)' is a term for culpability which merits execution; see the phrase 'his blood (guilt) is upon him' in the cultic-legal formulations of Lev. 20.[a] Israel's cultic perversion deserves the sentence of death. It is a shameful reproach against the Lord (Hosea uses $'^a d\bar{o}nayw$ only here), so the one who rules Israel will turn the reproach back on the guilty as a revelation of his lordship.

32. TODAY WITH BAAL—NO TOMORROW: 13.1–3

13 [1]When Ephraim spoke, (there was) dread;[b]
    he was exalted[c] in Israel,
      but he incriminated himself by the Baal – and died.
    [2]Now they keep on sinning;
      they have made a molten image for themselves,
    idols according to their notion[d] from their silver;
      everyone is the work of artisans.
    'To them sacrifice,'[e] they say.
      Men kiss calves!
    [3]Therefore they shall be like morning mist,
      like dew that quickly vanishes,
    like chaff blown[e] from the threshing floor,
      like smoke from the vent.

The past (v. 1), present (v. 2), and future (v. 3) of Ephraim pass in review in the course of this oracle of judgment. The indictment (vv. 1f.) of Ephraim is introduced by a historical preface which sets the stage for understanding the present conduct of the nation (as in 9.10; 10.1; 11.1ff.; 12.3f., 12f.). 'Now' makes the transition from history to the present and connects Ephraim's guilt by Baal with the worship of idols. 'Therefore' introduces Yahweh's verdict (v. 3) on Ephraim's idolatry. Ephraim, once feared and respected, shall disappear without a trace. The text offers no clue about the style, whether the oracle is a

[a] H. Reventlow, 'Sein Blut komme über sein Haupt', *VT* 10, 1960, pp. 311ff.
[b] $r^e t\bar{e}t$, only here in OT, appears in this meaning in 1 QH iv 33.
[c] Cf. BH.
[d] The noun is a variant form of $t^e b\bar{u}n\bar{a}$, or a miswriting of $t^e b\bar{u}n\bar{a}t\bar{a}m$.

divine or prophetic saying; since it is an announcement of judgment, the first is probably correct.

[1] The indictment begins with a reference to the time when Ephraim's position within Israel was so superior that even his speaking provoked apprehension and trembling among the rest of the tribes. Hosea generally uses 'Ephraim' as a name for the contemporary northern state, a synonym for Israel; for that reason a tradition from the lore about the tribe, Ephraim, can be applied to the whole nation. References to Ephraim's pre-eminence appear in such texts as the blessing of Jacob on Ephraim and Manasseh (Gen. 48) and in Judg. 8.1–4. Joshua (Josh. 24.30) and Jeroboam I (I Kings 11.26; 12.20) were Ephraimites. Whether Hosea knows some other tradition of Ephraim's early superiority, or refers to these, cannot be learned from the text. He simply makes the point that the people whom he now calls Ephraim are pitiful by comparison with the tribe whose name they bear. Their decline and fall is the consequence of worshipping Baal (the singular appears also in 2.8 and possibly 9.10). The fertility cult of Canaan was the source of Ephraim's guilt and death. The basic covenant requirement of Israel's relation to Yahweh was its rigorous exclusiveness. Yet since coming to the land Israel had worshipped Baal (9.10). Hosea sees Ephraim's present condition as the effect of guilt that invokes the death sentence upon itself. After 733 the nation was decimated in territory and population; its wounds and weakness were symptoms enough that it was already in the realm of death.

[2] In spite of the punishment they have suffered, Ephraim continues in the way of sin like zombies, the walking dead, who have lost control of their actions. The explanation lies in their false faith in Baal. They believe him to be the god of fertility and life, so in their desperate need they fervently prepare images for use in the adoration of Baal (cf. 11.2). They seek salvation by means of what is actually sin, and so hope to find life in what works death. 'Molten image' (*massēkā*) is a figure of a deity cast of bronze and overlaid with a precious metal (8.4). *Massēkā* is the name used for the golden calf in Ex. 32 (see vv. 4, 8 and Deut. 9.16). Hosea clearly has the bull-image of Bethel in mind; see the comment on 8.5f.; 10.5f. Whatever its makers intended it to represent, a pedestal for Yahweh or Yahweh himself, Hosea reckons it among the apparatus of Baal worship. It appears that figurines on the model of the bull-image are being struck for use in private and public ritual. The general use of images was

forbidden in the decalogic tables (Ex. 20.4) and the molten image specifically in Ex. 34.17; Lev. 19.4. Hosea is aghast that Ephraim cannot draw the consequences of the obvious fact that these images are man-made, the work of artisans (cf. 8.5). Yet the national cult is devoted to them and sacrifice offered to them. What irony! *men kiss calves*. Kissing the image of the deity was part of the ritual of Baal (I Kings 19.18).

[3] 'Therefore' introduces the verdict of Yahweh upon Ephraim's sin. Four metaphors are heaped up to reiterate one assertion: Israel has no future. Dead in their sins now, they will be gone on the morrow, vanished like mist, like dew, like chaff, like smoke. All four comparisons evoke the sense of evanescent impermanence; they are things that quickly disappear. On morning mist and dew, see 6.4 where the comparisons are used to describe Israel's devotion. Chaff is driven away by the wind that blows across the threshing floor (Pss. 1.4; 35.5). Smoke is another favourite image of the temporary (Isa. 51.6; Pss. 37.20; 68.2). The vent (*'aʳubbā*) is the hole left in the roof or wall for smoke to escape from inside fires. The Ephraim that once struck terror in the hearts of its neighbours has become a vanishing smoke.

33. THE SHEPHERD SHALL DESTROY THE FLOCK: 13.4–8

13 ⁴I am Yahweh your God
       from the land of Egypt.
   A God besides me you do not know;
       there is no Saviour except me.
   ⁵I it was who pastured[a] you in the wilderness,
       in a land of drought.
   ⁶When I pastured them, they were satisfied;
       they were satisfied and their heart was proud;
       therefore they forgot me.
   ⁷I have become like a lion to them;
       like a leopard I lurk upon the way.
   ⁸I will attack them like a bear bereaved (of her cubs),
       and I will tear away their breast.
   Dogs[b] shall then devour them,[b]
       wild beasts rend them.

[a] *reʿītīkā* with GS for MT's 'I knew you'.
[b] Cf. BH.

The oracle begins with a sketch of Yahweh's acts of deliverance and help (vv. 4–5), but ends with a portrayal of Israel's God as a ravaging beast (vv. 7–8). The saviour shall become the destroyer! Between these starkly contrasting pictures lies the report of Israel's proud and arrogant rejection of Yahweh (v. 6), binding the two and accounting for the incredible change. The oracle is an announcement of judgment with indictment (vv. 4–6) and verdict (vv. 7–8). The indictment is drawn by setting the salvation-history of Exodus and wilderness over against Israel's conduct in the land, as in 11.1–4. All of vv. 4–6 is a preparation for the specific accusation: 'They have forgotten me.' The punishing action of Yahweh is proclaimed in theriomorphisms which draw the most savage picture of Yahweh's wrath in Hosea's prophecy. The style of the divine saying persists throughout. The audience is addressed directly in vv. 4–5 where the salvation-history is reviewed. When Israel's own history of sin takes up in v. 6, and the accusation proper begins, Yahweh speaks of Israel in third person plural pronouns as though addressing a court concerning the accused. This terrible prophecy of Israel's end probably comes from the middle years of Hoshea's reign when it was all too clear that he would persist in seeking a solution for Israel's peril by political conspiracy and trust in the pagan cult.

[4] Yahweh begins by proclaiming his own identity as the election-God of Israel ('your God'), who is known to his people definitively through the deliverance from Egypt (11.1). This formula of self-presentation (see comment on 12.10) was used in Israel's covenant cult as an introduction to the proclamation of Yahweh's will for his people (Ex. 20.2; Deut. 5.6)[a] and comes as near as any element of the tradition used by Hosea to stating the central article of his theology. In the decalogic formulations the formula established the right of Yahweh as God of the Exodus and covenant to set his policy for the life of Israel. Here it is the basis for the assertion of Yahweh's exclusive role as God of Israel. Indeed, v. 4b is a narrative form of the first commandment. Israel is to have no other God than Yahweh because no other deity has participated in its history. 'Know' means 'experience the benefits and presence of another'. The 'helper' (*mōšia'*, 'saviour') is the one who acts in the time of peril to deliver the people from danger. Israel's history is revelation that Israel *has* no other God and that there *is* no other helper for them. This assertion that Israel is

[a] See W. Zimmerli, 'Ich bin Jahwe', in *Gottes Offenbarung* (Th. Büch. 19), 1963, pp. 11ff.

exclusively dependent on Yahweh is in Hosea's situation a polemic against all other forces to which Israel looked for deliverance: the king and his princes (13.10; cf. I Sam. 10.18f.), military power (14.3), and idols (14.3; 13.2). During the Exile Deutero-Isaiah raises the assertion to the level of an ontological denial that other deities are gods (Isa. 43.11; 45.5, 21).

[5] The acts of Yahweh in the wilderness (2.14; cf. 11.3; 12.9) further emphasize Yahweh's claim on Israel through the normative salvation-history and prepare for the description of Israel's response in v. 6. In the barren emptiness of the wilderness where there was neither water nor food, Yahweh was the good shepherd to his people. He led his flock to pasture and water. If MT's 'I knew you' is correct, 'knew' is used in the sense which it has in Amos 3.2, where it means the recognition extended by a suzerain through treaty to a vassal.[a]

[6] Against the background of Yahweh's deliverance and help, Israel's conduct appears in stark contrast (cf. 11.2). When their divine shepherd had brought them into the cultivated land they mistook its good things as the gifts of Baal (2.8). The self-understanding of Israel was unchanged by the revelation of their history. Their attention was focused alone on the satisfaction of their human desires, and when these were satisfied they dismissed the Yahweh of the Exodus and wilderness. Instead of living by the knowledge of Yahweh (4.1) they forgot him (cf. 'forget me' in 2.13). That Israel thought their own satisfaction exhausted Yahweh's purpose, that his acts led to their self-exaltation in pride against him, was bitterest frustration – and out of that bitterness the vehemence of the following sentences (vv. 7f.) unfolds. Warning against taking the bounty of the land as gifts of another god or against being sated and forgetting Yahweh is a favourite theme of Deuteronomic exhortations (Deut. 8.11-20; 6.10-19; 11.15f.); here again Hosea appears to be one of the early forerunners of Deuteronomic thought.

[7-8] In announcing the punishment which he will wreak on Israel, Yahweh turns to theriomorphisms to express the savage violence of his wrath. The God who played the role of shepherd in the salvation-history will act in such fury that only metaphors which cast him as the enemy of the flock suffice to portray the vehemence of his judgment. These metaphors have their background in the formulary

[a] So H. B. Huffmon, 'The Treaty Background of Hebrew *Yāda'*', *BASOR* 181, 1966, pp. 31ff. who finds here specific allusion to the Sinai Covenant.

treaty-curses of the ancient Near East which threaten those who break treaty; ravenous wild animals (lion, leopard, and bear are listed) are invoked in the curses which are listed as part of the treaty form to enforce its obligations. The curse of marauding animals appears in Lev. 26.22, and Jer. 5.6 is an example of a use of the curse in prophecy.[a] Hosea goes to the extreme of casting Yahweh himself in the role of the ravaging beasts. In his action he will become as lion and leopard and bear to the flock (I Sam. 17.34). Yahweh's punishing attack on Israel was compared to that of the lion in 5.14. Here leopard and bear are added. A she-bear robbed of her cubs was a particularly vivid image of fury (Prov. 17.12; II Sam. 17.8). The attack leads to the nation's death, not just its wounding! Israel will be left after Yahweh's judgment like the carcass of a sheep slain by a beast of prey – jackals and dogs will devour the leavings. The end is absolute. In this oracle, as in 13.3, Hosea sees no future but total annihilation for the Israel to which he speaks. They have refused to heed the chastisements of history and messages of his oracles, persist in idolatry and self-sufficient schemes; Yahweh himself will enforce the curses which their conduct invokes upon them.

34. IF GOD BE AGAINST US . . . : 13.9–11

13 [9]I destroy you,[b] O Israel!
   [c]Who then is your helper[c]?
[10]Where[d] now is your king
   that he may save you against all your foes,[e]
your rulers, of whom you said,
   'Give me king and officials.'
[11]I gave you kings in my anger,
   and I take (them) away in my wrath.

The stance of this divine saying indicates that it is a disputation-speech, an oracle delivered in the course of controversy between prophet and audience. Apparently the hearers of such messages as

[a] D. R. Hillers, *Treaty-Curses and the Old Testament Prophets*, 1964, pp. 54ff.
[b] Vocalizing MT's consonants *šiḥattīka*.
[c-c] Taking the opening *kī* as an emphatic and reading with BH in dependence on GS.
[d] *'ehī='ayyēh*, as in 13.14; cf. the versions.
[e] *ṣāreykā* with Rudolph; MT has 'your cities' (*'āreykā*).

13.3, 7f. demur at the announcement of the nation's end. Yahweh responds by the prophet's mouth: 'I will destroy you' and challenges them to produce any helper to prove the contrary (v. 9). The blunt assertion insists on a twofold recognition – that even now the destruction of the nation is under way and that Yahweh is the one who is bringing it about. The obvious 'helper' that should be available to deliver the nation from its foes is the king, so the challenging question of v. 9b is developed in the argumentative question of v. 10 and concluded with the assertion in v. 11 that the kings themselves are both instruments and objects of Yahweh's wrath. The disputation-speech may have been placed here because it belonged to the setting in which the two foregoing sayings were delivered; at least the collectors saw a connection between the description of Yahweh's destruction in vv. 7f. and the opening verb in v. 9, and between v. 4b and the questions in vv. 9b and 10.

[9] Verse 9a is savage and blunt. The Hebrew perfect verb states what has already become fact. Even though the nation is going under, the Israelites do not get the point that Yahweh is at work. They still blather about help and salvation. Since the destruction is Yahweh's work, just whom can they have in mind? The oracle, with its intense concentration of God's terrible purpose into one word, slams the door on any protest or hope for the Israel that hears the message. God's agenda for his dealings with this political and religious Israel is devastation. The question (v. 9b) simply makes the same point as v. 9a argumentively. The role of 'helper' ('ōzer) in Israel belongs to Yahweh alone. In the ancient theology of Yahwism wrought out in the experiences of Holy War, Yahweh disclosed his own identity and vindicated his election of Israel by acting as their help against every adversary (Deut. 33.26, 27). To trust in him as helper was to be set free of every reliance on kings and princes (Pss. 121; 115.9–11). But if it is Yahweh who destroys them, there is no helper to come when they lift up their eyes to the hills. Now Yahweh vindicates his role by a frightful contradiction; their helper destroys them. Note the reversal in 13.4, 8 where the shepherd-saviour becomes the ravaging beast. Just as there is no other helper for Israel, there is no one that can rescue from his hand when he becomes their enemy (2.10; 5.14). Judgment becomes the revelation of the role and rule of Yahweh.

[10] The questions in v. 10 make the point that the institution through which the people had expected Yahweh's help to come was mortally wounded. Israel had looked to the military competence of

the royal court for deliverance. For other oracles dealing with Israel's kings and predicting their fall, see 7.3–7; 8.4–10; 10.3f., 7, 15. In all the palace revolutions, assassinations, and anointings which punctuated every phase of the Assyrian crisis, Israel had been looking for salvation. The ruthless vehemence of Israel's royal politics was a testimony to their desperate belief that a proper king would save them. Hosea's taunting question may be simply a rhetorical scorn directed at Hoshea's helplessness; or it may imply that the son of Elah is already in the hands of Shalmaneser V (II Kings 17.4). The tradition about the history of Israel's kingship in which Hosea stands attributes their existence to the petition of the people. Having a royal court was their idea and the quotation sounds like an echo of the old anti-monarchical source in the early chapters of Samuel (I Sam. 8.6).

[11] Yahweh answered the petition of Israel and gave them kings, but one and all they were a gift of God's left hand, an answer which was punishment for the petition. The ruinous careers of the nation's rulers had been an expression of divine wrath, an action to bring his people back to a knowledge of his own kingship by which alone they could know salvation. In 8.4 Hosea said that Yahweh had no part in Israel's king-making. Here the assessment is even more negative. Yahweh has no responsibility for Israel's kings and all that his people can receive from him through them is his anger.

35. LET DEATH TAKE OVER: 13.12–16 (Heb. 13.12–14.1)

13 ¹²Ephraim's guilt is bound up,
   his sin is stored away.
¹³The pains of birth come for him,
   but he is a child without wisdom;
   when it is time he does not appear
   at the womb's opening.
¹⁴From the power of Sheol shall I ransom them?
   from death shall I redeem them?
   Where[a] are your plagues, O Death?
   where[a] are your scourges, O Sheol?
   Sympathy is hidden from my eyes!

---

[a] 'ehī='ayyēh, as in 13.10. For a decision in favour of 'I will be. . .', see Ward, pp. 220ff.

[15]Though he were to[a] flourish midst rushes[a]
the east wind of Yahweh will come,
arising from the wilderness.
His fountain shall go dry[b]
and his spring shall fail.
He shall plunder his store
of every desirable thing.
[16]Samaria shall bear her guilt,
because she has rebelled against her God.
By the sword they shall fall;
their babes shall be dashed down,
and their pregnant women split open.

This is Hosea's last and harshest announcement of Israel's end. At the conclusion the horrors of Samaria's fall to besieging troops is already in sight (v. 16b). The saying probably comes from the final years of King Hoshea's reign, when his revolutionary schemes were spreading hopes that the nation might yet escape the fate toward which recent events had steadily carried it. The saying begins with a warning that there will be no escape from punishment, because Ephraim's guilt is an imperishable record before God (v. 12). The situation of the reduced nation is like that of an unborn child who does not know its time and so has no hope for life (v. 13). Yahweh asks himself whether he should intervene and redeem them from death, and answers his own questions by calling for death to do its worst (v. 14). The certain end of the nation is described in vv. 15f., beginning with the metaphor of the hot east wind that blasts every living plant and shifting to outright military language to depict the plundering of the nation and the fall of the capital city. The oracle is a divine saying; the first-person style (v. 14) can be assumed throughout ('wind of Yahweh' (v. 15) is a locution better expressed so, than with a possessive pronoun; 'her God' (v. 16) is a way of emphasizing the magnitude of the guilt). The unity of vv. 12–15 is apparent in the dependence of all the pronouns and verb-subjects on the opening 'Ephraim' of v. 12. 'Samaria' introduces a new identity in v. 16, but the capital city is put in focus to particularize the punishment that will fall on it within the nation as a whole.

[12] The oracle begins directly with the assumption of Ephraim's

---

[a] Reading *'āḥū mapri'* for MT's *'aḥīm yapri'*; see the comment on the problem in v. 15a.
[b] Reading *weyibas* for MT *weyēbōš*.

guilt. The saying contains no specific reproach and uses only the general terms, guilt and sin, to refer to the basis of Yahweh's punishment which is the real concern of the saying. Behind these general terms are such specifics as those already identified in the immediately preceding sayings, which must have come from the same situation as this one: the apostasy to Baal (v. 1), idolatry (v. 2), trust in kings (v. 10) – all of which add up to the rebellion against Yahweh charged in v. 16. In spite of all the destruction and suffering that has already befallen the nation, the payment for that sin has not been made. It is still 'bound up and stored away'. The language comes from the practice of tying together papyrus and parchment documents and putting them in a depository for safe-keeping (cf. Isa. 8.16). The metaphor is a picturesque way of stating the formulary sentence: 'He will remember their guilt and punish their sin' (8.13; 9.9; so Wolff). Ephraim's guilt does not fade with the passing of time or the increasing desperation of the nation's circumstances. The record is kept in the heavenly court like legal documents preserved for evidence.

[13] The desperate urgency of Ephraim's situation is dramatized by depicting the nation as a foetus that does not emerge from the mother's womb in spite of her labour pains. See II Kings 19.3, where the inability of mothers to give birth is used as a sign of acute danger. Here the phenomenon is that of the child that lies in the womb in such a position that it cannot be born. The language of the comparison ('an unwise child') attributes judgment and responsibility to the foetus and may reflect a popular idiom used to describe such circumstances (Rudolph). It is the essence of wisdom to know the right time (Eccles. 8.5) and the mother's labour is the time of the child in the womb. The labour pains of a mother will be used repeatedly by later prophets as an image for the writhing of the nation under judgment (Jer. 13.21; 22.23; Isa. 26.17f.; 13.8). But the term of comparison here is not the mother, but the child. Ephraim's 'time' has come and he will not recognize it. The punishment suffered thus far was meant to bring about a return to Yahweh, and could be the occasion for birth, new life (cf. Isa. 66.7–9). Behind the image is Hosea's faith that Yahweh's chastisement was the crucible of renewal, the painful preparation for a new covenant and a revived people (2.15; 3.5; 11.8ff.). Now is the time! But alas, Ephraim does not know its own time – like a child that will not be born, it can only have death as its future.

[14] The predicament of the child that will not be born provokes the response of Yahweh. The exegetical tradition is divided on the problem of the significance of this verse. Does Yahweh resolve to intervene on behalf of the helpless nation, or does he leave them to the death they seem to choose? The parallel sentences in v. 14a could be either questions or assertions. The parallel questions in v. 14b can be construed as a summons to death to come and do its work, or as an invincible challenge flung against death by the God who saves Israel. The import of the final sentence (v. 14bβ) depends on the meaning of the Hebrew word (*nōḥam*), found only here in the Old Testament, translated 'vengeance' by some and 'sympathy, compassion' by others. This ambiguity in the written Hebrew text of the verse (it would not have been ambiguous in the spoken oracle because oral emphasis would have clarified the speaker's intention) has been resolved by interpreters in two basic ways. First, the verse is read as an announcement of salvation for Ephraim, in which Yahweh draws back from their annihilation; 11.8f. is pointed to as an anaology. This understanding appears in the translation in G and is used by Paul in his quotation of the passage (I Cor. 15.55). In this approach it is a matter of indifference whether v. 14a contains questions or assertions. Either Yahweh asks himself whether he will redeem because he is contemplating this action, or he announces his decision to redeem Ephraim. The questions in v. 14b are understood as rejections of death's threat against the nation. The final sentence is then an announcement that Yahweh has decided against *vengeance* as a course of action. If this interpretation is correct, then vv. 15f. cannot be a continuation of vv. 12–14. The second approach takes the verse as a word of judgment. This interpretation is adopted in the following comment as the more probably correct. It fits better with the sense of vv. 12f. and the larger context of ch. 12, which seems to furnish a historical setting for the saying. Ultimately, any decision depends upon *nōḥam* whose cognates point in the direction of 'sympathy, compassion'. Analogies with other texts cannot solve the question because there are examples enough of both judgment and salvation words in authentic sayings of Hosea.

The word-order of the Hebrew sentences in v. 14a clearly allows them to be construed as questions. 'Ransom' (*pdh*) and 'redeem' (*g'l*) are used as synonyms, as verbs for the action of God in behalf of his people when their existence is threatened. Yahweh is the only saviour of Israel (cf. the comment on 13.4); to him alone belongs the role of ransoming and redeeming the whole people. In their general use, 'ransom' and 'redeem' both denote an act in behalf of one who is helpless. *Pādā* means to free someone from legal or cultic obligation through the payment of a price. *Gā'al* is the act of a kinsman or related person to vindicate another in cases of blood-revenge, levirate marriage, and the reclaiming of bound property; the basic idea is protection.[a] The verbs were assimilated into the vocabulary describing Yahweh's historical acts of help, especially the deliverance from Egypt (Ex. 15.13; Micah 6.4). So the question is appropriate and urgent. Shall Yahweh fulfil his role as the God of the Exodus to save this people? The introduction of Sheol and Death as the threatening danger dramatizes the extremity of the nation's situation; the child that will not be born is already in the power of Death. In the Old Testament death is the state of those whose life is gone, and Sheol is the place where the dead are. The two are frequently paired as virtual synonyms (Prov. 5.5; 7.27) and are personalized in the imagery of poetry (Isa. 28.15, 18; 5.14; Ps. 49.14f.; Prov. 1.12), which may reflect the fact that in Canaanite mythology the god of the underworld was named *Mōt* (Death). Some OT texts seem to view the underworld as a place beyond the ken of Yahweh; he is not praised or remembered in Sheol (Isa. 28.18; Pss. 6.5; 30.9; 88.11). Death and Sheol are always inimical and foreign to Yahweh, but both Amos (9.2) and Hosea believe that Yahweh's power extends into Sheol. The questions clearly imply that Yahweh can rescue the nation from death.[b]

The questions in v. 14b are in effect commands to the alien powers of Death and Sheol to execute their terrible work on the nation. Plague and scourge are the weapons of death and belong to the arsenal of threats against the living (Ps. 9.13, 6). 'Sympathy' is the more probable translation of *nōham* (only found here; cf. 'compassion' [*niḥūmīm*] in 11.8; the predominant meaning of the verb *nḥm*; and G's translation by *paraklēsis*). Yahweh has his sympathy for this unwise people, but he will not consider it now in deciding his course of action. Ephraim's guilt still stands on the record (v. 12). The judgment that is already in progress has brought forth no new life of repentance (v. 13). In another time and place there may be occasion

[a] Cf. G. von Rad, *Theology of the Old Testament* I, 1962, p. 177, and the literature cited there.
[b] See G. von Rad in *TWNT* II, pp. 844ff.; 'Dead, Abode of' and 'Death' in *IDB* I.

for Yahweh's sympathy. But for now, this nation in its present form and mood is given over to death for punishment.

[15] Uncertainty about the meaning of the first measure (v. 15a) is an embarrassment to all interpretations of v. 15, especially of its relation to v. 14. MT means something like: 'Though (because, yea) he among brothers flourishes', which in the context is difficult to understand. Hosea does not use the name Ephraim for one tribe among the others, but for the contemporary northern kingdom. The reading adopted above requires only a slight adjustment in the received text and fits well with what follows. Though Ephraim (who must be the antecedent of 'he') were to be as flourishing as plants that grow among reeds where there is always water, Yahweh will nonetheless dry them up with his wind of judgment. The image of flourishing plants in marshes is not meant to be an allusion to Ephraim's current prosperity but is a comparison chosen in anticipation of the rest of the verse where the accent is on the east wind of Yahweh. The shift from the imagery of drought to the specific language of military conquest in the last line of the verse (v. 15bβ) uncovers the historical actuality behind the image. The east wind which Yahweh will send is Assyria (12.1). The ravaging army of Assyria will appear in answer to Yahweh's call for the plagues of Death and Sheol.

[16] This announcement of punishment for Samaria continues the description of what will take place because Yahweh has decided not to redeem Ephraim (v. 14). Samaria comes into focus because the capital city was the centre of King Hoshea's plot to revolt against Assyria, and therefore the source of hopes that the nation would not long have to submit to foreign power. In the prophet's eyes such hopes were the hope to escape Yahweh's punishment and only obscured the true nature of the situation. No one should look to Samaria in expectation for the city will itself bear its guilt. Especially Samaria, because the capital has been the driving power of the nation's rebellion against its God. The cult of the calves and the murderous revolutions and the vaccillating international politics all stemmed from Samaria's leadership. The Assyrian will be the instrument of the punishment. The prophet foretells the siege of the city in all its horror (II Kings 17.5). The picture is progressively more gruesome. The men will fall to the enemy's sword and then the ravaging of the city that resisted siege will follow. On the practice of slitting pregnant women in wars of territorial conquest and in punishment for rebellion see Amos 1.13; II Kings 15.16. The entire population of the city is doomed.

36. THE THERAPY OF LOVE: 14.1–8 (Heb. 14.2–9)

14 ¹Return, O Israel, to Yahweh your God,
    for you have stumbled on your guilt.
²Take words with you
    and return to Yahweh.
 Say to him,
    'Forgive all ª guilt.
Accept our speech ᵇ that we may make restitution
    with the fruit ᶜ of our lips.
³Assyria shall not save us;
    upon horses we will not ride.
 Nor will we say "Our God" any more
    to the work of our hands;
    in you the orphan finds compassion.'
⁴'I will heal their apostasy;
    I will love them freely,
    for my anger has turned from him.
⁵I will be like dew for Israel;
    he shall flourish like the lily.
 He shall strike root like the (trees of) Lebanon;
⁶   his shoots shall grow out.
 His beauty shall be like the olive tree,
    his fragrance like Lebanon.
⁷They shall once again dwell ᶜ in my ᶜ shade.
    They shall grow corn.
 They shall flourish like the vine,
    his renown be like the wine of Lebanon.
⁸Ephraim! what has he ᶜ to do any more with idols?
    It is I who answer and make him happy. ᵈ
 I am like a verdant fir,
    your fruit is found with me.'

14.1–8 contains two related but clearly distinct sections. The first (vv. 1–3) is a prophetic exhortation calling on Israel to return to their God (vv. 1–2a) and proposing a prayer of penitence as a way of approaching him (vv. 2b–3). The second is a divine saying in which Yahweh promises salvation to Israel (vv. 4–8). It begins with a direct declaration that he will heal their failure and love them freely (v. 4).

    ª *kol* is awkwardly placed, but see *GK* 128e.
    ᵇ *ṭōbēnū* with Rudolph; the suffix has been lost by haplography. For *ṭōb*= 'speech, word' cf. Neh. 6.14; Ps. 39.3 (R. Gordis, *VT* 5, 1955, pp. 89f.).
    ᶜ Cf. BH.
    ᵈ Reading *waʾaʾašśᵉrennū* with *KB*, p. 957.

Then following an image for his beneficence ('I will be like dew,' v. 5a), the effect of his love for Israel is described with comparisons from plant life (vv. 5aβ–6, 7b); the metaphorical language is apparently dropped in v. 7a. The oracle reaches its climax with the cry that Ephraim now has done with idols because all his needs are met by Yahweh (8a), and it concludes with a final image for Yahweh's love ('I am like a verdant fir'). This juxtaposition of prayer and answering oracle reflects the structure of the liturgy for a service of repentance.[a] But in contrast to 5.15–6.6, where the material also incorporates elements from a liturgy of penitence, no actual service of the people is presupposed. 6.1–3 is the prayer of the people and 6.4–6 the divine *negative* answer. Here Hosea proposes a penitential prayer as part of his prophetic exhortation and the divine oracle is the answer revealed by Yahweh to him as the response he will make to such penitence and even now waits to make. The setting of the unit is completely that of the prophetic message; the material does not yet have a place in the liturgical life of the people. Therefore the two parts must be held together. Yahweh will not bestow this saving beneficence upon Israel apart from the penitential return demanded. But the prophet would not call the people to penitence apart from his certainty that Yahweh wants them to return, wills to bless them. The demand is the call of love that wants a chance to bestow its healing. And the healing will enter into the penitence and bring it to complete freedom from every idolatry. The location of this oracle at the end of the book says nothing conclusive concerning its date or authenticity. Following his usual practice of balancing words of judgment with oracles of salvation, the collector has set a piece of hopeful outlook at the close of this final block of material. The many connections of its vocabulary, theme, and outlook with other Hosea material are noted in the following comment. Other sayings of exhortation in Hosea clearly are a summons to act in the crisis of imminent judgment (2.2f.; 4.15; 10.12; 12.7). But here the judgment seems to have done its work. Israel has already stumbled (cf. 5.5). It is possible to think of this summons as an oracle set in the final months of the northern kingdom's defeat by Shalmaneser V. The judgment upon the nation works its way toward the final scene; the end of Ephraim with its politics and cult is near. Once more Hosea calls for the repentance which he always believed would be the outcome of God's punishment.

[a] See Claus Westermann, *The Praise of God in the Psalms*, 1965, pp. 61f., for his analysis of the liturgical elements here and in the similar Jer. 3.21–4.2.

[1] The opening imperative is addressed to the entire people as if to a single individual (verbs and pronouns are singular). 'Return' (*šûb*) is Hosea's essential demand for a nation in apostasy (see the comment on 3.5) and here the summons to return is given its classic formulation. *Šûb* is a movement of life back along a route that was travelled away from Yahweh, a return to 'Yahweh your God' who by covenant said 'I will be your God and you will be my people.' It means the revival of exclusive loyalty to the God of Exodus and Torah. The call is addressed to a people who have already stumbled upon their guilt. What the primary items of this guilt are is declared in the renunciation in v. 3. Assyrian politics, trust in military solutions, idolatry have sent the people reeling toward their final fall. Their perilous position should at last make them see that the stone of their stumbling is their own guilt. Addressed to such a people the call to return is demand and gospel; it tells them what they must do if they are to survive, and declares that the door is open from their God's side. The basis of the call is his will to heal them, to be their God (v. 4).

[2] The address to the corporate Israel gives way to plural imperatives; every person is called as an individual to obey the summons. Verses 2f. direct the audience how the response is to be made. They are to take words, offer Yahweh their speech; so that they may do that properly the prophet teaches them a prayer which they are to make. Its elements of confession (v. 2b) and renunication (v. 3) are the outline of a service of penitence. The very language of Hosea's instruction shows that the prayer is set over against sacrifice as an alternative. An Israelite was not supposed to appear before Yahweh empty-handed (Ex. 23.15; 34.20); by offerings he was to make good his vows. But Hosea is categorically against the sacrificial approach to Yahweh (4.8; 5.6; 6.6; 8.13). Instead of sacrifice Israel is now to take words, make restitution with 'the fruit of our lips' (on the expression see Prov. 13.2; 12.14). Prayer is to be the means of their access to God. They are to bring the sacrifice of a broken and contrite heart (Ps. 51.17). The cult is to become the place and time in which Israel presents itself to Yahweh and puts itself at his disposal by a plea for forgiveness and rejection of dependence on all other powers. The prayer begins with the central problem – the iniquity upon which Israel has stumbled. The petition for Yahweh's forgiveness is both confession that they are sinners and recognition that he alone by his own act can overcome the failure of their past. Israel must cast him-

self wholly upon Yahweh in whom is the sovereign power both to punish and forgive (*nāśā' 'āwōn*, Ex. 34.7; Num. 14.18; Micah 7.18).

[3] The second element of the prayer is a series of vows by which Israel is to declare her total submission to Yahweh. The series is composed of renunciations which forswear the basic sins of court and cult, politics and worship, against which Hosea had repeatedly brought indictment. The first line covers the policy of trusting in international agreements and military power for deliverance. For Hosea's protests against Israel's attempt to escape its crisis by constant experiments in dealing with Assyria, see 5.13; 7.11; 8.9; 12.2. To 'ride on horses' refers to the use of war chariots. Similar locutions (Isa. 30.16; 31.3; Deut. 17.16) are associated with Israelite dependence on Egypt as a source of chariotry. Israel did turn to Egypt as an ally against Assyria during Hosea's career (7.11; 12.1; II Kings 17.4) and possibly the rejection of chariotry contains an allusion to Egypt in parallel to Assyria. 'Our God' is the confessional cry which in Israel should be addressed only to Yahweh, the electing God. That cry shall not be used any more in a cult at whose centre stands a man-made image, whether it is thought to be representation of Yahweh or not (8.6; 13.2; 4.12; 10.5f.; 11.2). Worship which centres on an object fashioned by man is an open invitation for the worshipper to suppose that he has the deity at his disposal. The intention of the threefold vow is to put Israel wholly in the hands of Yahweh. He is the only God that Israel knows and they have known him in his historical acts, not by cultic media; he is their only Saviour and no other powers in history can be the object of their trust (13.4f.). The affirmation of trust (3b) is attached to the vow sequence quite awkwardly in the Hebrew text, and looks like an addition to the original saying. Yet it supplies just the element of confidence and praise expected in the penitential prayer. Yahweh is a God whose compassion (1.6, 8; 2.3, 25) is especially given to those without strength to gain their own rights (Ex. 22.22f.; Deut. 27.19). Israel, now desolate as an orphan, can only appeal to the compassion of a God whose special concern is the helpless.

[4] The prophetic summons with its proposed prayer of repentance ends, and Yahweh's word of salvation begins. He stands ready and waiting to practise the physician's art in unqualified love upon the sickness of Israel. 'Heal' belongs to Hosea's vocabulary of salvation (5.13; 6.1; 7.1). Israel's sickness is their apostasy (*mešūbā*, 11.7), the demented proclivity for rebellion and against return to Yahweh. The term is a favourite of Jeremiah's for diagnosing the intractable

character of Israel and Judah (Jer. 2.19; 3.22; 8.5, etc.). When the sick one knows his illness (expressed in the prayer), Yahweh will remove the malady by the therapy of love given without obligation or restraint (on God's love in Hosea, see 3.1; 11.1). He will take up once more the love and healing of the wilderness days (11.1, 3) and bind the heart of the people to him with the acts of love depicted in the metaphorical language of vv. 5–7. The salvation-word expresses the intention of God, but the execution of the intention waits upon the return of Israel. God's wrath uncovers the recalcitrance of Israel and his love will heal it. The promise of salvation is thus part of the summons, the wooing of a people who have stumbled and fallen (cf. 2.14f., and the sequence in Jer. 3.12f., 22). The suspicion that v. 4b is a later addition (BH, HAT, ATD, BK) is based in part on the shift from plural to a singular pronoun for Israel, but the shift could anticipate the singular in vv. 5–8. God's wrath (9.15; 8.5; 13.11) has done its work in Israel's fall and now will give place to love. Love and wrath are more anthropomorphisms for the action of God than emotions raging irrationally in the person of God.

[5] The promise of v. 4 is translated into an image of nature; Yahweh will be like dew for Israel. The effect of Yahweh's love and healing is then described in terms of flourishing plant life, using one comparison after another to develop an overwhelming impression of the luxuriance of the blessing that will come through Yahweh's love (vv. 4aβ–6, 7aβb). The technique of using comparisons with plant life to describe prosperity was cultivated in Wisdom circles; the motifs in the metaphors are to be found in unusual concentration in the love songs in the Song of Solomon (BK). Unless the capacity of the Hebrew to use such images in the speech of love is appreciated, the degree to which the motif of love penetrates the description of Israel's flourishing will be missed. There is also in the use of plant imagery a polemic against the fertility religion of Canaan. Yahweh is the one who confers every blessing on his people, who therefore have no need of Baal (cf. v. 8a); but note – it is the people who flourish, not the crops, for it is the people on whom the God Yahweh concentrates. His salvation-history is the cultivation of a church, not a plantation. So Yahweh's love will work on Israel as the dew does on the dry earth of summer. During the long rainless summer the nightly dew waters the vegetation of Palestine. Its presence brings fruitfulness (Gen. 27.28) and supports life (Pss. 110.3; 133.3) so that dew can come to represent the difference between death and life (Isa. 26.19). By the

succour of Yahweh Israel will live in an abundance whose richness is like that of flourishing plants. His fast growth will be like the lily. His permanence will be like the giant trees of the Lebanon range [6] whose roots strike deep into soil and rock. His beauty will compare to the olive tree (Jer. 11.16) and his scent to the slopes of Lebanon where constant moisture nourishes an abundant growth of fragrant flowers and shrubs.

[7] In the first poetic line of v. 7 the description of Israel as a flourishing plant seems to be dropped. The picture of the people sitting or dwelling under Yahweh's shade is an anticipation of the second image for Yahweh's beneficence: 'I am like a verdant fir' (8b). The effect of the images overlaps in the portrayal of Israel's revival. The shade of Yahweh is a famous locution for his protection and sphere of rule (Pss. 17.8; 36.7, etc.). On dwelling in the land as a salvation theme in Hosea, see 2.15, 18, 23. Cultivation of corn is a sign of the restoral of Yahweh's favour (2.8f., 22).[a] The second poetic line resumes the imagery of vv. 5f. Once Israel flourished like a luxuriant vine (10.1); in the future its growth will bring it renown like that of the famous wine from the vineyards on the slopes of Lebanon.

[8] Ephraim is Hosea's usual personal name for the contemporary northern kingdom. In the midst of Yahweh's promise the name is cried out to introduce a great exclamation that mingles protest and relief. The idols have been the greatest sin of the nation (v. 3; 13.2; 8.4). The penitence of the people and the ministry of Yahweh will combine to liberate Israel from its dependence on them. Ephraim will be free at last from subservience to other gods because the people will know the abundant work of Yahweh for them. He is the one who responds to their prayers and bestows good fortune upon them; they have no need of any other. The oracle concludes and sums up with a second image for Yahweh's work of love. He is for them like a verdant fir. This sentence is the only place in the OT where Yahweh's relation to Israel is depicted by the image of a tree. Once again Hosea exploits the fertility cult to appropriate the role of sacral tree (4.12f.) for Yahweh. The fir ($b^e r \bar{o} \check{s}$) could be any one of several coniferous trees.[b] The metaphor's accent is on the fir's constant greenness which is not diminished with changing seasons. Since the fir does not bear fruit,

---

[a] Admittedly the text of v. 7a is uncertain; for another construction of this line which attempts to preserve the continuity of the imagery from vv. 5f., see J. Ward, pp. 226ff.

[b] See 'Pine' in *IDB* III, p. 818.

it is used not so much as a particular species as a type of the tree of life
(Gen. 3.22). In Yahweh alone Israel may find life! That has been the
message of Hosea in all his oracles – and the word from the Lord
which he leaves as a heritage for all who read his prophecy.

37. INSTRUCTION FOR THE READER: 14.9 (Heb. 14.10)

14 ⁹Whoever is wise, let him understand these things,
    and whoever is perceptive, let him know them.
  For the ways of Yahweh are right,
    and the righteous walk in them;
    but the rebel stumbles therein.

The final verse is an evaluation of the entire book. Its author sees
in the book of Hosea a Witness to the ways of Yahweh which the wise
may interpret as a guide for a righteous life. The saying is formulated
in the style and vocabulary of Wisdom. The first line (v. 9a) is similar
to Ps. 107.43 and Jer. 9.12. For counterparts to the antithetical
parallelism and diction of v. 9b, see Prov. 10.29; 24.16. 'The ways of
Yahweh' are the commandments of his covenant law; the phrase is a
favourite of Deuteronomic writers (Deut. 8.6; 10.12; 11.22, etc.;
Judg. 2.22). The verse was written specifically as a conclusion to the
book of Hosea; 'rebels' ($pō\check{s}e^{\varsigma}îm$) replace the 'wicked' ($r^e\check{s}\bar{a}^{\varsigma}îm$) as the
counterpart to the righteous, and the theme of 'stumbling' of 14.1 is
echoed. It is the last addition to the written form of the book and was
added in the exilic or post-exilic period. Some reader of the period
schooled in the reflections of Wisdom, and painfully aware that
Hosea's prophecy had truly disclosed Yahweh's will, commends the
book to the wise and perceptive of all generations. The book reveals
the ways of Yahweh. They are right ($y\bar{a}\check{s}\bar{a}r$) and life depends on knowing them. The righteous obey what they learn and find the way to life,
but rebels stumble in disobedience and fall (Ps. 1).